UPRISING OF 1857

A New Survey of Historical Facts

AIJAZ AHMAD

Dedicated to the memory of my Father Late Chaudhary Shafaat Mohammad

Preface

The Indian Uprising, which lasted for more than two years from the rising at Meerut in May, 10, 1857 to the fall of General Bakht Khan and Nana Sahib in June 1859 in the Terai border of Nepal, is the most written about an event in the world history. However, still many of its dimensions seem to be enveloped. Particularly distinct perspectives such as popular, national, military, religious, etc. should be analysed in the modern context and independent research and thinking. The role of different personalities also needs to be re-evaluated in the light of contemporary and primary sources. By writing this history the author has presented a new look of the Uprising based on critical analysis of the historical facts. This book is a humble attempt to remedy the deficiency which the author has felt after long experience of reading and writing history.

In the seventeenth century, the merchants of the East India Company, whose chief aim was to make money out of the Indian resources, made the Indian subcontinent as their commercial abode. Slowly, and gradually they snatched the political power of India by imposing several treaties upon the Native rulers who were always engaged fighting to each other. The whole of Hindustan between the sea and the Himalayas was brought within a ring fence under the sway of England. The East India Company and its workers were more concerned with their trade and commerce and had been little to do with the affairs of Indian population. However, as the time passed, great and wide-ranging steps were taken towards the moral improvement and material development throughout the country. However, on the pretext of moral improvement, the British Government adopted intolerant religious policy, which led to the conversion from oriental religions to Christianity. Both Hindus and Muslims of this country began to feel that their religion was in danger, and particularly the Muslims due to their fanatical pride, and resented the Christian supremacy.

The prophesy of the 12th century Saint, that after hundred years' rule of Christianity in India, they would be vanished, created a mindset that British rule would definitely come to an end in 1857. Right from the beginning of 1857 the Indians began to wait the doom's day of the Christian ruler in India. Nevertheless, the infamous policies of Lord Dalhousie further ablaze the revolutionary atmosphere throughout the country. According to some contemporary English historians, the revolutionaries, Sepoys, and Native rulers fixed the day of Uprising as 31st May 1857. However, there were a lot of movements both in the army and in the civilians in the form of Chapati and red Lotus but the fixation of the date does not receive much support from the historical research It is being proven by throwing light on many revolutionary incidents from different centres that the day of Plassey 23rd June was fixed for Uprising by the Sepoys and also by various chiefs of Northern India.

Whatever the date was fixed by the revolutionaries, but the nature could not wait for that fixed date and due to the greased cartridge episode and the treatment meted out by the Sepoy prisoners, the Sepoys of Meerut rose into the revolt and headed towards Delhi, the only symbol of national unity. The titular Emperor Bahadur Shah Zafar was enthroned in the Red Fort, and Delhi was made, once again, the capital of India. It was appealed, through the proclamations, to the Sepoys, public and Native rulers to join the National Government which has intended to give independence in every respect. The Sepoys, general masses, and the rulers, accordingly, rushed to Delhi and joined the new Government. Thomas Lowe, a contemporary British chronicler, wrote in 1860: "The infanticide Rajput, the bigoted Brahmin, the fanatic Musalman, had joined together in the cause; cow-killer and the cow-worshiper, the pig-hater and the pig-eater… had revolted together."

Although most of the Europeans cried a single voice of Mutiny, but they were sure that the petty military grievances of the Sepoys were not at all the sole reason of the Uprising. It was definitely the common national cause which bound the Indian masses against the common hatred enemy, the British. After the failure of the Uprising, the heavy hand of the British Government fell upon the Indian people and millions of people butchered in the process of retribution.

The entire history covered under different chapters of this book shows the real picture of the revolt. The whole topics are quite interesting, full of knowledge, and based on authentic sources with little hypothetical narrations. This book restlessly engaged me about two years during which I accessed a lot of reputed libraries, met different individual scholars to get the research materials and information to complete this book. There is much scope to write on this topic as my work is not complete in all respects, but I am sure that my readers would enlighten with the subject and surely appreciate the work.

As mentioned in the contents, the whole book is divided into fourteen chapters, which have covered comprehensively all the events, facts, and aspects in a very easy way. The last one is a conclusive chapter which is the author's own opinion based upon the facts mentioned within the book. The readers could easily access the facts which have been analysed assuming contemporary records and the research of the following periods.

I am thankful to my teachers and well wishers Professor Mohammad Tariq, Professor Ali Athar, Professor Farhat Hasan, Mr. S.M. Javed, Dr. Mohammad Isa Gauhar, Dr. Hasan Imam, Dr. Basheer Hasan, etc. for boosting my will power and encouraging me whenever I lose my hope. My acknowledgements are due to my ever loving friends Dr. Waseem Raja, Mr. Wahid Ali, Mr. Mazharul Haq, etc. for the support, they rendered me in every step of completing this book. Lastly, I express my gratitude to my wife Imrana Anjum, my kids Lubna, Iram, Anam, and Sadaf whose sweet smiles and happiness encouraged me to work constantly to complete the book, and freed me from all domestic assignments.

Aijaz Ahmad
Associate Professor in History
YMD College, Nuh, Mewat, Haryana

Contents

Chapter 1

Causes, Nature and Beginning of Uprising

After the downfall of the Mughal Empire, a British company of traders with the Government of England as a sort of sleeping partner dashed in India. This company known as the East India Company with an army of some thirty to forty thousand Europeans, permanently and peacefully maintained an oppressive system of domination and monopoly over the country of such a vast extent, inhabited by one hundred and fifty million of people of different religion, language, manner and custom. It does not mean that Indians had no idea of governance but history proves that the great masses of India, both Hindus and Muslims were strongly attached to their Native system of Government and devoted to their modes of faith with an obstinate and inveterate bigotry which has no parallel in the British system of Government.

The Company's Government which was uniformly oppressive, treacherous, and unjust, not ever tried to win over the inhabitants of this country rather it attacked upon their religion and social customs, which had tied them since long into uniformity. The Christian Missionary activity further infuriated the Indian population and ultimately united them against the British East India Company. The British were also afraid of the unknown danger and perhaps fully aware of the military dissatisfaction.

The debate over the causes and nature of the Uprising of 1857 continues till today, mainly because of its unique position and remains one of the most sensitive and highly controversial issues of modern Indian history. It was not only the first widespread resistance to British rule, but it also brought about fundamental changes in the relations between the rulers and the ruled and left far-reaching effects on the future political system of India. The Uprising of 1857 was more multifarious in its nature and causes. There were the series of factors, such as political, social, economic, military and religious, made for an explosive mix, which burst forth like a volcanic eruption in 1857. All the factors are analysed in full details in this chapter and also in the forthcoming chapters with its nature and perspective.

Scholars of distinctive ideology have given different theories regarding the Uprising. Some have contended that it was the revolt of a class, which had long been injudiciously pampered and petted into insubordination. Some have declared it to be the result of a national movement, to free the country from foreign Government. The Annexation Policy of Lord Dalhousie has been assigned by others as the primary cause. John William Kaye quotes a statement of Sir James Outram that the rebellion was set on foot by the Muslims long before the British took Awadh from its rulers. An impression has been created by some writers, that the Native army was corrupted by agents of the old princely houses and that these agents had wandered from city to city, sowing the seeds of sedition. Another writer believes the mutiny to have been the result of fanaticism, created by a Royal Proclamation, emanating from the Court of Persia, copies of which undoubtedly were circulated throughout India. Some have contended it was a purely Muslim rebellion, others a joint Hindu and Muslim revolt; and that in order to create a sympathetic movement of both Hindu and Muslim in a collective resistance to the British power; the cartridge grievance and military infidelity were the other factors raked by the Imperialist historians.[1]

The scholars generally divide into groups regarding the controversies over the nature and causes of the Uprising. British House of Commons's opposition leader Benjamin Disraeli called it a National Revolt rooted in deep mistrust. V. D. Savarkar declared it as the fight for Swadharm and Swaraj or First War of Independence. S. B. Chaudhary called it a Civil Rebellion. R. C. Majumdar tried to prove it neither first nor national nor a war of independence. He says that all the leading figures in this great outbreak were alienated from the British for private reasons. Marxists called it a soldier-peasant struggle against foreign and feudal bondage. British scholars Kaye and Malleson called it a Sepoy Mutiny which broke out due to the use of greased cartridges.

There are a lot of scholars who by their close study on the situation and conditions of the Indian people opined that any single cause or perspective was not fully responsible for Uprising, but it started due to the multiple causes. Martin Richard Gubbins, Member of the British Commission at Awadh states the following causes which embrace all the causes, that stave been adduced, so far as he heard or read:[2]

Firstly- It has been attributed to Russian intrigue.

Secondly- It was a long-matured conspiracy upon the part of the Mohammedans.

Thirdly- It was viewed by others as a national revolt.

Fourthly- Some attribute the mutinies to the British annexation of the Province of Awadh.

Fifthly- Some regard it to be a religious outbreak of the soldiery, aroused by our interference with their prejudices and religion, in which the people sympathized. Lastly- It was regarded by others as chiefly attributable to the absence of a sufficient European force; to the condition and management of the Bengal Army having been unsound and bad; and to the Sepoy having been too much freed from the bonds of discipline, and having become discontented.

All the Uprisings right from the July 1806 to the end of 1858, caused by the headgear, and greased cartridges, were having a lot of hidden causes infused with sentimental and national consciousness. In the Vellore Uprising, the reason for the outbreak was never satisfactorily ascertained. At least, no reason was found out, which would seem to an intellect to be at all adequate. A more probable supposition, and one which render some approach to a reasonable cause of the Uprising, was that the sons of

Tipu Sultan, the deposed ruler of Mysore, along with many distinguished Muslims, who had been deprived of office, in consequence of his deposition, were at that time in Vellore; and these influential personages would, no doubt, while using other arts to alienate the Native troops from the Company's service, arouse them to this murderous mutiny by inflaming their suspicions regarding any endeavour to tamper with their religious usages.[3]

In the Uprising of 1857, although the immediate cause was the greased cartridges' episode but the Uprising could not stop even after allowing the Sepoys to grease the cartridges by their own substances. It was confined to North India, and the armies of Madras and Bombay did not join it. It was basically associated with the matters related to the North India, and South Indian didn't have any connection with it. The Muslim rulers, who had established their dynasties in the Deccan, were not akin to the Mughals of Delhi and North India, against whom they had fought long and stubbornly. Actually, the dethroning and exilement of Nawab Wajid Ali Shah and treatment of Mughal Emperor Bahadur Shah Zafar filled the national and religious passion among the Natives, and the remedial measures of the Company could not stop the national enthusiasm and hatred against the British. Wherever one could see, there were only option, *Maro Firangi Ko* and *Dilli Chalo*.

The revolutionaries, who took part in the Uprising of 1857, consisted of many groups: the Sepoys, the feudal nobility, rural landlords, the peasants and the Muslim fanatics who were associated with the old rebel groups popularly called as Wahabis and Faraizis. By studying the first group, one can call it a Mutiny, by second it could be called as the War of Independence and followers of the third group called it as Popular Uprising by quoting the socio-economic reasons. The very recent study added another one, which may be quoted as the fourth group as the War of Religion. The new thinkers advocated this theory by close study of mutiny papers found within the rebel camp and the Red Fort.

Undoubtedly, the revolt of 1857 was the result of the multiple causes, but it also could not be ignored that the battle of Plassey and later the war against the British waged by Hyder Ali, and his son Tipu Sultan were first and second points on which it was discussed that whether India should belong to the Indians or to the English. These incidents created a general mindset on every Indian that the British had forcefully occupied their motherland. On the 23rd of June in 1757, the matter of sovereignty of India was not only discussed, but the seed of revolution was sown. Savarkar mentions that if Plassey had not been there, the War of 1857 also would not have taken place. Though a century had rolled by, the memory of that day was fresh in the heart of Hindustan. Savarkar continues that in proof of this, witness the terrible scene on the 23rd day of June 1857, in Northern India, in the vast country from the Punjab up to Calcutta, wherever there was an open field, thousands of revolutionaries were fighting the English simultaneously in different places, from morning till evening, after openly challenging them, saying: "To-day we are going to avenge Plassey!"[4]

Indian considered that in the battle of Plassey, Clive with his 3,000 forces utterly routed Sirajuddaula, the Nawab of Bengal, and his army of 60,000 men. It was nothing a battle but a treachery which the Europeans generally used to apply with Indian rulers. Now after 100 years it was the turn of the Indians to apply the same treachery and insubordination against the British to uproot the Company's Government. This treachery was applied by Indian rulers by alluring the Sepoys, which were the backbone of the British paramountcy. This time they had to settle the matter from Plassey to Awadh via Shrirangapattam and Delhi.

Above all, the infamous policies of Lord Wellesly, Lord William Bentinck, and Lord Dalhousie created a havoc scene in the political drama of religion, and nationalism played upon the stage of India. Initially, the blood of the youths of Native armed forces boiled in Vellore, Barhampur, and Barrackpur and lastly the national volcano erupted from Meerut and destroyed the tyrannical setup of the British. Undoubtedly, Vellore may be considered the dress rehearsal of the Uprising and very closely connected to the Indian discontents which were boiling after Plassey and Shrirangapattam disaster. It was the first time before the world that Indian Sepoys including rulers and subjects celebrated the hundredth anniversary of Plassey in a great style at home.

The general perception that the *Purbea* Sepoys raised their arms against their masters, as the British Government annexed the Awadh province, does not seem the healthy factor. No doubt many Sepoys belonging to Awadh province were stationed at various centres of Northern India and definitely their emotional attachments were with the ruling dynasty of Awadh province, but moreover, they had much sympathy with the Emperor of Delhi. Alexander Duff quotes the statement from an officer who escaped from Faizabad, that, in a conversation with the Subedar of his own regiment, the latter said, "...... You English have been a long time in India, but you know little about us. We have nothing to do with Wajid Ali (the ex-King of Awadh) or any of his relations. The Kings of Lucknow were made by you; the only ruler in India empowered to give *Sunnuds* (titles to Kingship) is the Emperor of Delhi; he never made a King of Awadh, and it is from him only that we shall receive our orders."[5]

The main cry of the revolutionaries was to save their religion and motherland, which were since long on the stake. The other factors which were also added during the passage of time make the matter more complex to understand the Uprising more easily. By analyzing and deeply studying different perspectives, it would be easy to understand the various sects of the revolutionaries and their mentality, their love and passion regarding their goal.

No doubt the urge of independence or freedom from the foreign yoke was one of the strongest among all the important, secondary, temporary, and accidental causes, which also played the leading role in the Uprising.

The fateful year of 1857, which finally grew on 10th May from Meerut, covered hastily the whole of Northern India. The British Government authorities also began to feel the sign of the tide, which was about to overthrow everything. Malleson mentions that Lord Dalhousie on his journey to homewards have written a minute, in which he painted in roseate hues the condition of India, the contentment of the Sepoys, and the improbability of disturbance from any cause whatever. However, this minute itself shows the doubt of disturbance, apart from the positive clarification of Dalhousie. In August, 1855, Lord Canning, at the farewell banquet given by the Directors, gave warning that "We must not forget that in the sky of India, serene as it is, a small cloud may arise, at first no bigger than a man's hand, but which growing bigger and bigger may at last threaten to overwhelm us with ruin."[6]

In the year of 1857, there was a whispering among the Indian people about the old Indian prophecy. It was represented to contain a prophecy made by a Punjabi Fakir in the twelfth century, seven hundred years ago, so the people were informed. It had been foretold that after various dynasties of Muslims had ruled for some centuries, the Nazarenes, or Christians, should hold power in India for one hundred years; that the Nazarenes would then be expelled. The prophecy was clearly indicating the hundred year's gap, dating from 1757 to 1857. According to prophesy there were many chances of a change of Government in 1857 after a hundred years. Plassey had been in 1757 and in the hundredth year after the battle, it seemed everyone was waiting for a change.[7]

Besides the rumour of hundred years' British rule, many other exciting rumours were filled in the air such as Russia was to avenge the Crimea by the invasion of India and the re-establishment of the Mughals. Persia will also help the Indians in establishing the Mughal rule and in this connection a proclamation, posted at the gates of the Great Mosque in March, 1857, announcing that the King of Persia was marching to the destruction of the British Raj, and that it behoved the faithful to be ready to fight the infidels.[8]

The British were well informed by their secret agents about the rumours and daily happenings and public grievances; however the British made little impression and rather mistrusted their informers and avoided in the pretext that the Natives have an unfortunate habit of sending anonymous information to the authorities to the view of injuring some personal enemy.

Sir Syed Ahmad Khan says that for a long period, many grievances had been rankling in the hearts of the people. In a course of time, a vast store of explosive material was collected. It wanted but the application of a match to light it, and that match was applied by the mutinous army. The English were living over a volcano ready to burst into deadly violence at any moment, but they could not, or would not, apprehend their danger. Even the English historian Martin has described that the bad governance of the British was one of the main causes of the revolt. He says, "India is, in truth, a mine of wealth, and if we are permitted to see the sword of war permanently sheathed, it may be hoped that we shall take a new view of things; especially, that the leaders of our large manufacturing towns, Birmingham and Manchester, Glasgow and Belfast, will take up the question of good Government for India".[9]

It was frequently admitted even by the British authors that in India, the British rule had always maintained a certain aloofness from the Natives, which was unfortunate, and galling to the Native pride. However, at the time of Uprising all the administrative follies were evaded and according to the British authors, India was ruled by many able bodies like Lord Canning in Calcutta as Governor General; General Anson as the Commander-in-Chief; Elphinstone at Bombay and Harris of Madras as Governors of distinguished ability. Three celebrated brothers governed the areas of Northern India, which was considered most dangerous by the British- John Lawrence in Punjab; George Lawrence in Rajputana; Henry Lawrence in Awadh with headquarters in Lucknow.

After the hundred years oppressive British rule, the Uprising of 1857 given a chance of revenge to the Indian masses for which they were awaiting. This war mobilized all sections irrespective of race and religion and gradually converted the revolt into the War of Independence. The Hindus and Muslims rose simultaneously to protect their 'Dharma' and 'Din' and to 'save their country'. The Sepoys (from Persian Sipahi, meaning Native infantry but the term Sepoy was generally used for every Native troop, whether they were belonged to infantry, artillery or cavalry) sparked at Meerut and proved the prophecy true.

The Uprising started from Meerut, covered almost all North and Central India. Alexander Duff narrates that take the map of India, and look at the extent of country that has been the scene of actual mutinies. Beginning with the far North, in the Punjab, there are Peshawar and Jhelum; southward, Noshera, Jallandhar, and Sialkot; crossing the Satlaj, Ferozpur, Hamirpur, Pilhaur, and Ludhiana; emerging from Sirhind to the West, there are Hansi, Sirsa, and Hissar; then the great cities of Meerut, Delhi, and Agra, with Mathura, Aligarh, Bulanshahar, Etawa, Mainpuri, and Muradabad; along the Ganges, before its junction with the Jumna, there are Fatehgarh, Kanpur, Fatehpur, and Allahabad; to the North-east, Bareilly in Rohelkhand. In the Kingdom of Awadh, Lucknow, Shahjahanpur, Sitapur, Sultanpur, Faizabad, with Dariabad, Dhaurahra, and Gonda. Southward from Awadh and eastward, there are Banaras, Asimgarh, Jaunpur, Gorakhpur, Segowli, Dinapur, Bhagalpur; and running to the south-west from Bhagalpur through Bihar, and skirting Bengal, there are Gaya, Hazaribagh, Ranchi, Puruha, Chota Nagpur, and Chaibasy, with many other places ripe and ready for a rise at the falling of the feeblest spark. In Central India there are Mhow, Indore, Neemuch, Naseerabad, Asingarh, Saugar, Japalpur, Naugaon, Banda, Jhansi, Gwalior, Angur, Sipru, etc.[10]

The Indian Uprising of 1857 occurred as the result from the accumulation of factors over time, rather than any single event. Although the factors were socio-religious, economic, administrative, military, etc. but these were the Sepoys or Native troops which refused to use the cartridges allegedly greased with animal fat and dared enough to raise their arms against the East India Company's rule. The Sepoys were in the superiority complex and according to Karl Marx, 200,000,000 Natives being curbed by a Native army of 200,000 men, officered by Englishmen, and that Native army, in its turn, being kept in check by an English army numbering 40,000, only.[11]

There was the resentment in Sepoys regarding the service rules such as the overseas service, promotions, pensions and the newly General Service Enlistment Act. Many Indian officers did not reach commissioned rank until they were too old to be effective. The final spark of unrest was due to the new Enfield rifle introduced in the Indian army in 1853. Pre-greased cartridges were used in these rifles. The cartridge of the Enfield rifle was heavily greased with wax and tallow made of cow and in certain lots, the swine fat. The grease was necessary in order to improve loading speed and so that during firing, the gases did not escape ahead of the bullet thereby reducing the range and accuracy of the weapon. The cartridges had to be bitten by the teeth or opened by finger nails before being loaded. The new rifles began to manufacture at Damdam, Ambala, and Sialkot. When the complaints and suspicions of the Sepoys were made known, firstly, from Damdam, inquiries were sent to England for exact particulars relating to the obnoxious missiles. It was ascertained that the new cartridges were made at the Royal Laboratory at Woolwich; and that Captain Boxer, the superintendent of that department, was accustomed to use for lubrication a composition formed of five parts tallow, five parts stearine, and one part wax containing, therefore, the ox or cow's fat, but none from pigs. He had no prejudices on the matter to contend against in England, and used; therefore just such a composition as appeared to him most suitable for the purpose. The cartridges were not sent out to India ready greased for use; as, in a hot country, the grease would soon be absorbed by the paper. Therefore, a part of the process left to be accomplished when the cartridges reached their destination. In January 1857 on which the new weapon was to be issued to the Sepoys rumours started spreading about the swine/cow fat in the cartridges.[12]

As the story goes back in January 1857, a Khallasi or workman of a low caste attached in the Arsenal at Damdam (Artillery Station near Calcutta, where the school for musketry practice with the new Enfield rifle was then established), asked a Brahmin Sepoy of the 3rd Native Infantry (on some accounts 2nd Bengal Granadier): "Brother, lend me your brass pot, so that I may drink, for I have walked far in the sun." The Brahman Sepoy replied, "Do you not know, swine-begotten, that your hog's lips would contaminate my lotah?" Laskar smiled and told the Brahmin Sepoy, "Contaminate! By holy Ganga, it is your lips that are contaminated, not mine. Are not the Governments greasing your cartridges with cow's fat? And can you load your rifle without biting the forbidden thing? Learn more about your own caste, brother, before you talk so proudly to others." The Brahmin Sepoy rushed horror-stricken to his comrades and told them the story, which was soon widely spread throughout the Native army. The Native troops were afraid that when they would go to their home, their friends would refuse to eat with them.[13]

When the rumour spread the Native commissioned officer and Captain Wright at Damdam assured the soldiers that the grease was composed of mutton-fat and wax but the soldiers were not satisfied. They replied, "It may be so, but our friends will not believe it; let us obtain the ingredients from the bazaar and make it up ourselves; we shall then know what is used, and be able to assure our fellow soldiers and others that there is nothing in it prohibited by our caste." Captain Wright also observed the same when some of the depot men in conversing with him on the subject had stated that the cartridge report had spread throughout India, and when the Sepoys went to their homes, their friends refused to eat with them. McLeod Innes mentions another theory that in the present case the contractor had managed, without detection by the authorities, to introduce as one of the lubricants, cows' fat, the use of which would have involved contamination to a Hindu; though no lard or any other material that would have contaminated Muslims had been used.[14]

The rumour of greased cartridges soon spread like wild fire all over the Bengal Army from Calcutta to Peshawar. The matter was immediately reported to the Government on 22nd January. Major General J.B. Hearsay commanding the Presidency Division Barrackpur, immediately responded and reported the matter to the Governor-General with some suggestions. On the 27th, the Governor General in Council not only approved General Hearsey's recommendation, but issued special orders to the Inspector-General of Ordnance that, "with the least possible delay, he was to submit any suggestions for removing the objections raised by the Sepoys "that" means must be taken to satisfy them that nothing which may interfere with their caste was used" and that in the meantime the cartridges were to be issued without any grease at all. On the morning of the 28th, the order of the Government, allowing the Sepoys to choose for themselves the grease required for their ammunition, was made known to every regiment in the cantonment.[15]

A modification was made with the drill for loading so that the cartridge was torn from the hands and not bitten. The officers also attempted to convince the Sepoys. However, the damage had been done, and the Sepoys now started suspecting everyone and everything. General Hearsey wrote to the Government on the 11th of February that they had been dwelling at Barrackpur "on a mine ready for explosion."[16]

Another military station which was badly affected by greased cartridge was Barhampur, near Murshidabad (100 km North of Calcutta). The town is on the left bank of the river Bhagirathi, a great offset of the Ganges, and on the high road from Calcutta to Murshidabad. The military cantonments were large and striking; the grand square, the excellent parade-ground, the quarters of the European officers all were handsome. Before the Revolt, Berhampur was included within the presidency division in military matters, and was usually occupied by a body of infantry and another of artillery. Barhampur, a few years before the Uprising, was a manufactory of the silk bandana handkerchiefs once so popular in England. At that time there were cantoned in it the 19th Regiment Native

Infantry, a corps of Irregular Cavalry, and two 6-pounder guns manned by Native gunners under Colonel Mitchell.

On 25th of February, a portion of the 34th regiment of Bengal infantry changed its station from Barrackpur to Barhampur, where it was greeted and feasted by the men of the 19th Native Infantry, the only Native regiment stationed there at that time. During their feasting, the newcomers narrated all the news from Damdam and Barrackpur concerning the greased cartridges. Next day at the parade, when ordered to exercise with blank cartridge, the men all refused to touch the unclean thing! In the night of 27th February, the Sepoys revolted and seized their arms, drumming and shouting defiance. As a result, they were warned and ordered for the 19th Native Infantry to march to Barrackpur where they were disbanded, but before they reached that station, the first blood had been shed in the Indian Mutiny.[17]

The next station which was caught by the cartridge fire was the Barrackpur. It was situated along the banks of the Hooghly, sixteen miles from Calcutta. It was at that time the headquarters of the Presidency Division of the army, and four Native regiments were quartered there; the 2nd Grenadiers, the 34th Native Infantry, the 43rd Light Infantry, and the 70th Native Infantry. The station was commanded by Brigadier Charles Grant; and the General of the Division was John Hearsey. On the 24th of January 1857, the telegraph office in Barrackpur was burnt down and this was the first act of open insubordination in the events of the Uprising 1857. It followed the burning of the Sergeants bungalow in Raniganj. On March 29, 1857, Mangal Panday of the 34th Native Infantry at Barrackpur having intoxicated himself with bhang openly mutinied and called his colleagues, "Rise! ye brethren, rise! Why do you hold back, brethren? Come, and rise! I bind you by the oath of your religion! Come, let us burst forth on the treacherous enemies for the sake of our freedom."[18]

Mangal Panday fired at Sergeant Major Hewson, but his fire was missed. He also fired at Regiment Adjutant Lieutenant Baugh and killed his horse with his second shot. This was followed by a hand to hand sword fight in which Baugh was wounded. Mangal Panday meanwhile was overpowered by Shaikh Paltu, a Sepoy of the same regiment. This enabled the wounded European Sergeant Major and the Adjutant to escape. Mangal Panday tried to commit suicide with his musket but was only wounded. In due course, Mangal Panday was hanged on 8th of April, and his sympathizer Jamadar Ishwary Panday was also court marshaled and hanged on the 21st of April, 1857. The seven companies of the 34th Native Infantry were disbanded in the presence of all the troops. Shaikh Paltu was promoted and rewarded with proprietorship of a confiscated village.[19]

The revolutionaries entered Delhi without any pre-planning and shocked the Europeans as they could not be able to do any defensive measure. Their occupation of Delhi on 11th May, proved to be the decisive general signal for the whole army to revolt. It is also said that the date of the revolt was fixed by the revolutionaries on Sunday the

31st of May in their council, but the circumstances forced the Sepoys to explode several days before.[20]

The other area which caught the fire of the Uprising was Rohelkhand where important stations like Bareilly and Moradabad, Badayun and Shahjahanpur rose against the British. Savarkar has very beautifully quoted the daring words of the Sepoys of Moradabad. He says that on the morning of the 31st of May; however, all the Sepoys began to form on the parade-ground. The English were about to ask the reason of their assembling thus without permission, when the Sepoys spoke authoritatively in the following manner: "The rule of the Company is at an end. Therefore, you should leave this country immediately and go away, or else you will be massacred! If you cannot go at once we will allow you two hours to prepare for departure. But you must vacate Moradabad as soon as the two hours are over."[21]

Allahabad was another important place, which was clung into the Uprising after Meerut and Delhi. On the night of the 6th of June, the Native regiment in Allahabad mutinied, butchered the British officers with their wives and children, attempted to seize the fort. The British in Allahabad received aid from Colonel Neill on 11th June, coming up with the Madras Fusiliers from Calcutta. Neill occupied the fort and garrisoned the place only with the British. Neill, on his way Allahabad, had occupied Banaras and defeated 37th Native Infantry in the first stage of mutiny. The English troops flowed from all sides into Allahabad. The fortress of Allahabad, occupying a most commanding position on the Jumna, considered the gateway to the North-West India.[22]

The unexpected and unplanned eruption of the soldiers and civilians greatly shocked the European authorities. The Governor General Lord Canning mobilized the European forces as Henry Lawrence had suggested him to get every European from China, Ceylon, and elsewhere; furthermore all the Gorkhas from the hills. John Lawrence also requested that he might raise Punjabi levies and make use of the Sikh Rajas of the Cis-Sutlej and Trans-Sutlej States. At that time, an Indian force under Outram had been sent to Persia, and an army from England was on the sea, on its way to China. Canning recalled Outram's regiments and intercepted the fleet, though he had no authority over the China Expedition. With the permission of the Governor General Lord Canning, Henry Lawrence invited Jang Bahadur, the Prime Minister of Nepal, to form an army of 10,000 men and 24 guns, to clear the districts North of Awadh, and to co-operate in the attack on Awadh. The request was at once complied with, and Jang Bahadur in response, arrived in Lucknow with his 10,000 Gorkha soldiers.[22]

References:

1. Metcalfe, Charles Theophilus, *Two Native Narratives of the Mutiny in Delhi,* (Eng. Trans. of *Roznamcha Mainudin Hasan Khan* and *Munshi Jeewan Lal*) , London, 1898, pp. 5-6 (Hereafter cited as *Two Native Narratives*)

2. Gubbins, Martin Richard, *An Account of the Mutinies of Oudh and of the siege of the Lucknow Residency; With some Observation on the Condition of the Province of Oudh and of the Causes of the Mutiny of the Bengal Army*, London, 1858, pp. 49-50 (Hereafter cited as Gubbins)

3. Kofoid, Charles Alwood, *The Story of the Indian Mutiny, 1857-58*, Edinburgh, 1898, p. 18

4. Savarkar, V.D., *The Indian War of Independence of 1857*, London, 1909, p. 13, (hereafter cited as Savarkar) (Alexander Duff writes about the effects of centenary of battle of Plassey, "... The centenary day of the battle of Plassey (23rd instant), which laid the foundation of our Indian empire, and which Native hopes and wishes, and astrological predictions, had long ago fixed on as the last of British sway, has passed by; and, through God's overruling Providence, Calcutta is still the metropolis of British India. But, alas! throughout the whole of the North-West provinces, all Government is at present at an end. The apparently settled peace and profound tranquility which were wont to reign throughout British India in former years, once called forth from an intelligent French traveler the somewhat irreverent but striking remark, that the Government of India was "like the good deity: one does not see it, but it is everywhere." So calm, serene, and ubiquitous did the power of British rule then appear to be! How changed the aspect of things now! Throughout the whole of the North-West, Government, instead of being in its regulating power and influence everywhere, is, at this moment, literally "nowhere." Duff, Alexander, *The Indian Rebellion: Its Causes and Results, in a Series of Letters*, New York, 1858, pp. 36-37)

5. Duff, Alexander, *The Indian Rebellion: Its Causes and Results, in a Series of Letters*, New York, 1858, p. 52

6. Malleson, George Bruce, *The Indian Mutiny of 1857*, New York, 1891, p. 23, see also, Frazer, R. W., *British India*, New York 1896, pp. 274-275, and Cunningham, Henry Stewart, *Earl Canning*, Oxford, 1891, p. 53

7. Kofoid, Charles Alwood, *The Story of the Indian Mutiny, 1857-58*, Edinburgh, 1898, p. 20

8. Malleson, George Bruce, *The Indian Mutiny of 1857*, New York, 1891, p. 23, see also, Frazer, R. W., *British India*, New York 1896, pp. 274-275, and Cunningham, Henry Stewart, *Earl Canning*, Oxford, 1891, p. 53 (The proclamation pasted on the wall of the Great Mosque at Delhi, which purported to be a manifesto from the Shah of Persia addressed to the people. "All the Faithful in India! The infidels had brought troops to the soil of a power of Islam. They desired to destroy the religions of Islam in Persia in like manner as the religion of the Muslims of India. It was incumbent on the Faithful to rise against them everywhere. Let them unite all differences, and remember that they had but one Quraan and one Qiblah, and extend the hand of brotherhood, remembering the words of the Prophet, 'Verily all true believers are brothers.' Let them all take part in the *Jihad*, or Holy War. Let the Faithful in Hindustan unite with him (the Shah) against this tribe of wanderers from the path of righteousness, and have no friendship with a tribe of whom the Prophet said, 'Verily they do not love you, and neither do you love them. Let all the Faithful in Hindustan consider it incumbent upon them to follow the precept, 'Slay, in the name of God, those who wish to slay you'; and let the

old and the young, the small and the great, the wise and the ignorant, the ryot and the Sepoy, all without exception arise in the defense of the orthodox faith of the Prophet, and, having girt up the waist of valour, adorn their persons with arms and weapons. And for the purpose of settling the quarrel, it is necessary that not only a small number of true believers should stand forth in defense of the faith, but that the whole should answer our call. And the victory should be with them, to make manifest the decree of God, 'Verily the Almighty will weigh the wicked in different scales from the pure." Forrest, Robert Edward, *Eight Days; A Tale of the Indian Mutiny*, London (ND), pp. 34-35, hereafter cited as *Eight Days*)

9. Khan, Syed Ahmad, *Asbab-e-Baghawat-e-Hind*, (Eng. Trans.), Patna, 1999, p. 3, (Hereafter cited as *Asbab-e-Baghawat-e-Hind*), see also Martin, R. Montgomery, *The Indian Empire*, Vol. II, London, 1858, p. 37

10. Duff, Alexander, *The Indian Rebellion: Its Causes and Results, in a Series of Letters*, New York, 1858, pp. 91-92

11. *New York Daily Tribune*, July 15, 1857

12. Dodd, George, *The History of the Indian Revolt and of the Expeditions to Persia, China, and Japan, 1856-7-8*, London, 1859, p. 38, (Hereafter cited as Dodd), see also Kofoid, Charles Alwood, *The Story of the Indian Mutiny, 1857-58*, Edinburgh, 1898, p. 25, Forrest, George. W., *A History of the Indian Mutiny; Reviewed and Illustrated from Original Documents*, Vol. I, London 1904, p. 2, (Hereafter cited as *A History of the Indian Mutiny*)and *Defense Journal*, Vol. 3, No. 9, Islamabad, December,1999

13. Tracy, Louis, *The Red Year; A Story of The Indian Mutiny*, New York 1907, p. 1, see also Argyl, Campbell, George Douglas, Duke of, *India Under Dalhousie and Canning*, London, 1865, p. 77, Surridge, Victor, *Romance of Empire, India*, London, 1909, pp. 249-50 and Wright, Charles H.H., *Memoire of John Lovering Cooke*, London, 1873, p. 29

14. *A History of the Indian Mutiny*, p. 2, see also Innes, McLeod, *Lucknow & Oude in the Mutiny: A Narrative and a Study*, London, 1895, p. 10 (Hereafter cited as *Lucknow & Oude in the Mutiny*)

15. Argyl, Campbell, George Douglas, Duke of, *India Under Dalhousie and Canning*, London, 1865, pp. 78-79, see also, Dodd, p. 38, *The Living Age*, Volume 0055, Issue 702, New York, November 7, 1857, pp. 325-326, Beveridge, Henry, *A Comprehensive History of India*, Vol. III, London, 1962, p. 556, 557-561, and *New York Daily Tribune*, July 15, 1857

16. Mead, Henry, *The Sepoy Revolt: Its causes and its Consequences*, London, 1858, p. 53

17. *A History of the Indian Mutiny*, pp. 11-12&18, see also Dodd, p. 40

18. Edward, Gilliat, *Heroes of the Indian Mutiny; Stories of Heroic Deeds*, London 1914, p. 25, see also Kaye, John William, *A History of the Sepoy War in India, 1857-58*, Vol. I, London 1875, pp. 539-540, and Savarkar, p. 87

19. *The Living Age*, Volume 0055, Issue 702, New York, November 7, 1857, p. 326, see also *A History of the Indian Mutiny*, pp. 20-21, Wood, Evelyn, *The Revolt in Hindustan 1857-59*, London, 1908, p. 9, Norman, Henry Wylie, *Delhi - 1857; The Siege, Assault, and Capture as given in the Diary and Correspondence of the Late Colonel Keith Young*, London 1902, pp. 5-6, Mead, Henry, *The Sepoy Revolt: Its*

causes and its Consequences, London, 1858, pp. 57-58, and Malleson, George Bruce, *The Indian Mutiny of 1857*, New York, 1891, pp. 53-56, (It has become the custom to call all those who fought for religion and country in the war of 1857 by the appellation of "Panday". Savarkar, p. 89)

20. Kaye, John William, *Kay's and Malleson's History of the Indian Mutiny of 1857-8*, Vol. II, London, 1910, pp. 81-82, see also Edward, Gilliat, *Heroes of the Indian Mutiny; Stories of Heroic Deeds*, London 1914, p.141, (Kaye quotes the report of Mr. Cracroft Wilson, "Carefully collating oral information with facts as they occurred, I am convinced that Sunday, 31st of May, 1857, was the day fixed for mutiny to commence throughout the Bengal Army; that there were committees of about three members in each regiment which conducted the duties, if I may so speak, of the mutiny; that the Sipahis, as a body, knew nothing of the plans arranged; and that the only compact entered into by regiments, as a body, was, that their particular regiments would do as the other regiments did. The committee conducted the correspondence and arranged the plan of operations, viz., that on the 31st of May parties should be told off to murder all European functionaries, most of whom would be engaged at church; seize the treasure, which would then be augmented by the first installment of the rubbie harvest; and release the prisoners, of which an army existed in the North-western Provinces alone of upwards of twenty-five thousand men. The regiments in Delhi and its immediate vicinity were instructed to seize the magazine and fortifications. . . . From this combined and simultaneous massacre on the 31st of May, 1857, we were, humanly speaking, saved by Lieutenant-Colonel Smyth commanding the 3rd Regiment of Bengal Light Cavalry, and the frail ones of the Bazaar. . . . The mind had been prepared, and the train had been laid, but it was not intended to light the slow match for another three weeks. The spark, which fell from female lips, ignited it at once, and the night of the 10th of May, 1857, saw the commencement of a tragedy never before witnessed since India passed under British sway." Kaye, John William, *Kay's and Malleson's History of the Indian Mutiny of 1857-8,* Vol. II, London, 1910, pp. 81-82)

21. Savarkar, p. 142

22. Marx, Karl, *Notes on the Indian History (664-1858),* Russian Edition, Moscow, 1947, pp. 152-153, Malleson, George Bruce, *History of the Indian Mutiny of 1857-58, Commencing from the Close of the Second Volume of Sir John Kaye's History of the Sepoy War,* Vol. III, (Contemporaneous with Sir John Kay's Third Volume), London, 1878, p. 12

23. Gibbon, Frederick P., *The Lawrences of the Punjab,* London, 1908, p. 256, (Hereafter cited as Gibbon), see also Sedgwick, F.R., *The Indian Mutiny 1857: A Sketch of the Principal Military Events,* London, 1920, p. 107, (Hereafter cited as *A Sketch of the Principal Military Events*)

Chapter 2

Meerut in the Uprising

Meerut, standing on the small river popularly known as Kali Nadi, is about equidistant from the Ganges and the Jumna, twenty-five or thirty miles from each. It came in British occupation in 1830. The cantonment was two miles north of the town, and was divided into two portions by a small branch of the river, over which two bridges had been thrown. The Northern half of the cantonment was containing lines for the accommodation of a brigade of horse-artillery, a European cavalry corps, and a regiment of European infantry. The opposite or southern half of the cantonment was mainly occupied by the huts for Native troops, and by the detached bungalows for the officers who command them.[1]

Meerut was the largest cantonment in India, and as it contained the greatest proportion of British troops of all branches of the service. There were the 6th Dragoon Guards (Carabineers) under Colonel H. Jones; 1st Battalion 60th Rifles under Colonel J. Jones; a troop of Horse Artillery under Major Tombs; a Light Field Battery under Major Scott; 3rd Bengal Light Cavalry under Colonel Smith, 11th Native Infantry under Colonel J. Finnis; 20th Native Infantry under Major Taylor. The brigade was commanded by Colonel Archdale Wilson, and Major-General W. Hewitt commanded the division. Meerut, in some respects, was one of the last towns in which the mutiny might have been expected to commence as there was at the time about 2200 English troops.[2]

Here in Meerut the rumours afloat in the markets and among the Native troops, especially those regarding the use of polluting grease in the preparation of the new cartridges. Another rumour which gained ground that the mixture of ground bones in the flour sold at the market, by which it was said that the British Government intended to destroy caste and the religion of the people. Early in April 1857, it was decided to use the new cartridges at Meerut cantonment most probably in order to check the spirit of the men. It was ordered to 3rd Bengal Light Cavalry troopers to use the new cartridges. A trooper, by name Brijmohan, announced to his comrades that he had used them and requested his comrades to use them without hesitation. The result was that Brijmohan's house was set on fire on the 13th of April. Anyway, the 24th of April was fixed for a parade of the 3rd Bengal Light Cavalry, and on the preceding day the troopers, both Hindu and Muslim, bound themselves by an oath not to use the cartridges when called out to exercise.[3]

On 24th April, the 3rd Bengal Light Cavalry was ordered to parade and perform firing drills. The parade took place and there were ninety men present furnished from each troop. The Colonel Smyth explained to them the reason for ordering the parade, and commanded the Havildar-Major to show them the new way of loading, which he did and fired off his carbine. Colonel Smyth then ordered the cartridges to be served out; only five (3 Muslim 2 Hindus) namely Heera Singh Havildar, 4th Troop. Parshad Singh Havildar, 5th Troop, Ghulam Nabi Khan Havildar, 6th Troop, Shaikh Ghulam Mohammad, Naik, 6th Troop, Dilawar Khan accepted them and remaining 85 refused to accept their cartridges.[4]

All the 85 troops (49 Muslims and 36 Hindus) were ordered to return to their barracks. General Officer Commanding, Major General Hewitt ordered a Court of Inquiry composed of a president and six members, three of whom were Native officers of the Infantry and three Native officers of the Cavalry. The names of the members were as follows:[5]

President
Subedar-Major Thakur Awasthi, 20th Regiment, Native Infantry
Members
Subedar Ganga Deen Dubey, 20th Regiment, Native Infantry
Subedar Ram Charan, 3rd Regiment, Light Cavalry
Subedar Gunesh Singh, 20th Regiment, Native Infantry
Subedar Ghulab Khan, 3rd Regiment, Light Cavalry
Subedar Bakshish Singh, 20th Regiment, Native Infantry
Jamadar Faiz Khan, 3rd Regiment, Light Cavalry

Colonel G. M. C. Smyth, Commanding the 3rd Regiment, Light Cavalry, was called into Court of Inquiry who reported that firstly it was ordered to the Havildar-Major, Shaik Baksh Ali to load and fire his carbine, to show them how it was to be done; he immediately did so. Then it was ordered the cartridges to be served out to the 90 men on parade. The first man to whom the cartridge was offered was Shaikh Peer Ali, Naik. He said that he would get a bad name if he took it. It was said to him, "You see the Havildar-Major has taken and fired one"; he replied: "If all the men will take the cartridges, I will." He assigned no reason for not taking it, but still refused to do as he was ordered. The next man Ameer Qudrat Ali, Naik, who stood in the rear of Shaikh Peer Ali, was ordered to do so, but he also refused, saying, "If all the regiment will take cartridges, I will." After this, it was ordered to each man in succession to take his cartridges, but except for five men, all refused.[6]

In the Court of Inquiry, all 85 troopers of the 3rd Regiment of the Light Cavalry were charged and placed in confinement. They were as follows:[7]
Matadin, Shaikh Peer Ali, Ameer Qudrat Ali, Shaikh Hashmuddin, Shaikh Noor Mohammad, Sheetal Singh, Jahangeer Khan, Meer Mohsin Ali, Ali Noor Khan, Meer Hussain Baksh, Mathura Singh, Narain Singh, Lall Singh, Shivdin Singh, Shaikh Hussain Buksh, Sahibdad Khan, Bishan Singh, Baldeo Singh, Shaikh Nandu, Nawab Khan, Shaikh Ramzan Ali, Ali Mohammad Khan, Maukun Singh, Durga Singh, Nabi Baksh Khan, Nasrullah Beg, Meer Akib Khan, Durga Singh, Nabi Baksh Khan, Jurakhan Singh, Najju Khan, Jurakhan Singh, Abdullah Khan, Kasam Khan, Zabardast Khan, Murtaza

Khan, Badjor Singh, Azeemullah Khan, Azeemullah Khan, Kalla Khan, Shaikh Sadullah, Salar Baksh Khan, Shaikh Rahat Ali, Dwarka Singh, Kalka Singh, Raghubeer Singh, Baldeo Singh, Darshan Singh, Imdad Hussain, Peer Khan, Moti Singh, Shaikh Fazal Imam, Heera Singh, Sewak Singh, Murad Sher Khan, Shaikh Aram Ali, Kashi Singh, Musharraf Ali Khan, Khudadad Khan, Shaikh Rustam, Bhagwan Singh, Meer Imdad Ali, Shiv Baksh Singh, Lakshman Singh, Shaikh Imam Baksh, Usman Khan, Maksood Ali Khan, Shaikh Ghazi Baksh, Shaikh Umed Ali, Abdul Wahab Khan, Ram Sahai Singh, Panah Ali Khan, Lakshman Dubey, Ramsaran Singh, Shaikh Azad Ali, Shiv Singh, Sheetal Singh, Mohan Singh, Vilayat Ali Khan, Shaikh Mohammad Ewaz, Inder Singh, Fateh Khan, Miku Singh, Shaikh Qasim Ali, Ramcharan Singh, and Dariyaw Singh.

Based on the findings of this Court of Inquiry, a General Court Martial was assembled. The prisoners were then confined in an empty hospital, and a guard of their own regiment was placed over them. The tribunal before which they were to be brought up for trial was composed of fifteen Native officers, of whom six were Muslims and nine were Hindus. Ten of these members were furnished by the regiments at Meerut Artillery, Cavalry, and Infantry; five came from the Infantry regiments at Delhi. On the 6th of May, the Court commenced its sittings, and continued its proceedings on the two following days. The Court, by a vote of fourteen members against one, found the Eighty-five guilty, and sentenced them to imprisonment and hard labour for ten years. It was a sentence doubtless designed to vindicate discipline and quell the rebellion in a bud. This sentence was recommended by the Judge Advocate General and approved by the Commander-in-Chief. Major General Hewitt requested for mercy for the condemned men on the grounds that the men were of good character and had been misled by rumours. Keeping this mercy appeal in view sentence of 11 men who had less than five years service were reduced to five years hard labour. The sentence was to be carried into effect at daybreak on the 9th of May.[8]

On 9th May 1857, the entire Meerut garrison was assembled on the European Infantry parade ground. The 85 accused were marched in front of the hollow square formed by the whole garrison. The sentences were read out; the uniforms and badges were removed; boots were taken off, and each convicted was fitted into a pair of leg-irons, fitted there and then, on to his ankles by blacksmiths. The operation lasted for several hours. The prisoners, on seeing their hands and feet manacled, looked at their medals, and wept. They remembered their services and thought how they had been recompensed, and their pride caused them to feel the degradation all the more keenly. Most of the condemned Sepoys kept silent but some shouted threats and taunted their comrades who had not mutinied and stood as the observer, some of them threw their boots at their Commanding Officer Colonel Smith. The 85 condemned prisoners were lodged in the new jail near the Suraj Kund under a guard of the 20th Native Infantry.[9]

The inner sense of the Sepoys condemned their cowardice, and they decided to revenge the torture and humiliation of their brethren. When they strolled out in the markets, the womenfolk of the town said to them scornfully, "Your brothers are in prison, and you are lounging about here killing flies! Fie upon your life!" All over the lines, that night there were a number of secret meetings of the Sepoys and it was decided to rise against the British in the evening of the next day. On 10th of May, when most of the Europeans were attending the Church prayers on Sunday evening, the Indian troops led by the 3rd Cavalry together with the two Native regiments, the 11th and 20th, seized the weapons, burnt the barracks and attacked and killed many of their officers by shouting the war cry "*Maro Firanghi Ko*" (kill the Europeans). They galloped to the jail and broke it open releasing all the prisoners, including their 85 comrades (including 85; total number of Sepoys was 1200). The markets soon thronged with crowds armed with sticks, staves, spears, and swords eager for the coming carnival of riot, plunder, and unrestrained license.[10]

The city people of the revolutionary mentality also joined the Sepoys and were responsible for most of the loot, plunder, and atrocities committed against the women and children. The most famous among these brutalities was the killing and hacking to pieces of a pregnant British lady. Subsequently, it was discovered that she had been killed by a Muslim butcher from the city who was caught and hanged at the same place where he had killed the lady. There was a complete breakdown of law and order in the city. An eye witness Mackenzie writes that "shouts of '*Maro! Maro!*' (kill! kill!), began to be heard among them, and we all thought the end was approaching .... the whole cantonments seemed one mass of flames." Colonel Finnis of the 11th, who had approached to pacify them, was cut down; the next victims were Captain Macdonald of the 20th who tried to control them and Mr. Tregoar of the Education Department, who had unfortunately gone along the lines. Besides Colonel Finnis, seven officers, three officers' wives, some children, and many other European men, women, and children were massacred. The death toll of the revolutionaries and Native Sepoys who were killed in the counter actions was six times more than the Europeans. According to an estimate, some 300 Europeans and Natives were killed during the conflict. Out of them, about 50 European men (including soldiers), women and children were killed in Meerut by Sepoys and local crowds.[11]

Mackenzie writes, "Our women and children and unarmed civilian refugees were given shelter in the 'Damdama,' an often-described walled enclosure. The Generals and their staffs and many other officers took refuge in a barrack, over which a guard was duly mounted. Piquets, in lying and outlying, were told off, and every precaution was taken to prevent the cantonments being rushed by the 'budmashes' of the 'Burra Bazaar' or the Goojars of the neighbouring villages!"[12]

As there were only two Sepoy regiments of infantry and one of the cavalry, while there was a complete riflemen battalion and a regiment of dragoons of Europeans there; besides, the whole of the artillery was in the hands of the Europeans; the Sepoys had no chance of success. Therefore, immediately after the rising, the Sepoys went away towards

Delhi, leaving the work of revenge to the townsmen of Meerut. Soon, however, the cry was raised— "Quick, brother, quick, Delhi, Delhi," and the revolutionaries fled across the road towards the Mughal capital, expecting every moment that the white soldier would pursue and overwhelm them. They crossed the Jumna; some going straight to the palace by way of the bridge of boats, while others forded the river came to Delhi and asked the Emperor to give his blessing to their war against the British. As a letter sent out by the revolutionary leaders subsequently put it: "The English are people who overthrow all religions ... As the English are the common enemy of both (Hindus and Muslims), we should unite in their slaughter ... By this alone will the lives and faiths of both be saved."[13]

Kaye narrates the quotes of the Commander-in-Chief that it was natural that the safety of the cantonment was his first care; nevertheless, Hewitt commanded the whole Meerut Division, including the great station of Delhi, with its immense magazine, and not a single European soldier to guard its profusion of military stores. The danger was not local, but national; danger no less portentous in its political than in its military aspects. However, not an effort was made to intercept the fatal flood of mutiny that was streaming into Delhi. General Hewitt ignored the fact that the whole of the Meerut Division was under his military charge, and thinking only of the safety of the place in which lie himself resided; he stood upon the defensive for many days, whilst the rebels of the Lines, of the Gaols, and the Bazaars, were rejoicing in the work that they had done with impunity equal to their success.[14]

Here it needs to be mentioned that when the Sepoys mutinied, there were a large number of Europeans and loyal Sepoys at Meerut, but they didn't follow the mutineers. Kaye narrates that the military commanders at Meerut believed that it was their primary duty to protect life and property in the Cantonment. Forrest quotes the portions of a letter, written by Major- General A. Wilson in Meerut, that European force then stationed at Meerut consisted of the 6th Dragoon Guards (Carabineers), half of whom were recruits unable to ride, Her Majesty's 60th Rifles, about 800 strong, a troop of horse artillery, a light field battery, and 200 artillery recruits, who had been learnt nothing beyond the initial principles of foot drill, being totally unacquainted with gun drill or the use of the carbine.[15]

Kaye further says by quoting the writings of Henry Lawrence, "How unmindful have we been that what occurred in the city of Kabul may someday occur at Dehli, Meerut, or Bareilly........ There were troopers without horses, troopers that could not ride — artillerymen without guns, and artillerymen who did not know a mortar from a howitzer, or the difference between the round-shot and grape. This was not the fault of General Hewitt or Brigadier Wilson; it was the fault of the system — the policy."[16]

According to General Hewitt's witness report, the 20th, 11th Regiments, Native Infantry, with 3rd Regiment, Light Cavalry, and shot down the officers who were on parade and galloped down to the jail to rescue the 85 men of the corps and at the same time liberated all the other prisoners, about 1,200 in number. The mutineers then fired nearly all the bungalows' including Mr. Greathed's, the Commissioners, and his own, together with the Government cattle-yard and commissariat officer's house and office. In this, they were assisted by the population of the bazaar, the city, and the neighbouring villages. Every European man, woman, and child fallen in with was ruthlessly murdered. The loss of life at Meerut was about forty, including Colonel Finnis, 11th Regiment, Native Infantry; Captain Taylor and Captain Macdonald, 20th Regiment, Native Infantry, together with the wife and two children of the latter; Henderson, Lieutenant Pattle Macnabb, Veterinary-Surgeons Phillips and Dawson, together with the wife of the latter.[17]

Before returning of the Europeans from the Church, the rebellious Sepoys rushed towards Delhi. The European forces instead of following the fugitive Sepoys in every remained to guard the burning bungalows, the corpses of the slain and their own barracks. Frazer says that although there were enough English troops, artillery, rifles, and carbineers to scatter the mutineers and all the badmashes of the city from out of Meerut, but there was no head to guide them, no Gillespie as at Vellore, no Hearsey as in Barrackpur, to lead them forth and save Europeans from the horrors that ensued.[18]

The British took the precaution within a few hours of the Meerut rising; the Electric Telegraph was carrying the evil tidings to all parts throughout the country. The note of warning was sounded across the whole length and breadth of India; and wherever an Englishman was stationed there was the stem preparation of the defence. Apart from all the precautions taken by the Europeans, the Sepoys and the civilians totaling about 2000 in number, entered Delhi, massacred every Christian man, woman, and child they could find and formed their own Government under 82-year-old last Mughal Emperor Bahadur Shah Zafar.

References:

1. Dodd, pp. 49-50
2. Handcock, Arthur Gore, *The Siege of Delhi in 1857: A Short Account*, Allahabad, 1897, p. 3
3. Nevill, H. R., *District Gazetteers of the United Provinces of Agra and Oudh*, Vol. IV, Allahabad, 1904, p. 163
4. Forrest, George W., *Selections from the Letters Dispatches and other State Papers Preserved in the Military Department of the Government of India 1857-58*, Volume I, Calcutta, 1893, (Hereafter quoted as Forrest), pp. 227-228
5. *Ibid*, p. 230
6. *Ibid*, p. 231
7. *Ibid*, pp. 239-240
8. Kaye, John William, *A History of the Sepoy War in India, 1857-58*, Vol. II, London 1874, pp. 48-51 see also *Defense Journal*, Vol. 3, No. 9, Islamabad, December,1999, *The Living Age,* Volume 0055, Issue 702, New York, November

7, 1857, p. 329, and Qasmi, Ataur Rahman, *Hindustan Ki Pahli Jang Azadi 1857 Me Musalmanon Ka Hissa*, New Delhi, 2008, p. 40

9. Kaye, John William, *A History of the Sepoy War in India, 1857-58*, Vol. II, London 1874, p. 51, see also Nevill, H. R., *District Gazetteers of the United Provinces of Agra and Oudh*, Vol. IV, Allahabad, 1904, p. 164, Forrest, Volume I, Calcutta, 1893, p. Introduction 20, and Mackenzie, A. R. D., *Mutiny Memoirs: Being Personal Reminiscences of the Great Sepoy Revolt of 1857*, Pioneer Press, Allahabad, 1892, p. 6 (The same day in the evening, Lieutenant Bough visited the jail to meet the imprisoned Sepoys, who had spent 30 to 40 years of their lives fighting for the British. Many of the prisoners wept bitterly before the British officer. Most of the senior officers including the Governor General viewed the sentences as too harsh. But main villain was the Judge Advocate General who persuaded the Commander-in-Chief to confirm the sentences. *Defense Journal*, Vol. 3, No. 9, Islamabad, December,1999, see also *The Living Age*, Volume 0055, Issue 702, New York, November 7, 1857, p. 329)

10. Nevill, H. R., *District Gazetteers of the United Provinces of Agra and Oudh*, Vol. IV, Allahabad, 1904, p. 164, see also Savarkar, p. 94, (It was really strange that the army (Native and European) stationed at Meerut was almost equal in number (2,028 Europeans against 2,057 Natives), yet the mutineers originally few hundred could not be controlled. The General Officer Commanding Major General William Henry Hewitt answered when he once asked the reasons for his inaction at Meerut, "As soon as the alarm was given, the artillery, carabineers, and 60th Rifles were got under arms, but by the time we reached the Native parade ground, it was too dark to act with efficiency in that direction; consequently the troops were retired to the North of the nullah." *Defense Journal*, Vol. 3, No. 9, Islamabad, December,1999)

11. *Ibid*, p. 164, see also Edward, Gilliat, *Heroes of the Indian Mutiny; Stories of Heroic Deeds*, London 1914, p. 133, Mead, Henry, *The Sepoy Revolt: Its causes and its Consequences*, London, 1858, p. 97, and Mackenzie, A. R. D., *Mutiny Memoirs: Being Personal Reminiscences of the Great Sepoy Revolt of 1857*, Pioneer Press, Allahabad, 1892, p. 15

12. Mackenzie, A. R. D., *Mutiny Memoirs: Being Personal Reminiscences of the Great Sepoy Revolt of 1857*, Pioneer Press, Allahabad, 1892, p. 36

13. Argyl, Campbell, George Douglas, Duke of, *India Under Dalhousie and Canning*, London, 1865, pp. 88-89, see also, Savarkar, p. 96, Forrest, Volume I, Calcutta, 1893, p. Introduction 22, Anderson, Clare, *The Indian Uprising of 1857-8: Prisons, Prisoners and Rebellion*, London, 2007, p. 3, and Tracy, Louis, *The Red Year; A Story of The Indian Mutiny*, New York 1907, p. 42

14. Kaye, John William, *Kay's and Malleson's History of the Indian Mutiny of 1857-8*, Vol. II, London, 1910, p. 77

15. *Ibid*, see also Forrest, Volume I, Calcutta, 1893, p. 260

16. Kaye, John William, *Kay's and Malleson's History of the Indian Mutiny of 1857-8*, Vol. II, London, 1910, p. 78

17. Forrest, Volume I, Calcutta, 1893, pp. 249 & 255

18. Frazer, R. W., *British India*, New York 1896, p. 282

Chapter 3

Delhi, the Centre of Uprising

Delhi, the ancient capital of India, also known as the Rome of Asia was large and well-fortified city, high up on the banks of the Jumna. It was having eleven huge gates, each a small fort in itself, and a massive wall of seven miles long and twenty-four feet in height. The wall was protected by a dry fosse, or ditch, twenty-five feet wide and about twenty feet deep; this, in turn, was guarded by a counterscarp and glacis. Delhi had seven gates on the land-side, named, respectively, the Lahore, Ajmer, Turkman, Kabul, Mori, Kashmiri, and Agra Gates; while along the riverfront were four others, the Rajghat, Negumbod, Lall, and Kala Gates. Besides this, the glories of Delhi are the Jama Masjid and Red Fort. Delhi enjoyed the glorious periods from Prithvi Raj Chauhan to the Mughal Emperor Aurangzeb and the later rulers under the protection of Rohillas, Marathas, and the British. In 1803, British occupied the city by driving the Marathas. They stationed their Native brigade 38th, 54th, 74th Native Infantry and a battery of Native Artillery in the cantonment about two miles from the western wall of the city situated on and below the Ridge and commanded by Brigadier Graves. During the British period and just before the Uprising of 1857 Delhi, comprising the 160,000, population, witnessed the communal harmony, religious toleration, and fraternity.

Robert Edward Forrest has very beautifully described the daily morning atmosphere in Delhi, "Sweet the sound of English church bells, strange the moaning of the Hindu conch-shell, mellow the vibration of the disk of metal sonorous of the great Burmese gong; but of all such sounds the finest is the voice of the high-placed muezzin loudly proclaiming the greatness of God: 'Allah-ho-Akbar!'—'Allah-ho-Akbar!'"[1]

He again describes the beauty of Chandni Chawk, "…. main street of the town, named Star Street, in order to give expression to the sense of its excessive brightness, of its sparkling beauty. In it were to be found congregated the shops of the superior classes of tradesmen, whom the ancient splendour of the Court of Khizrabad had brought into the city in such numbers — the diamond merchants, and the shawl merchants, and the dealers in cloth of gold; and the shops of the higher classes of handicraftsmen — the goldsmiths, and the silversmiths, and the workers in enamel, and the miniature-painters who have preserved to us the faces of the celebrated men and women of the East — of Akbar, of Roshanara Begam, of Shah Jahan, and of Sheikh Sadi of Shiraz; here were to be seen the gay, tinsel-covered skullcaps of muslin or bright silk for the men, the gold-embroidered, spangle-covered petticoats and trousers for the women; here were shops full of bright-coloured paper kites'; shops full of bright soft muslins, and the chintzes on which the same patterns have been imprinted for thousands of years; here were to be seen the gleaming braziers' shops."[2]

On the eve of the Uprising, there was a deep hatred against the British in Delhi, which has been quoted by various historians. It was a coincident that at the same time a war between England and Persia was going on, and the Shah of Persia was in open correspondence with the Emperor Bahadur Shah Zafar. It resulted in the change of the mentality of not only the palace but the whole city as well. The Shah of Persia was in the hope that a simultaneous rising in India would be helpful to Persia. In the Declaration of the Emperor Bahadur Shah Zafar, it had been made quite clear that a confidential agent had been sent to Persia from the Delhi Darbar. While this intrigue was going on at the Darbar of the Shah, right in the city of Delhi agitation had begun to stir public feeling to its very depths. For this work, even public proclamations were sometimes posted up on the walls of the town. V.D. Savarkar mentions a proclamation which was pasted in public places at the beginning of 1857. According to the proclamation, "The army of Persia is going to free India from the hands of the Firangis. So, young and old, big and small, literate and illiterate, civil and military, all Hindustani brothers should leap forth into the field to free themselves from the Kafirs." The Indian newspapers used to publish these Proclamations and to criticize them in a mysterious language. The various Shahzadas and their retainers in the palaces of Delhi openly and secretly spread disaffection, and were engaged in weaving a network of conspiracies.[3]

V.D. Savarkar quotes some examples of hatred against the British on the eve of the Uprising of 1857. He mentions that in the grounds of Prince Nawab Bakht, for six years, Sergeant Fleming's son had been practicing riding. However, at the beginning of April 1857, the prince, excited beyond measure, said, "Away, get away from here. I boil with rage when I see the face of any Firangi" So saying, he spat on him! Savarkar again quotes that Mrs. Aldwell says in her evidence, that she had personally heard Mohammad Jan's mothers asking their children to pray that the English should be destroyed root and branch.[4]

Meerut Sepoys of the three Native regiments and rioters numbering more than two thousand from the Meerut city and other nearby places reached to the Delhi in the morning of 11th May. They marched to Red Fort by crossing Jumna through the bridge of boats and killing the toll keeper and firing the toll house. The Kashmiri gate and Calcutta gate were opened, and the Sepoys entered the city with shouting of *Deen! Deen!* and 'Long live the Emperor, Victory to the Emperor'. They assembled on the ground in the river bed, under the walls of the Emperor's apartments, known as the '*Zer Jharokha*' and demanded admittance. The Emperor heard the noise and sent Captain Douglas, commandant of the Palace Guards, to see the matter. Douglas stepped to the balcony overhanging the courtyard and saw thirty or forty of the troopers standing below. He ordered them to depart, as their standing opposite to the monarch's private apartments was an act of disrespect to the King. They dispersed gradually, but as they spread over the palace, they roused the inmates with their religious cry, *Deen! Deen!*[5]

They again came and forcibly admitted into the Palace. They killed all white men and women they found within the fort wall. They cut down the Commissioner of Delhi, Mr. Fraser, Captain Douglas, the Collector, Mr. Hutchinson, the Chaplain Mr. Jennings, his daughter, and Miss Clifford. The fury soon spread from the palace to the city. Delhi bank was attacked first, its manager, Mr. Beresford was slain, and the bank was stormed and gutted. The church and every house occupied by Christian or Europeans were attacked and rifled and no quarter was given to age or sex. They not even left the Indians who were converted to Christianity. The revolutionaries, in the city, were greeted with lotus flowers and chapatis and were urged to clear Delhi by the British. A slogan of '*Prithvi Raj Ki Jai*' was again raised after many hundred years.[6]

Indian regiments of the Sepoys at Delhi were in wait of the Meerut Sepoys and they welcomed them after their arrival. The 38th NI was first who united with the revolutionaries. The officers of the 54th Native Infantry led their men towards the city gates and ordered the Sepoys under him to fire on the Meerut troopers, but they refused with insulting expressions, and instead some fired on their own officers. Colonel Ripley, Smith, Burrowes, Edwards, and Waterfield were shot dead. The colonel of the 74th also ordered his soldiers to fire on the Meerut Sepoys but they also followed the example of 54th. Gordon of 38th, the field-officer of the day, fell dead from his horse; Smith and Reveley of the 74th met the same fate. The 74th NI also joined the revolutionaries. They galloped on the Ridge, the cantonment, and the Metcalfe House near the Qutub Minar. However, for them neither the cantonment nor the Metcalfe house were safe refuges, so they ran away throwing each and every belonging. The officers ran in different directions. Many were cut down, but some went off together.[7]

Munshi Jeewan Lal[8] in his Roznamcha narrates the story of 11th May as follows:[9]

"On the morning of the 11th May, between eight and nine o'clock, a wonderful report reached me as it spread through the city, that some cavalry and foot soldiers had arrived from Meerut, and were in the bazaar plundering and killing the people..... Europeans were being killed in every direction, and their property plundered. The Bank had been broken into and robbed; Mr. Bensford, the Manager, and Mr. Hara murdered, others had hid themselves. Mr. Nixon, Head Clerk of the Commissioner's Office, had been killed, and his body was lying on the road; Mr. Neil, the Second Clerk, together with Mr. Peppe and the children, had concealed themselves, but the soldiers had managed to find out their hiding place, and had killed them all. .... Next came news that Mr. Simon Fraser, the Commissioner, and Mr. Henderson had escaped and that Sir John Metcalfe, the joint Magistrate, and Mr. Le Bas, the Judge, had also got away, no one could tell where. Sir John was thought to have gone to the Kutub.... .Budmashes were naming me as being the Mir-Munshi (Chief Writer) to the Agent of the Governor General, and as one worthy of death… and had killed the surgeon, Dr. Chuman Lal, who had been as usual attending his patients in the Daryaganj Hospital."

After a large massacre of the Europeans and in the late hours of 11th May, two Subedars were admitted to a private audience to the Emperor Bahadur Shah as the representatives of the crowds of soldiery and asked the Emperor to give his blessing to their war against the British. As a letter sent out by them subsequently put it: "The English are people who overthrow all religions … As the English are the common enemy of both (Hindus and Muslims), we should unite in their slaughter … By this alone will the lives and faiths of both be saved." They were directed to take their orders from Hakim Ahsanullah Khan. According to Munshi Jeewan Lal, Hakim Ahsanullah Khan asked them: "You have been long accustomed under the English rule to regular pay. The King has no treasury. How can he pay you?" The officers replied: "We will bring the revenue of the whole Empire to your treasury." Subsequently, a regiment of the cavalry arrived and took up a position in the courtyard of the Dewan-i-Khas. In order to restore normalcy, the orders were issued by Ahsanullah Khan directing, the different Princes to assume command of the several regiments.[10]

Mughal Emperor Bahadur Shah Zafar, on hearing the intention of the Sepoys, showed some hesitation but lastly agreed to give his countenance to the rebellion. The 82 years-old Emperor was formally declared the Emperor of Hindustan. The formal court was held, which was abandoned 15 years ago. The court was attended by many excited or unruly Sepoys who were unaware of the etiquettes and royal assembling. He named Mirza Mughal as Commander-in-Chief, and gave the title of General of Cavalry to Mirza Abu Bakar; he posted about eight or nine thousand mutineers and volunteers at the several gates of the city and also cantoned in the Daryaganj Bazaar. Additional guns were placed on the ramparts; and the Native sappers and miners were placed in command of the cannon in the old fort of Salimgarh. Hakim Ahsanullah summoned the leading men of Delhi, and it was decided to send the letters to the Rajas of Patiala, Jhajjar, Ballabhgarh, Bahadurgarh, and Alwar to march at once upon Delhi with all their forces to join the King's army, and to repel any attack on the city by the English. Mughal Emperor Bahadur Shah Zafar also mounted on an elephant, passed in procession through the streets and personally appealed to allay the fears of the citizens and order the people to resume their ordinary occupations. Most of the Native states also joined the Uprising and taken oath of allegiance to the Emperor.[11]

Just after enthroning Mughal Emperor Bahadur Shah Zafar, revolutionary felt it necessary to capture the city arsenal. In this arsenal, there was a vast quantity of ammunition useful for war. At least 900,000 cartridges, 8 to 10 thousand rifles, guns, and siege-trains were there. Without its capture, the life of the Uprising was not safe for a moment; so thousands of Sepoys made ready to carry out the task. They sent a message by the name of the Emperor to the officers of the arsenal, asking them to surrender. However, the Commissary of ordnances Lieutenant Willoughby did not even condescend to reply to the note. At this insult, many of the infuriated Sepoys began to mount the walls of the arsenal. To their aid came also hundreds of the citizens of Delhi. Within the walls were nine Englishmen and some Natives. The British ultimately blew the magazine which resulted nine British soldiers, twenty-five Sepoys and about three hundred men in the neighbouring streets blown to pieces![12]

After the arsenal blast in which hundreds of Indians were killed, the Sepoys determined to revenge the slavery and arsenal. They started massacring of hundreds of Europeans, and wherever the Englishman was found, he was killed. The massacre which was started on 11th May, ended on May 16. A small number of the Europeans left the cantonment near Ridge and after suffering terrible privations, some reached Meerut, 40 miles, others Karnal, 80 miles, and a few got to Ambala, 140 miles distant, exhausted and half dead. In the long way, the fugitives hid themselves by day and walked by night, and, though frequently robbed and beaten by villagers, they were in some cases kindly received. Evelyn Wood quotes the words of Captain Holland that how Jumna Dass, a Brahman, housed and fed him for a week; and Paltu, a sweeper living near, went daily to other villages to procure milk for the Europeans. There were some of all classes who risked their own lives to secure the European unfortunate people.[13]

For the protection of their capital Delhi, the Sepoys posted their heavy guns on the Ridge near Delhi, about two miles in distance from the walled city, which later became the base of the British camp. But the Delhi was free from any attack for the whole month of May as the British forces marched towards the city very slowly.

After hearing the great disaster of 11th May, many of the Europeans, gathered themselves in one of the largest and strongest houses, occupied by the Christian people. They barricaded themselves in that strong house. However, the defence was impossible for long; the house was stormed, and the defenders were dragged to the Palace and thrust into an underground chamber. About forty nine Christian people; men, women, and children were huddled together. After four or five days of this suffering, a servant of the King asked one of the ladies in the dungeon how, if they were restored to power, the English would treat the Natives; and the answer was, "Just as you have treated our husbands and children." On the following day, they were led forth to die. According to Kaye & Malleson, the Palace-guards came to the prison-door and told them to come forth, as they were to be taken to a better residence. They were taken to a courtyard; the appointed shambles; where great crowds of people were gathered together to witness the massacre of the Christians. So on 16th May, they were killed in spite of the objections of the Emperor. Their bodies were taken away in carts and pitched into the muddy flowing Jumna. After that 16th of May, there were no more Christians left in Delhi.[14]

Once the Sepoys seized Delhi on 11th May 1857, and persuaded or pressurized or coerced the Mughal Emperor Bahadur Shah Zafar into leading them, they changed their status from mutineers to that of freedom fighters. The Meerut revolutionaries were followed by the other mutinous Sepoy regiments which steadily revolted against the

British, in the succeeding months, estimating about 100,000 out of the 139,807 Sepoys of the Bengal army. The 3rd Light Cavalry provided a blueprint of action to all the Sepoys of the entire Bengal Army, and they established a pattern which was followed by the Sepoys at Lucknow on 1st July, in Kanpur on 4th June, in Bareilly and Shahjahanpur on 31st May and in Jhansi on 5th of June. The Sepoys stationed at Sitapur rebelled on 3rd June 1857. The 9th Awadh Irregular Infantry stationed in Sitapur also joined the rebellion. On the 4th of June 1857, Sepoys at Khairabad mutinied. The 17 Native Infantry stationed at Azamgarh also joined the rebellion in June. Troops in Faizabad the major town of Awadh apart from Lucknow rebelled on 8th June 1857. The troops of Nawab Ganj, Chinhat, and Bara Banki also joined the revolt in mid June of 1857. The remaining troops of Lucknow by 30th June also mutinied and Sir Henry Montgomery Lawrence, British Commissioner of Awadh, left Lucknow Residency. In the Doab area, the Sepoys rebelled on 20th May 1857 at Aligarh, on 22nd May at Mainpuri, on 23rd May at Etawa and on 24th May at Bulandshahar. Allahabad Sepoys joined the Uprising on 6th June 1857. Badaun and Moradabad joined the rebellion on 1st and 3rd June. At Nimach, the Sepoys rebelled on 6th June and Gwalior, Mehidpur (Malwa) and Nowgong the Sepoys revolted on 9th June. The Sepoys of Indore revolted on 1st of July 1857. Although Rajputana remained loyal to the British, there is evidence of troopers who rushed to Delhi from different areas of Rajputana. At Punjab, the Sepoys of Ambala, Amritsar, Lahore, Peshawar, Mardan, Dera Ismail Khan, and Mianwali were dispersed and disarmed. The Sepoys at Ferozpur and Jallandhar were mutinied on 14th May and 7th June 1857. At Jaunpur, Ghazipur and Mirzapur, the Sepoys were disarmed. The Sepoys of Dinapur rebelled on 25th July 1857 and joined Kunwar Singh of Jagdishpur. The 12th Irregular Cavalry at Segowlee on the Nepal border rebelled in June 1857 and 32 Native Infantry in Orissa also rebelled in June 1857.[15]

According to one estimate one-fifth of the Indian population in 1857 directly or indirectly participated in the Uprising. By the popular support, different centres like Delhi, Patna, Arrah, Azamgarh, Allahabad, Gorakhpur, Faizabad, Fatehpur, Jhansi, Lucknow, Kanpur, Etawah, Fategarh, Gwalior, Shahjahanpur, Agra, Bharatpur, Rohilkhand, Mathura, Agra, Hathras, Delhi, Meerut, Bareilly and Roorki, etc, emerged as storm-centres of the Revolt. In this entire region, the dispossessed tallukdars and impoverished peasants and artisans, including Muslim fanatics known as *Jihadi, Ghazi,* or *Mujahideen* joined the Sepoys to contest the English authority. Almost all the areas of North and Central India were burning in the flame of the Uprising. Massacre of European's looting and plundering of their property was common throughout the period of the Uprising. According to Karl Marx, "It is the first time that Sepoy regiments have murdered their European officers; that Musalmans and Hindus, renouncing their mutual antipathies, have combined against their common masters." He further says, "disturbances beginning with the Hindus, have actually, ended in placing on the throne of Delhi a Mohammedan Emperor."[16]

The neighboring areas of Delhi like Mewat, the choudharies of the villages controlled the administration by the name of the Emperor Bahadur Shah Zafar. Muslim religious leaders like Maulana Fazlul Haq Khairabadi, etc. declared *Jihad* against the British and joined the Sepoys. The civil population in this revolt who were also fighting shoulder to shoulder with the British consisted of three groups, the feudal nobility, rural landlords and the peasants and all these three groups had their own grievances against the British. Emperor Bahadur Shah Zafar through the Court of Administration and other office bearers tried to control the administration, issued *Farmans* and coins in his name. The contemporary and modern accounts suggest that he was coerced by the Sepoys and his courtiers to sign the proclamation against his will to which the Emperor also accepted in his trial. In fact, these forcible decisions were perhaps situation based but many times Emperor took the independent decisions and unapproved the advice of the most powerful Court of Administration.

The loss of Delhi was a crushing blow to British prestige and the symbolic associations of the capital of the Mughals becoming the center of the revolt was something the British could not ignore. It took British nearly two months to regroup, and then they set out to reclaim Delhi. On the 27th of May, Brigadier Archdale Wilson, accompanied by Mr. Greathed, marched out of Meerut in the direction of Delhi with the object of uniting with the Ambala forces, which were to be concentrated in Karnal, and effect a junction by way of Baghpat. The column to attack Delhi was to consist of three brigades. The 1st Brigade under Brigadier Halifax consisted the forces of 75th Regiment, 1st Bengal Europeans, two Squadrons 9th Lancers, one Troop Horse Artillery. The second Brigade under Brigadier Jones consisted the forces of 2nd Bengal Europeans 60th Native Infantry, two Squadrons 9th Lancers, one Squadron 4th Bengal Lancers, one Troop Horse Artillery. The third one Meerut Brigade under Brigadier Wilson consisted of four Companies 60th, two Squadrons Carabineers, one Battery Field Artillery, one Troop Horse Artillery, one Company Native Sappers, 120 Foot Artillerymen. The total strength of the British force according to the siege plan was about 400 European Cavalry, 100 Native Cavalry, 2200 European Infantry, 900 Native Infantry, 22 Field Guns.[17]

They arrived at Ghaziuddin Nagar (Ghaziabad of Uttar Pradesh) on 30th of May and halted their camp until 4th of June to wait the incoming enforcement. They further halted at Baghpat on 6th June. On the 7th of June, the European forces like Sirmuri Battalion of Gorkhas, Nabha Contingent, Farquhar's Baluchis, Jind Horse, Kashmiri Contingent, Multani Horse, Kumaon Battalion, Coke's Pathan Borderers, and lastly, a day after Punjab Guides reached over Delhi and encamped at Alipur, 12 miles from Delhi.[18]

Stationing at Alipur, the British forces met with tough resistance from the revolutionaries of Delhi in the battle of Badli ki Sarai, 6 miles to the North of Delhi, on the 8th June, 1857. Commander-in-Chief, Henry Barnard moved towards the Ridge overlooking Delhi, drove thence the revolutionaries posted there, and encamped in the position whence he could best direct his attacks on the proud city of Delhi. Thus, the

British forces find the Ridge, the most suited place, firmly established a base camp on the Ridge. The Ridge was the thin spur of high ground to the North of the city of Delhi, and a continuous fight started from June to September, 1857. The British forces drove the revolutionaries within the walls, with a loss to them of about 350 men, twenty-six guns, and some serviceable ammunition. The gain of the British under Henry Bernard, in the battle of Badli ki Sarai, was the occupation of the Ridge, the finest base of operations against the city, a position open in the rear to the reinforcements which he hoped to receive, whilst commanding the plain right up to the walls.[19]

Greathed quotes a letter, written from Delhi Cantonments near Ridge on June 8, "We fought our way to Delhi this morning, accomplishing everything that was proposed, capturing twelve guns and routing the enemy. .... The fire was very heavy, but our Infantry advanced on the position, and the Artillery and Cavalry took it in flank, and after a severe contest the enemy fled, and we advanced without further opposition to the Delhi Parade Ground. The enemy then opened from the ridge behind cantonments; they were attacked by two columns, the right advancing through Shabzi Mandi, and the left through cantonments. Wilby was with the former and I with the latter, and we were glad to see each other again at Hindu Rao's House where the two columns met after scouring the ridge and driving off the enemy......"[20]

After setting up of European forces at Ridge, a daily fight started in places like Shabzi Mandi, Alipur, Hindu Rao's House, Metcalfe's House, Kisanganj, Najafgarh, Paharipur, Eidgah, Paharipur, Flag Staff Tower, Teliwara, etc. with heavy loss for both the sides.

These were the very challenging days of the British in the history of their occupation of Indian Territory. On 23rd June, the centenary of Plassey, the revolutionary came out with all their available men and guns for the final decisive battle as there was a prophecy which had long been quoted that on this day, they were destined to overthrow the Firangi rule. The astrologers calculated it; the holy Brahmins read it; the spirits of the conjurors and the dice of the soothsayers all told the same tale. It was written that assuredly on this day the reign of the white people would be over. Unfortunately, on the side of the British, the Sikh corps arrived from the Punjab on the same day and gave the specimen of their fighting powers to the revolutionaries. All day long, the fight went on under a burning sun which knocked over many officers and men; Hodson was in the saddle most of the day and bears testimony to the conduct of his old Guides and his new Sikhs and Gorkhas. In this battle, the British suffered a lot from this fierce sortie. The revolutionaries were also met a heavy loss. In the village Shabzi Mandi around 400 dead bodies were found. The total loss of the revolutionaries was about 1600 men.[21]

This was the period when both the parties suffered from the deadly heat. It affected a lot to the Europeans who were encamped on the Ridge, which was the hottest place in the surroundings of Delhi. Thousands of Europeans fell by sun stroke and invalided to fight against the revolutionaries. They suffered a lot from sun stroke, Cholera, and fever than bullet shots. Henry Barnard was also died out of Cholera.

While the revolutionaries were active in fighting the British, the worst role, they played was the loot and plunder of the city of Delhi. The helpless Emperor Bahadur Shah Zafar issued order after order that the inhabitants of the city must not be plundered. However, unfortunately, no order was obeyed and there was no omen to enforce them. Fortunately, on 1st July 1857, a very experienced Bareilly leader, field battery commander Mohammad Bakht Khan, arrived in Delhi with a large military contingent and joined the revolutionaries. He assured the Emperor that he shall drive away the English out of Delhi and Meerut. A shield, a sword, and the title of General were bestowed on Mohammad Bakht Khan, and he was appointed Commander-in-Chief of the whole Native forces. General Bakht Khan also received the title of *Farzand* later on. A proclamation was issued ordering the attendance of all officers in command of regiments to receive instructions from Mohammad Bakht Khan. Mirza Mughal was appointed Adjutant General.[22]

Mohammad Bakht Khan inflicted strict law and order. He informed even the Emperor that if any of the Princes attempted to plunder the city, he would cut off their noses and ears. He also informed the Kotwal of the city that if any more plundering took place, he would be hanged. Soldiers plundering were to be arrested. The General Mohammad Bakht Khan ordered a proclamation, by beat of drum, that all shopkeepers were to keep arms, and that no one should leave his house unarmed. Persons having no arms to apply to headquarters for them, and they would be given them free of charge. Any soldier caught plundering was to have his arm severed from his body. The General ordered to fine all those plundering, and to give compensation to the plundered victims. He was also instructed to arrange for the civil administration, the police, and revenue departments. By order of the Emperor Bahadur Shah Zafar, the royal princes were relieved of all further duties connected with the army.[23]

In order to weaken the position of the enemy, the revolutionaries tried their best to persuade the Gorkhas, the most trusted regiment of the British. However, these infidels never came in terms of revolutionaries. On the 10th June during a battle near Ajmeri Gate, the Gorkhas of Sirmur Battalion played a very worst role. On the advance of the Gorkhas the revolutionaries called, "We are not firing; we want to speak to you, we want you to join us." The little, stubborn Gorkhas replied: "Oh yes, we are coming, wait a bit — we are coming to you." Then, when within twenty paces of the Sepoys they fired a volley and killed nearly 80 of them.[24]

On 4th July, a large body of revolutionaries marched past to the right flank of the British along the Alipur road. Major Coke, with a force 300 cavalry 800 infantry and 12 guns, was set out to intercept the revolutionaries and had to struggle through swamp and marsh. The British met a heavy loss in both men and horses and could hardly crawl back to camp. About this attack Hodson writes, "I was mercifully preserved, though I am sorry to say my gallant Feroza was badly wounded twice with sabre-cuts, part of his bridle was cut through and a piece of my glove shaved off."[25]

On 6th of July, General Barnard was died and General Reed assumed the command in his place. Under him first most important battle was fought on 9th July in which the British met a heavy loss. The British loss on this date was 52 killed and 168 wounded. Another battle was held on 14th July, in which about 10,000 revolutionaries attacked the right flank of the enemy in the Shabzi Mandi area. At last, the revolutionaries were driven back but the Europeans suffered a lot from grape fired on them from the town. Eventually, the Shabzi Mandi was evacuated by the revolutionaries. The Adjutant-General, Chamberlain, of the British force was very severely wounded in the shoulder, the bone of his arm being shattered; and young Walker, an excellent engineer officer, was also critically wounded in the thigh. The European loss was 280 killed and wounded.[26]

On the 17th July, General Reed was invalided and Brigadier Archdale Wilson assumed the command. On the following day, especially on 18th, 20th, and 23rd July the Europeans were again attacked. On the first occasion, the British troops lost 81 men killed and wounded, including many fine class officers. Among the others was Colonel Seaton, a musket-ball striking him with some force on the breast, but glancing off; and Mr. Money of the artillery, who was shot through the knee. It was thought his wound would prove fatal, as injuries from shot were so difficult to heal. The battle held on July 23rd was also a hard nut for the Europeans and met the same suffering as usual. The revolutionaries occupied the Ludlow Castle, but they lost in the last. As a result of the battle, the British needed further assistance to the British. Sir John Lawrence again sent on 25th July, 4000 good and reliable troops from Punjab under Nicholson, of whom 1200 were the Europeans, who reached Delhi on 14th of August, 1857. Besides all the reinforcement of the British, their numerical strength was nominal in comparison of the revolutionaries which were very gallant under the command of General Bakht Khan.[27]

The date of 1st of August was very important for the revolutionaries as it was the day of Bakrid (Muslim festival of sacrifice). In the afternoon, the revolutionaries poured forth from the city gates with religious enthusiasm. Their zeal rekindled by the loud cries which rang from the minarets of the city mosques. The British force checked their advance. Again and again, the revolutionaries rallied and rushed upon the breastworks to the whole night. The air rang with the cries of the *Jihadis* and the rolling of musketry. The day dawned and the fight still continued, and it was past noon when the revolutionaries retired with heavy loss. The revolutionaries could not drive the British from the Ridge. Forrest writes that the revolutionaries made a well-planned and desperate assault in the following days and for the six weeks, day after day they cannonaded the British batteries and attacked their breastworks were forced to go back to the walls.[28]

Undoubtedly, General Bakht Khan's ability played important role in the war against the British, but it equally proved injurious to him. Slowly and gradually he began to be victimized as soldiers of many contingents raised their finger on his loyalty. According to Munshi Jeewan Lal, it was 23rd of August when the officers of the Nimuch force accused Bakht Khan of negotiating with the English, and of withholding his soldiers until the English should receive sufficient reinforcements from England. Although, General Mohammad Bakht Khan, in the presence of all the principal officers of the army, and of Mirza Mughal, swore upon the Holy Quraan that he had opened no negotiations with the English. Nimuch forces also induced to the Emperor to issue an order that General Bakht Khan should not be admitted to the Palace. They further suggested that they should be allowed to disarm the Bareilly troops, which they offered to do with four regiments of infantry and one of the cavalry. Emperor Bahadur Shah Zafar gave no answer to this proposal, but later in the day he issued orders to all the officers to obey neither the orders of Mirza Mughal nor of any other General, but approved the appointment of a council (Court of Administration) of twelve members. Out of twelve Court members, six were appointed by the Emperor and six by the army. They were responsible for the future conduct of the siege. The army was to obey all orders issued by the Court.[29]

Notwithstanding that many attacks were made on British forces vigorously and simultaneously at Badli ki Sarai, Shabzi Mandi, Alipur, Mubarak Bagh, Bada Hindu Rao, etc. and dispersed their forces and lost thousands of lives. However, Delhi proved a hard nut for the Europeans and there was constant pressure from the British Parliament on Governor General about the siege of that very historic city.

John William Kaye quotes a letter of General Wilson to Colonel Baird Smith written in August, "My dear Smith, — A letter has been received from the Governor General urging our immediately taking Delhi, and he seems angry that it has not been done long ago. I wish to explain to him the true state of affairs: that Delhi is seven miles in circumference, filled with an immense fanatical Musalman population, garrisoned by full 40,000 soldiers armed and disciplined by ourselves, with 114 heavy pieces of artillery mounted on the walls, with the largest magazine of shot, shell, and ammunition in the Upper Provinces at their disposal, besides some 60 pieces of field artillery, ……… but that it was considered, from the state of preparation against such an attack on the part of the rebels, such an attempt would inevitably have failed, and have caused the most irreparable disaster to our cause; and that, even if we had succeeded in forcing our way into the place, the small force disposable for the attack would have been most certainly lost in the numerous streets of so large a city, and have been cut to pieces. It was, therefore, considered advisable to confine our efforts to holding the position we now occupy, which is naturally strong, and has been daily rendered more so by our engineers, until the force coming up from below could join to cooperate in the attack…………"[30]

Although the great majorities of the Sepoys were Hindus, in Delhi a flag of *Jihad* was raised in the principal mosque, and many of the insurgents described themselves as *Mujahideen* or *Jihadis*. They flooded towards Delhi from various parts of North India to save their religion and nation. Indeed, by the end of the siege, after a significant proportion of the Sepoys had melted away, hungry and dispirited, the proportion of *Jihadis* in Delhi grew to be about half of the total revolutionary force, and included a regiment of "suicide *Ghazis*" from Gwalior who had vowed never to eat again and to fight until they met death at the hands of the *Kafirs*, "for those who have come to die have no need for food".[31]

After many battles and the loss of men and money outside the wall of Delhi, the serious work of the siege of Delhi from the side of the British was commenced from the 7th of September. From the night of September 7 to the day of assault, all the artillerymen in the force, European as well as Native, were constantly employed in the batteries and trenches. All reinforcements that could possibly arrive had reached to the British with siege train, and the effective force which was available for operations before Delhi consisted of the following troops:[32]

European Artillery- 580
Cavalry- 514
Infantry- 2,672
Total- 3,766

Native Artillery- 770
Cavalry- 1,313
Infantry- 3,417
Engineers, Sappers, Miners, etc.- 722
Total- 6,222

Kashmir Contingent- 2,200
Cavalry, Raja of Jind- 400
Total- 2,600
Grand Total- 12,588

From the 7th September, the continuous fight started and at last the British became successful to enter the walled city on the 14th of September, through Kashmiri Gate without serious opposition, gained possession of the large buildings in its neighborhood, and advanced along the ramparts to the Mori and Kabul Gate. For this assault, the Europeans divided themselves into five columns:[33]

1- Brigadier General Nicholson,
75th Regiment;
1st Bengal Europeans;
2nd Punjab Infantry;
Total 550 Europeans and 450 Natives. It was to storm the Kashmiri Bastion.
2- Brigadier Jones
The 8th Regiment;

The 2nd Bengal Europeans;

The 4th Sikhs;

Total 500 Europeans and 350 Natives. It was to storm the Water Bastion.

3- Colonel Campbell

52nd Light Infantry;

Kumaon Battalion of Gorkhas;

1st Punjab Infantry;

Total 250 Europeans, 750 Natives. It was to blow in and storm the Kashmiri Gate.

4- Major Reid

Sirmur Battalion of Gorkhas;

The Guides;

Some of the piquets;

The Kashmir contingent;

Total 100 Europeans and 2,000 Natives. It was to attack Kishanganj and Paharipur, and support the main attack by demonstrating against the Lahore Gate, which it was to enter after the walls were captured.

5- Brigadier Longfield (Reserve Column)

61st Regiment;

4th Punjab Infantry;

Baluch and Jind contingents;

Total 450 Europeans and 1,000 Natives. The 60th Rifles were to cover the front of the three storming columns. The remainder of the force remained in camp under arms.

In the decisive days from 14th to 20th of September, there were only 50,000 fighters, including 25,000 Sepoys and a similar number of the *Mujahideen* and city fighters. Under the command of Major Nicholson and with the support of Sikh and Gorkha army, the British were able to reclaim Delhi. The first attempt to storm the city through the breaches and the Kashmiri Gate was launched on 14th September. The attackers gained a foothold within the city but suffered heavy casualties, including John Nicholson. The 15th was employed by the British troops within the walls in securing the positions gained and preparing the means to shell the city. On the 16th, the revolutionary Sepoys evacuated Kishanganj, and the British took the magazine, full of guns and ammunition. On the 17th and 18th, the Delhi Bank and other houses were occupied by the British forces. On the 19th, the Burn bastion was taken, preparatory to an attack on the Lahore Gate. The artillery had been set up in the main mosque in the city, and the neighbourhoods within range were bombarded. These included the homes of the Muslim nobility from all over India, and contained innumerable cultural, artistic, literary, and monetary riches. Colonel John wrote to General Wilson announcing the capture of the palace in these words, "Blown open the gate, and got possession of the Palace."[34]

On the 20th, Sunday, a cry was raised, "To the Palace! To the Palace!" the British troops advanced to the Red Fort where they find some *Ghazis,* by their religious enthusiasm, to die at their posts in the Palace. Except a sentry found at each gate, there was none found left alive in the imperial premises. The British troops entered the famous fort-palace of Emperor Shah Jahan. That same day the Jama Masjid was captured by Brind, as also the Lahore Gate of the city by Brigadier Jones. The same afternoon Wilson took up his quarters in the Imperial palace.[35]

The British standard was hoisted, and a royal salute was fired in honour of the capture of Delhi and on Sunday, 20th September, a thanksgiving service was held in Dewan-i-Khas followed by dinner in the Elysium of the Dewan-i-Khas. The entire city of Delhi was occupied on Sunday, the 20th September 1857 and the revolutionaries left the city at 3 a.m. on the same day, and escaped over the bridges of boats in the direction of Rohelkhand. The British succeeded in recapturing Delhi, but this victory was not much praised as it was not due to the bravery of the soldiery but due to the desertion of the revolutionaries.[36]

The casualties of the British force day by day were most serious. In the fight commencing from 8th June, the daily average of casualties among the soldiers averaged from thirty to forty, and on occasions of vigorous combats, the loss rose from 100 to 150. Sedgwick estimates that during the three months' siege being 992 killed, and 2,845 wounded. Some of the actual regimental casualties were very severe. The 60th casualties were 389. The Gorkhas lost 319 from a total of 540. The Artillery lost 365 out of a total of 1,600. The effective strength of the troops at Delhi on the 11th September was 7,794; by the 20th, they had lost 1,674 or 21.5 per cent. Another casualty of fully 1,200, perished from cholera and other diseases, during their stay on the Ridge, was additional to those of the killed and wounded in the encounter of the revolutionaries.[37]

H.C. Fanshawe also narrates that there were 992 killed and 2845 wounded, besides hundreds who died of disease and exposure. John Kaye remarks that the total loss of the army, from the 30th May to the final capture on the 20th September, amounted to nine hundred and ninety-two killed, two thousand seven hundred and ninety-five wounded, and thirty missing, out of a force never numbering ten thousand effective men. Nevertheless, in addition to these, many died from disease and exposure.[38]

From the side of the revolutionaries of Delhi, it was estimated that the total Sepoys fought with the British were around 30,000 to 40,000. In addition to the Sepoys there were similar numbers of the undisciplined armed hoards of fanatics known as *Ghazis* and *Mujahideen* and the city patriots called by Europeans as rabbles. They were also in double of the Sepoys in numerical strength. They all fought very bravely but unfortunately as the time passed the Sepoys in order to unavailability of their salaries or wages, they started mass level desertion from the city.

In the last days or after Kashmiri Gate assault, there were only the *Mujahideen* in the city to resist the disciplined British force. However, unfortunately, they could not harm a lot to the British soldiers and martyred while fighting both in the front and in the streets. The total loss of lives of the revolutionaries was innumerable and the property which was looted and burnt was estimated in hundreds of crores. Even after six days continuous street fighting and complete occupation of Delhi, cleansed by almost all the revolutionaries and thousands of its residents, the British didn't stop their butchery and genocide.

Thousands of people fled away to the distant places leaving their old and sick men to underground apartments of their houses. Griffiths narrates, "The tai-khanas, or underground rooms of houses, scattered all over the city, were found to be filled with human beings those who, by age or infirmity, had been unable to join in the general exodus which had taken place during the last days of the siege. Hundreds of old men, women and children, were found huddled together, half starved, in these places, the most wretched-looking objects I ever saw. There were no means of feeding them in the city, where their presence also would have raised a plague and many would have died; so, by the orders of the General, they were turned out of the gates of Delhi and escorted into the country. It was a melancholy sight, seeing them trooping out of the town, hundreds passing through the Lahore Gate every day for a whole week."[39]

H. C. Fanshawe narrates that the town was nearly empty of inhabitants, many of whom indeed (principally women and children of baniyas) had been passed out by our guards subsequent to the assault. Now and then Sepoys or fanatical Muslims, wounded or hiding, were discovered by parties of our troops, dragged out and shot.[40]

Emperor Bahadur Shah Zafar along with his family members took shelter in the Humayun's Tomb. In a letter of Colonel Keith Young to his wife, it is said, "The King, unfortunately, has gone away, so I suppose the first thing will be to try and catch him; he is said to be either at Hamayun's or Nizamuddeen's Tomb, and whether the mutineers are with him or not I don't know. I have just been all over the Palace, which is now occupied by us in large force." The Emperor and his family surrendered peacefully. Most of the Emperor's 16 sons and grandsons were tried and hanged, while three princes, of whom two sons, Mirza Mughal, Mirza Khizr Sultan, with the grandson, the son of Mirza Mughal, by name Mirza Abu Bakr, were shot in cold blood, having first freely given up their arms, then were told to strip naked.   Captain William Hodson wrote to his sister the following day. "In 24 hours I disposed off the principal members of the house of Taimur the Tartar, I am not cruel, but I confess I did enjoy the opportunity of ridding the earth of these wretches. I intended to have had them hung, but when it came to a question of 'they' or 'us,' I had no time for deliberation."[41]

Aitchison narrates that Delhi after the capture became like a city of the dead. Not an inhabitant remained. He quotes an account of the eyewitness, "for miles not a creature was to be seen save a half- starved cat, and here and there a withered hag groping about among the old papers and rags with which the city was strewn. The European artillery were quartered in the Arabic college. The Great Mosque, one of the finest works of the reign of Shah Jahan, unsurpassed in beauty by any building of the kind in India, became a barrack for the Sikhs. Military law was proclaimed, and a military governor appointed.

The houses of the leaders and active participators in the rebellion were confiscated. Hindus were allowed after a time gradually to come back to their homes. The Muhammadan population was altogether excluded. In May, 1858, it was estimated that the population did not amount to one-fourth of its former number. Not till 1859 was the attachment taken off the houses of the Muhammadans, and the order for their exclusion removed."[42]

Aitchison further gives the details that many clamoured for the destruction of Delhi; raze it, raze it, even to the foundations thereof. Charles Raikes describes that Mr. Philip Egerton, the Magistrate of Delhi gave a more moderate proposal, which found much favour at the time, was to convert the Great Mosque into a Christian church, and on each of the thousand compartments of its marble floor to inscribe the name of one of the Christian martyrs of the Mutiny. It was the general opinion that it would be madness to restore this noble building to the Muslims. An officer of the Government drew on himself the wrath of the newspapers because he took off his hat when he went into the chamber where the old Emperor was kept a prisoner.[43]

This defeat was due to the reinforcement of the British forces, their spying in the Red Fort and empty ammunition of the revolutionaries. This defeat forced the remaining national guards to flee from the field leaving the Delhi people and the Emperor on the mercy of the British marauders. Nevertheless, this was not the end of the war but in the different areas of Northern India, including Mewat, Agra, Jhansi, Lucknow, Kanpur, Allahabad, Shahjahanpur Jaunpur, etc. it continued until 1858, and the revolutionaries showed their chivalry and patriotism and happily met the fate of martyrdom. The last revolutionaries were defeated in Gwalior on 20th June 1858. By 1859, revolutionary leaders Bakht Khan and Nana Sahib were fled over the Nepal border of Terai forest and met the same fate of other revolutionaries. Many British soldiers started their merciless by hanging the revolutionaries and even butchering the innocent civilians. Many revolutionaries were tied over the mouths of cannons and blown to pieces when the gun was fired.

Although the Uprising was a very painful experience but it generated new national ideas among the Indian masses. The communal harmony shown during the Uprising by the rebel leaders visualized a new national order. The novel ideas of establishing a kind of elective military rule', assured economic relief to the zamindars, peasants and artisans alike and promises of better service conditions for the Sepoys were their excellent piece of work. The revolutionary leaders certainly deserve credit for nursing this national vision at a time when nationalism in the modern bourgeois sense had been yet to develop. They raised the standard of rebellion when the English power in India was at its ascendant height, and fought relentlessly shoulder to shoulder for a national cause till the last hour, ignoring religious, ethnic, and local divides.

References:

1. *Eight Days*, pp. 7-8
2. *Ibid*, p. 11, see also Fanshawe, H.C., *Delhi Past and Present*, London 1902, p. 184
3. Savarkar, p. 65
4. *Ibid*, pp. 65-66
5. Gilliat Edward, *Heroes of the Indian Mutiny; Stories of Heroic Deeds*, London 1914, p. 137, see also Savarkar, p. 99,
6. Forrest, Volume I, Calcutta, 1893, pp. Introduction 24-25, see also Gilliat Edward, *Heroes of the Indian Mutiny; Stories of Heroic Deeds*, London 1914, p. 138, Wagnor, Kim A., *The Great Fear of 1857, Rumours, Conspiracies and the Making of the Indian Uprising*, Witney (UK), 2010, p. 201, and Fanshawe, H.C., *Delhi Past and Present*, London 1902, pp. 96-103
7. *Ibid*, pp. 263-265, see also *Two Native Narratives* pp.81-82, and Norman, Henry Wylie, *Delhi - 1857; The Siege, Assault, and Capture as given in the Diary and Correspondence of the Late Colonel Keith Young*, London 1902, p. 17
8. Munshi Jeewan Lal was a writer by caste and profession; he recorded each day's events as they happened in the Palace and the intrigue among its household. His information was basically for the British Resident at Delhi. During the rebellion, he was residing within the walls and wrote a detailed record of what occurred in the city. Although he attached the Red Fort during the Uprising but remained a trustworthy and reliable source of information for the British. When the British power was re-established, Munshi Jeewan Lal was made an honorary Magistrate and a Municipal Commissioner. (*Two Native Narratives*, pp.2-3)
9. *Ibid*, pp. 75-79
10. *Ibid*, pp. 83-86, see also Anderson, Clare, *The Indian Uprising of 1857-8: Prisons, Prisoners and Rebellion*, London, 2007, p. 3 (Savarkar says that the Meerut revolutionary officers came in attendance to the Emperor and told him, "Khavind! the English are defeated at Meerut, Delhi is in your hands, and all the Sepoys and people, from Peshawar up to Calcutta, are awaiting your orders. The whole of Hindustan has risen to break the chains of English slavery, and to acquire God-given independence. At this time, take up the flag of Liberty in your own hands, so that all the warriors of India may assemble to fight under it! Hindustan has begun to fight to get back Swaraj and if you accept her leadership, in a moment, we will either drown all these Firangi demons in the oceans or give them as food to the vulture!" The Emperor said to the Sepoys, "I have no treasury and you will get no pay!" The Sepoys replied, "We will loot the English treasuries all over India and lay them at your feet!" Savarkar, p 100)
11. *Ibid*, pp. 83-86, see also *The Guardian*, 10th May, 2007 (Kaye & Malleson says, "The courtyards and the corridors of the Palace were swarming with the mutineers of the 3rd Cavalry and of the 38th, and soon the Meerut Infantry Regiments began to swell the dangerous crowd, whilst an excited Mohammedan rabble mingled

with the Sipahis and the Palace Guards. The troopers stabled their horses in the courts of the Palace. The foot-men, weary with the long night march, turned the Hall of Audience into a barrack, and littered down on the floor. Guards were posted all about the Palace. And the wretched, helpless King found that his royal dwelling-house was in military occupation." Kaye, John William, *Kay's and Malleson's History of the Indian Mutiny of 1857-8,* Vol. II, London, 1910, p. 61)

12. Savarkar, p. 102, (Ascott Hope writes that in an instant the building was hurled into the air, with hundreds of its assailants, and it is said that five hundred people were killed in the streets by the far-reaching explosion. A great number of revolutionaries, lookers on, and city residents were killed. Kaye states that in hours after this first great explosion, the Electric Telegraph was carrying the evil tidings to all parts of the country. The note of warning was sounded across the whole length and breadth of the land; and wherever an Englishman was stationed there was the stem preparation of the defence. Hope, Ascott R., *The Story of the Indian Mutiny*, London, 1896, p. 38, see also Kaye, John William, *A History of the Sepoy War in India, 1857-58,* Vol. II, London 1874, p. 111)

13. Wood, Evelyn, *The Revolt in Hindustan 1857-59*, London, 1908, p. 27, see also Norman, Henry Wylie, *Delhi - 1857; The Siege, Assault, and Capture as given in the Diary and Correspondence of the Late Colonel Keith Young,* London 1902, p. 17, and Mead, Henry, *The Sepoy Revolt: Its causes and its Consequences,* London, 1858, p. 101

14. Kaye, John William, *Kay's and Malleson's History of the Indian Mutiny of 1857-8,* Vol. II, London, 1910, pp. 74-75

15. *Defense Journal*, Vol. 3, No. 9, Islamabad, December,1999

16. *People's Democracy, (The 1857 Revolt in India: Lessons for Us-*Jyoti Basu) Vol. XXXI, No. 10, March 11, 2007 see also *New York Daily Tribune*, July 15, 1857

17. *A Sketch of the Principal Military Events*, p. 25

18. Vibart, H.M., *Richard Baird Smith: The Leader of the Delhi Heroes in 1857*, Westminster, 1897, pp. 10-11, see also Argyl, Campbell, George Douglas, Duke of, *India Under Dalhousie and Canning*, London, 1865, pp. 100-101, see also, *New York Daily Tribune*, July 15, 1857, Handcock, Arthur Gore, *The Siege of Delhi in 1857: A Short Account*, Allahabad, 1897, pp. 10-11, and Greathed, Harvey Harris, *Letters Written During the Siege of Delhi*, London, 1858, pp. 6-25

19. *Ibid*, p. 12, see also Malleson, George Bruce, *The Indian Mutiny of 1857*, New York, 1891, pp. 125-126, Handcock, Arthur Gore, *The Siege of Delhi in 1857: A Short Account*, Allahabad, 1897, pp. 11-12, and Roberts, P.E., *A Historical Geography of the British Dependencies: India*, Vol. VII, London, 1914, p. 371, (Greathed quotes the letter written from Delhi, Alipur on June 7, "We had a tempestuous ride from Bagpat to this, last evening ...... The force is in great spirits, and awaits anxiously the order for attack; and our next move must bring us under the walls of Delhi. ....I am glad to find here a Native named Rajab Ali, who was George Clerk's head munshi: he had been pensioned and had been living in retirement; but being sent for he came at once. He is a first-rate man. The camp is very large and well formed; and we have certainly a very perfect force and

unusually strong in Artillery." Greathed, Harvey Harris, *Letters Written During the Siege of Delhi*, London, 1858, pp. 26-29)

20. Greathed, Harvey Harris, *Letters Written During the Siege of Delhi*, London, 1858, pp. 29-36

21. *New York Daily Tribune*, August 4, 1857, see also, Gilliat Edward, *Heroes of the Indian Mutiny; Stories of Heroic Deeds*, London 1914, p. 82, Adam and Charles Black, *History of the Siege of Delhi*, Edinburgh, 1861, p. 120, and Grant, Hope, *Incidents in the Sepoy War 1857-58*, Edinburgh, 1873, p. 74 (Greathed quotes the letter written from Delhi Camp on June 24, "I MISSED writing yesterday, — I had nothing very pleasant to say, and the continued roll of musketry and booming of cannon, from 6 a.m. to 5 p.m., distracted my attention from other matters. The enemy came out with the object of intercepting a convoy, and then attacking us in the rear, ... the mass then got into the Shabzi Mandi and gardens on our right, and made repeated attempts on the rear of Hindu Rao's house and on the mound. .... It was a tiresome action, knowing that nothing could be gained beyond driving them away …….. It is said in the city 400 were killed and 300 wounded. We lost nearly 100 killed and wounded. Jackson of the Fusiliers was killed; Welchman and Captain Jones of the Rifles wounded. Our troops fought admirably, and showed an utter disregard not only of danger, but of fatigue, but it is a pity they had to endure so much to gain so little...." Greathed, Harvey Harris, *Letters Written During the Siege of Delhi*, London, 1858, pp. 68-69. Cave-Browne writes, "our loss this day was one officer and forty men killed; eight officers and one hundred and sixty-three men wounded; eleven men missing. The enemy must have lost near five hundred men, most of whom were killed on the spot." Cave-Browne, J., *The Punjab and Delhi in 1857*, Vol. II, Edinburgh, 1861, pp. 21-22, hereafter cited as Cave-Browne)

22. *Two Native Narratives* pp. 134-136, see also Spear, Percival, *Twilight of the Mughals: Studies in Late Mughal Delhi*, Cambridge, 1951, p. 206

23. *Ibid*, p. 134-136, see also Spear, Percival, *Twilight of the Mughals: Studies in Late Mughal Delhi*, Cambridge, 1951, p.206, (Cave-Browne states, "The clever and ambitions Mohammad Bakht Khan, dared to beard the old King in his own palace, and to dictate terms for himself in the council chamber, as an equal in power with the royal princes, who now commanded the army. This claim was first of all met by a compromise, and General Mohammad Bakht Khan was appointed Commandant of the Magazine and Commissary-General of Ordnance, and Commander-in-Chief....." Cave-Browne, p. 38)

24. Forrest, Volume I, Calcutta, 1893, p. 294, see also Gilliat Edward, *Heroes of the Indian Mutiny; Stories of Heroic Deeds*, London 1914, pp. 153

25. *A Sketch of the Principal Military Events*, p. 68, see also Gilliat Edward, *Heroes of the Indian Mutiny; Stories of Heroic Deeds*, London 1914, pp. 83, and Hodson, George Herbert, *Hodson of Hodson's Horse or the Twelve Years of a Soldiers Life in India: Being Extracts from the Letters of the Late Major W. S. R. Hodson*, London, 1889, p. 174

26. Grant, Hope, *Incidents in the Sepoy War 1857-58*, Edinburgh, 1873, p. 82, see also *A Sketch of the Principal Military Events*, pp. 68-69, and Cave-Browne, pp. 24-25

27. Grant, Hope, *Incidents in the Sepoy War 1857-58*, Edinburgh, 1873, p. 84, see also, *A Sketch of the Principal Military Events*, pp. 69-70, and Gilliat Edward, *Heroes of the Indian Mutiny; Stories of Heroic Deeds*, London 1914, pp. 113, and Cave-Browne, pp. 28-31, (Cave-Browne writes that on the 15th a council of war was held; all the Native officers of the rebel force attended. Each one threw a pinch of salt into a lotah of water, thereby pledging themselves that, as the salt dissolved in the water, so might each one perish who proved faithless or a coward; to do or die was their vow. Cave-Browne, p. 139)

28. Handcock, Arthur Gore, *The Siege of Delhi in 1857: A Short Account*, Allahabad, 1897, pp. 16-17, see also Forrest, Volume I, Calcutta, 1893, pp. Introduction 68-69

29. *Two Native Narratives*, p. 205, see also Gilliat Edward, *Heroes of the Indian Mutiny; Stories of Heroic Deeds*, London 1914, p. 153

30. Kaye, John William, *A History of the Sepoy War in India, 1857-58,* Vol. III, London 1876, p. 551

31. *New Statesman,* October, 16, 2006

32. Griffiths, Charles John, *A Narrative of the Siege of Delhi with an Account of the Mutiny at Firozpur in 1857*, London, 1910, pp. 140-141

33. *A Sketch of the Principal Military Events*, pp. 72-74, see also Julius George Medley, *A Years Campaigning in India from March 1857 to March 1858* , London 1858, p.102

34. Kaye, John William, *A History of the Sepoy War in India, 1857-58,* Vol. III, London 1876, p. 630, see also Rotten, J.E.W., *Captains Narratives of the Siege of Delhi from the Outbreak at Meerut to the Capture of Delhi*, London, 1858, p. 316

35. Handcock, Arthur Gore, *The Siege of Delhi in 1857: A Short Account*, Allahabad, 1897, p. 23

36. Kaye, John William, *A History of the Sepoy War in India, 1857-58,* Vol. III, London 1876, pp. 633-634, see also Tracy, Louis, *The Red Year; A Story of The Indian Mutiny*, New York 1907, p. 40

37. *A Sketch of the Principal Military Events*, p. 76, see also Vibart, H.M., *Richard Baird Smith: The Leader of the Delhi Heroes in 1857*, Westminster, 1897, p. 31, and Malleson, George Bruce, *Kay's and Malleson's History of the Indian Mutiny of 1857-8,* Vol. IV, London, 1911, pp. 58-59

38. Fanshawe, H.C., *Delhi Past and Present*, London 1902, p. 217, see also Kaye, John William, *A History of the Sepoy War in India, 1857-58,* Vol. III, London 1876, p. 630

39. Griffiths, Charles John, *A Narrative of the Siege of Delhi with an Account of the Mutiny at Firozpur in 1857*, London, 1910, pp. 199-200

40. Fanshawe, H.C., *Delhi Past and Present*, London 1902, p. 184

41. Norman, Henry Wylie, *Delhi - 1857; The Siege, Assault, and Capture as given in the Diary and Correspondence of the Late Colonel Keith Young,* London 1902, p. 299, see also Hodson, George Herbert, *Hodson of Hodson's Horse or the Twelve Years of a Soldiers Life in India: Being Extracts from the Letters of the Late Major W. S. R. Hodson,* London, 1889, p. 224
42. Aitchison, Charles, *Rulers of India: Lord Lawrence,* Oxford, 1892, pp. 101-102
43. Raikes, Charles, *Notes on the Revolt in the North-Western Provinces of India,* London, 1858, p. 78, see also Aitchison, Charles, *Rulers of India: Lord Lawrence,* Oxford, 1892, p. 105

Chapter 4

Uprising in Awadh

Awadh, known as the garden, the granary, and the queen province of India, was founded by Nawab Saadat Ali Khan in 1722 with its capital at Faizabad. It lied between the Himalaya Mountains of the foreign territory of Nepal on the North, and the river Ganges on the south. Nawab Saadat Ali Khan was succeeded by most influential rulers like Nawab Safdar Jang in 1739 and Nawab Shujauddaula in 1754. The rulers of Awadh were initially acknowledged as Nawab Wazir under the Mughal suzerainty. Awadh came under influence of the British when its ruler Nawab Asafuddaula assumed power in 1775, he hastened to strengthen himself by an alliance with the British and gave up to them some territory. Under Nawab Asafuddaula's rule the capital of Awadh was changed from Faizabad to Lucknow.[1]

Asafuddaula was succeeded by Wazir Ali in 1797, and in a very short time in 1798, he was succeeded by Saadat Ali. Nawab Saadat Ali faced ill-will of the British Government in 1801 and rather its fate was decided when they imposed subsidiary alliance and forcefully took the security of the Kingdom by putting the huge British army and a resident in its capital Lucknow. Under this treaty, Lord Wellesley obtained the rich districts of Allahabad, Azamgarh, Gorakhpur, and the Southern Doab, estimated to yield net annual revenue about two crores of rupees and forced him to accept the services of this extensive army of English soldiers.[2]

In 1814, Saadat Ali was succeeded by Ghaziuddin Haider. He was the first ruler of Awadh, who became first King of Awadh after renouncing the title of Nawab Wazir. Ghaziuddin Haider was completely under the protection of the British Government. The British also provided him a certain contingent of troops, for which the new King was to pay an annual sum of sixteen lakhs. By such forced protection and voluntary compulsion, the treasury of the Nawab was rapidly emptied. After the Nepal War, Ghaziuddin Haider lent the Company, two millions sterling, and received in return the Terai or Jungle-country between Awadh and Nepal. In 1819, the Company allowed Ghaziuddin Haider to renounce the vassal title of Nawab Wazir, which was a mockery as connected with the suzerainty of the now powerless Emperor of Delhi, and to become King of Awadh. In 1827, the throne of Awadh was ascended by Nasiruddin Haider. In his rule in 1831, Lord William Bentinck threatened to depose the King unless the affairs of the State were amended. When Mohammad Ali Shah ascended the throne, Lord Auckland drew the attention of the King to the willful oppression, anarchy, and insecurity, which prevailed in Awadh, and declared his intention of assuming the management of the country if the misrule did not cease. In 1837, the treaty of 1801 was renewed with more cunning intentions of the British. In 1842, Amjad Ali Shah became King of Awadh after his father's death.[3]

Nawab Wajid Ali Shah (30th July 1822-1st September 1887), was ascended the throne of Awadh on 13th February 1847, and again, the territory attracted the British. V. D. Savarkar mentions that this new Nawab determined from the first to destroy the poisonous white worm which was killing the life out of the state, and with that object began reforms in the army which was the life of the Kingdom. In November, 1847, the Governor General, Lord Hardinge, visited Lucknow and held a conference with the King. A memorandum was read and explained to him. In the memorandum, Nawab Wajid Ali was enjoined to take timely measures for the reformation of abuses and for the rescue of his people from their present miserable condition. If the King, within the following two years, should fail in checking and eradicating the worst abuses, then the Governor General would assume the Government itself.[4]

Colonel Sleeman was appointed as Resident of Awadh in 1849, and was authorised by Lord Dalhousie to make a tour throughout Awadh, and report upon the general condition of the people. Colonel Sleeman reported in 1851, but no immediate result followed the report of the Resident; for the Burmese war of 1851-52 occupied the attention of Government, and gave Wajid Ali Shah the advantage to rule the Awadh State. The report of the Colonel Sleeman was as follows:[5]

"The whole presented a revolting picture of the worst type of misrule, of a feebleness worse than despotism, of an apathy more productive of human suffering than the worst forms of tyrannous activity. In the absence of all controlling authority, the strong carried on everywhere a war of extermination against the weak............ There was hardly, indeed, an atrocity committed from one end of the country to the other, that was not, directly or indirectly, the result of the profligacy and corruption of the Court. Such being the state of the country, it was impossible long to resist active interference in its affairs, it was necessary that the British Government should take upon itself the responsibility of governing it properly. .... But even its annexation was not so unjustifiable and unrighteous an act as has been maintained by some. It produced, however, a deep feeling of dissatisfaction in many Native circles throughout India............ a large proportion of the men of the Sepoy regiments came from the territories of the King of Oude, and that they were peculiarly liable to be affected by whatever disturbed the political arrangements of their own country."

Due to the Sleeman's illness, General Outram was sent as Officiating Resident to Lucknow, in December, 1854, and desired to furnish a report with a view to determine whether public affairs continued in the state described from time to time by his predecessor. This he did, at considerable length, in February, 1855; and made a full report on the anarchy that prevailed, the vile life of the King, and the misery of the unprotected cultivators, seventy-eight of whose villages were on an average yearly, burned and plundered, the inhabitants tortured, slain, or sold into slavery.[6]

It was clear from his report that Colonel Sleeman was not in favour of complete annexation of Awadh and had fully suspected the mutiny on the condition of annexation. He had only reported about the mal-administration, and lawlessness prevailed in Awadh gave the details of the wishes of the people and suggested to provide better governance by British assistance. In one of his letters, he says, "Lucknow affairs are now in a state to require the assumption of the entire management of the country." In another letter, he says, "The present King ought not certainly to reign. What the people want and most earnestly pray for is that our Government should take upon itself the responsibility of governing them well and permanently."

In one of his private letters, Sleeman says, "Lord Dalhousie and I, have different views, I fear. If he wishes anything done that I do not think right and honest, I resign, and leave it to be done by others. I desire a strict adherence to solemn engagements with white faces or black. We have no right to annex or confiscate Oude; but we have a right, under the treaty of 1837, to take the management of it, but not to appropriate its revenues to ourselves. To confiscate would be dishonest and dishonourable. To annex would be to give the people a Government almost as bad as their own, if we put our view upon them."[7]

Gibbon describes that on June 18, 1855, Lord Dalhousie signed the Minute in which he advocated that, though the King might retain his crown, all powers, jurisdiction, rights, and claims were to be vested in the Company, and the surplus revenue to be at the disposal of the Company. Nevertheless, the Home Government declared for annexation pure and simple and in February 1856, Awadh became a British province. Duke of Argyl describes that the matter was discussed in the Cabinet of Palmerstone and finally on 2nd January 1856; the Court of Directors gave its nod about the annexation to Lord Dalhousie, "to assume authoritatively the powers necessary for good Government throughout the country." The Officiating Resident Outram was assigned the duty to take over the administration of Awadh.[8]

Duke of Argyl had very beautifully described the scene which happened between Outram and Nawab Wajid Ali Shah. He writes, "He (Nawab Wajid Ali Shah) resolutely refused to sign the instrument of his own humiliation. Uncovering himself, he placed his turban in the hands of Outram, declaring that now his titles, rank, and position were all gone, it was not for him to sign a treaty, or to enter into any negotiation......" Lastly Resident announced the Proclamation that the Government of the territories of Awadh is henceforth vested exclusively and for ever in the Honourable East India Company.[9]

V.D. Savarkar has rightly described the mal-intention of the British Government regarding the annexation of Awadh. He says that, nor could there be any excuse, as in the case of Nagpur that the Nawab had no direct heir; the palace was full of the Nawab's legitimate children. Nor was there trouble about adoption as in the case of Jhansi, for the present King was the legitimate son of the late King and had, further, sat on the throne for years. In short, the Nawab of Awadh had not committed any of the above "crimes" which lost other princes their Kingdoms. However, though the Nawab had thus avoided every other "crime", still the demented fool had committed one unpardonable crime! What crime could cry louder than this, that the land of Awadh was very fertile, teeming with crops and rich in every way?[10]

V.D. Savarkar further describes that on the instruction of Lord Dalhousie; the Resident went to the Nawab's palace and began to insist that the Nawab should sign a document stating that he was perfectly willing to give over his dominions to the Company. The Nawab read the document and flatly refused to sign. To make the Nawab sign this document, the Resident began attempts to bribe the Rani and the Wazir and the threat was also given that a refusal by the Nawab to sign the document would result in even his pension being stopped. The Nawab was overwhelmed with grief at this and began even to weep. However, it was of no use. Seeing at the end of three days that the refusal was still persisted in, the British army, insolently setting aside the Nawab's authority entered Lucknow and took forcible possession of the whole territory, including his palace. The Zenanas were looted; the Begams were insulted; the Nawab was hurled from the throne, and palaces were turned into stables for the soldiers of the English and thus began a happy beginning of the good administration of the so-far-badly-managed Kingdom of Awadh.[11]

Nawab Wajid Ali Shah dethroned by the British on 7th February 1856, before the 9th anniversary of his coronation. The excuse of mal-administration was only a drama, and the reality was entirely different. In fact, the Company had an eagle's eye on the whole province of Awadh from the last many years, and the excuse of mal-administration was the only way of annexation. In a real sense, Nawab was playing little more than a titular role, and the Resident was ruling the territory with the help of British army stationed at Lucknow. The army was composed mostly of British officers, while the purse strings were firmly under the control of the East India Company. If there was any misrule, then the Resident was responsible, not the Nawab. Overall, Awadh was neither as bankrupt nor as lawless as the British had claimed.

After the annexation of the Awadh province, the administration was formed on the Punjab model — a Chief Commissioner; a Judicial Commissioner, to look after justice, police, jails, etc.; a Financial Commissioner, to look after revenue, including the administration of the land, besides Divisional Commissioners and executive officers. Major-General Sir James Outram was appointed its first Chief Commissioner. Nawab Wajid Ali Shah was exiled to Garden Reach (Matia Burj) in the suburb of Calcutta with the pension of 12 lakh rupees per year, but most of his relatives and nobles remained at Lucknow. His Queen Mother and sons went to England in a hope to get back their territory annexed by the Company.[12]

It was described about the character of Nawab Wajid Ali Shah that his disposition was kindly, and himself indisposed to violence or cruelty of any kind. He possessed sufficient acuteness of understanding to enable him to acquire certain attainments, which mark the esteemed scholar. He was well read in Persian, and used frequently to write his orders on Native petitions with his own hand. His moral character was described by all to be extremely weak. He completely surrendered to his minister, Ali Naki, the entire control of public business. To rule Awadh, he regarded to be the business of Ali Naki, not of himself. How the public revenue was spent, he did not inquire, so long as his own expenses were provided for. He was a great bigot, and his bigotry is confined to the Shias, a peculiar creed of Islam which he professed.[13]

Martin states that the discharged soldiery of the Native Government, amounting to about 60,000 men, naturally regarded the new administration with aversion and hostility. Only 15,000 soldiers were given the service in the newly formed local regiments, and some found employment in the civil departments. The large proportion, for whom no permanent provision could be made, received small pensions or gratuities. Those who had served from twenty-five to thirty years, received one-fourth of their emoluments as pension; and those who had served from seven to fifteen years, received three months' pay as a gratuity. Under seven years' service, no gratuity whatever appears to have been given to the unfortunates suddenly turned adrift for no fault of their own.[14]

After the annexation of Awadh by the British Government, it had pursued an anti-landlord or anti-talluqdar policy. The first Chief Commissioner, James Outram's policy against the talluqdars was a little slow but his successor C. Coverley Jackson embarked on a harsher policy, taking away the rights of the talluqdars. The British Government's anti-talluqdari policy was prevalent in the adjoining North-Western Province right from its annexation in 1803. In the North-Western Province, James Thomason, who was Lt-Governor of the Province for a decade from 1843 to 1853, had steadily pursued a policy of reducing the authority of the talluqdars, had taken away their intermediary rights, had assumed some of their land, and had curbed their political and administrative power.[15]

This gave rise to discontent among the powerful landowning classes in Awadh. British Government remedied its folly by appointing Henry Lawrence as Chief Commissioner, who was sympathetic to the landed elite, in March 1857, but by that time things had already gone too far, and then within a few months the revolt broke out. At that time, Major Banks was the Commissioner, Mr. Ommanney Judicial Commissioner, and Mr. Gubbins Financial Commissioner, Dr. Fayrer Chief Surgeon. All tried jointly to normalise the harsher policy of Mr. Jackson, but they got very short time to restore the order.[16]

Cunningham in his book *Earl Canning*, writes, "the European officials regarded him (talluqdars) with no friendly eye, as an oppressor of the poor and a useless encumbrance of the soil. His title-deeds were strictly scanned; his vague prerogatives were disallowed. Tenant-rights, of which the tenant himself had scarcely dreamed, were boldly affirmed. Great dissatisfaction, accordingly, existed in the landed classes of Awadh. When the Mutiny came, the tenancy sided with their traditional lords against an alien protector, and the rebel soldiers, themselves for the most part drawn from the peasantry of Awadh, found in the strongholds and Jungles of the landholders their best refuge and in many of the landholders their warmest allies."[17]

This political conspiracy and allegation of misrule and eventually annexation by the British had far-reaching military consequences since Awadh was a major recruiting area for the East India Company's Bengal Army. The people of Awadh served the British army and gained their pension after their retirement. Under the Native rule, they enjoyed privileges, such as the exemption from some taxes, which were lost to them under that of the British rule. Even the Hindu soldiers were very much disgusted with the seizure of Awadh. They expressed their indignation in the most open manner, and told the King that, if he had resisted, they would have thrown down their arms and fought for him.

Around one-third of the Sepoys in the Bengal Army, numbering about 40,000, came from territories of the Kingdom of Awadh on the eve of the Uprising In every village were the families of men who wore the uniform and bore the arms of the English. The result was that widespread discontent against colonial exploitation in the countryside as well as in the cities, to which a large section of the rural poor and Sepoys flocked and added a glorious chapter of Lucknow Uprising in the history of modern India. All the Sepoys who rose in the Uprising in the Awadh area were known as *Purbeas* were in the real sense the peasants in uniform. The Bengal army which drew 60 per centum of its recruits from Awadh was deeply affected by the annexation of Awadh.[18]

At Lucknow, the British garrison was stationed at Residency (Bailie Guard), Machhi Bhawan (old small Sikh fort), Daulat Khana, Moosa Bagh, and Mudkipur in Lucknow. The headquarter of the Chief Commissioner was at the Residency, situated in the city close to the river Gomti. About a mile from this position were the barracks of the European regiment, Her Majesty's 32nd Regiment. Three miles from the Residency, on the other side of the river, was the cantonment, where the Native force consisted of a troop of Horse Artillery, two companies of Foot Artillery, the 7th Light Cavalry, seven regiments of Native Infantry, three field batteries of the Awadh Irregular Force, three regiments of Awadh Irregular Cavalry, ten regiments of Awadh Irregular Infantry, and three regiments of Police; in all, about 900 Europeans and 22,000 Natives in the heart of the Fatherland of the Sepoy race. On the eve of the Uprising, the Europeans chosen old fortress at Machhi Bhawan (a large building just outside the Residency enclosure), and the Residency (The Residency entrenchments enclosed a space of near 60 acres, and consisted of a number of well-built houses and buildings of various sorts connected by trenches and stockades) for their settlement under the tight security.[19]

Following the revolt in Meerut and Delhi, the favourable condition developed in Lucknow also and on 7th May, some happenings of disobedience were appeared, but it soon recovered. Nevertheless, there were the constant anxiety and resentment among the Sepoys of Lucknow cantonment, which lasted until the end of this month. During this period, the British Garrison consisted of British- 1008 (of whom 153 were civilian volunteers); Natives- 712 (of these 230 deserted during the siege). The non-combatants in the place were 1280, of whom about 600 were British and Eurasian women and children. This was truly felt by the military officers and the Chief Commissioner Henry Lawrence and the civilian Europeans, and the British officers were advised for their defense arrangements. He held Darbars and reminded the assemblies that under English rule, no sect had ever been persecuted; to the Muslims, he pointed out that in the Punjab, the Sikh yoke had been removed, and that in the cities of the Manjha, the muezzin again summoned the faithful to prayer; he asked the Hindu if his lot had not been made more easy in the Muslim states. However, all his efforts were in vain.[20]

Not only the annexation and humiliation of its Nawab was a curse for the people of Awadh but the discriminatory policy of the Company Government aroused its people to hold arms against the British. The Sikh regiments of Ranjit Singh, who had been defeated in 1840, had been incorporated into the British army. There were some 15,000 of these troops, and they were the first and largest force available to the British to move into the Northern plains and retake the areas which had risen in revolt. However, when they had taken over the Kingdom of Awadh, they did not recruit the army of the King in a similar manner. McLeod Innes states, "Though thousands of the soldiery had been brought into British service, other thousands had been discharged without the means of subsistence; and, in Oude, to discharge a Sepoy so was to create a bandit."[21]

Company tried to do certain measures to solve the unemployment problems of the Awadh troopers, but the Uprising broke out before any final decision taken by the British Government. The disbanded soldiers played very important role in the Uprising, particularly in the Awadh region. George Dodd quotes the Directors' minute of December 1856, just on the eve of Uprising: "The probable temper of the army, a force computed on paper at some 60,000 men of all arms, on the announcement of a measure which threw a large proportion of them out of employment, and transferred the remainder to a new master, was naturally a source of some anxiety to us. In your scheme for the future Government and administration of the Awadh provinces, drawn up on the 4th of February, you proposed the organisation of an Awadh irregular force, into which you suggested the absorption of as large a number of the disbanded soldiers of the King as could be employed in such a corps, whilst others were to be provided for in the military and district police; but you observed at the same time that these arrangements would not absorb one-half of the disbanded troops. To the remainder you determined to grant pensions and gratuities, graduated according to length of service."[22]

Apart from the discontent in the disbanded soldiers, there was also full doubt of infidelity from the side of Sepoys of British forces. The Sepoys had full faith that their religion was at stake under the British Government. Henry Lawrence called an assembly of the soldiers, addressed, and appealed them for fidelity. He said, "Soldiers! some persons are abroad spreading reports that the Government desire to interfere with the religion of their soldiers; you all know this to be a transparent falsehood; you, and your forefathers before you, well know and knew that for more than a hundred years the religion of your countrymen has never been interfered with. All Governments employ and cherish the faithful and the zealous, and punish the lukewarm and ungrateful. No army in the world has done better service than that of Bengal. I am a witness to this fact; so are these gallant officers.... We are all your friends, our interests are inseparable; if your faces are blackened, so are ours; if any dishonour befalls you do we not suffer? .... it freely permits all to worship at the altar before which their forefathers have bowed..... soldiers! it is my pleasing duty to reward, in the name of Government, those who have served it so well and so honourably."[23]

On 30th May 1857, Sepoys of the 71st Native Infantry and 7th Light Cavalry, in the area of Mudkipur mutinied. They burnt all the houses and bungalows in the cantonment except of Henry Lawrence, which was highly protected. It followed the murder and mass level destruction of the properties. Another fight took place in Husainabad area between the combined forces of mutineers and city people and British forces, but the attack of the revolutionaries was repulsed with some losses, and about forty in the number were arrested and lodged in the Machhi Bhawan. The defeated Sepoys were dispersed into the countryside, especially to Sitapur and many more fled towards Delhi. The arrested mutineers at Machhi Bhawan were Court Marshalled and hanged. On 30th of May out of four mutinous regiments no more than 437 i.e. 13th N.I. 200, 48th N.I. 57, 71st N.I. 120, 7th L.C. 60, remained loyal to the British. Most of the suspected regiments were disarmed, which reduced the Sepoys two-third in the British troops. Lucknow remained calm throughout the June but again rose on 30th of June with full vigour and force.[24]

The divisions and sub-divisions of Northern India like Sitapur, Shahjahanpur, Khairabad, Faizabad, etc. became centres of the revolt. The revolutionaries shot dead most of the European commanders of their Regiments and general destruction of the property, and murder followed. The revolutionaries on the outskirts of Lucknow overthrew the English, occupied the territory, and declared Nawab of Awadh as their ruler under Emperor Bahadur Shah Zafar. They galloped in Nawabganj, Barabanki, twenty miles from Lucknow. They slowly made their access in Lucknow and mobilized both the masses and the Sepoys. Their activities were known to the British only on 29th of June when they were about to fight on the next day.

At the time of Uprising in Awadh Nawab Wajid Ali Shah along with his Chief Minister Ali Naki Khan was in Calcutta. His Queen Mother and brother were in England on the fruitless mission to Queen Victoria where they died. The other relatives, the ex-Queen Begam Hazrat Mahal and son Brijis Qadr were in Lucknow. At Cacutta, the Prime Minister Ali Naki Khan played the same revolutionary role against the British, as Nana played at Kanpur. He tried his level best to seduce and organize the Sepoys in Bengal and to prepare them to join him at the right moment already determined upon. Confidential agents were sent by him, in the garb of Fakirs or Sanyasis, to preach revolutionary ideas to the Sepoys.

V.D.Savarkar writes that Ali Naki Khan opened correspondence with the Indian officers in the army to make them understand fully what immense advantages Swaraj could confer as compared to the service of the Company. How the English had committed an unpardonable crime in annexing Awadh, how the royal family of the Nawab had been treated with insult, and how the very Queen and Begams were expelled with violence from the palace— pictures of such heart-rending tyranny were drawn with such pathos that the brave Sepoys began to weep profusely. And, then and there, the Sepoys would take the water of the Ganges in their hands, or would swear by the Quran, that they would live only to achieve the destruction of the English rule. Savarkar further says that Ali Naki Khan, using such tactics, won over the whole army of Bengal; even in the Fort William itself, in Calcutta, his revolutionary agents moved silently.[25]

However, all the national efforts of Ali Naki Khan could not last long, and the British agents easily smell about his secret, extensive, and daring scheme. On June 15th 1857, Nawab Wajid Ali Shah was arrested along with his Chief Minister Ali Naki Khan, two principal members of the suit Ahsan Hussain Khan and his son, together with Tikait Rao, the Diwan of the Chief Queen. They were conveyed as state prisoners to Fort William. Kaye narrates that the British officer Edmonstone told to the Nawab Wajid Ali Shah that intelligence had reached the Governor General, which had satisfied his Lordship that emissaries using his Majesty's name had spread themselves in all directions over the British dominions, and had instigated many of the Native soldiers of the Army to swerve from their allegiance. The King in his reply said that he had not been guilty of the offence imputed to him. In the way to Fort William, he seemed suddenly to awaken to the misery and humiliation of his position. Bursting into tears, he spoke of the dignity of his ancestors, his own heavy fall, and wretched condition as an exile and a suspect. Nevertheless, nothing was brought to light to implicate the King in the alleged conspiracies against the British Government, and the King of Awadh restored for a time to Calcutta.[26]

Alaxander Duff writes, "early on Monday morning the ex-King of Oude and his treasonable crew were arrested and safely quartered in Fort William. Since then, various parties connected with the Oude family, and other influential Mohammedans, have been arrested; and on them have been found several important documents, tending to throw light on the desperate plans of treason which have been seriously projected. Among others has been found a map of Calcutta, so sketched out as to divide the whole of the town into sections. A general rise was planned to take place on the 23rd instant — the anniversary of the battle of Plassey. The city was to be taken, and the 'Feringhi Kaffirs,' or British and other Christian inhabitants, to be all massacred."[27]

When the Uprising re-started on 30th of the June 1857, the combined fighting force comprising Sepoys and the masses from the general rural populace fought to oust the British. It was the ties of loyalty that existed in the rural areas of Awadh, which resulted the thousands of men supplied by the talluqdars were not all just their retainers but also drawn from tenants, peasants and clansmen who lived on their land. The English were very much surprised that even the peasants whom the talluqdars oppressed were joined the rebel cause under the leadership of their respective talluqdars as they presumed that the peasants would appreciate the Company's anti-talluqdari measures, since these were supposed to be in the interests of the peasants. However, the British had perhaps forgotten that if the talluqdars were the oppressor, then the new British rule was defamed for its heavy taxation and harsh mode of revenue collection.

It was reported to the British that revolutionaries were preparing to fight at Chinhat on the outskirt of Lucknow, and the British soldiers moved accordingly with full preparation, but they met tough resistance near the village Ismailganj, near side of Chinhat. The battle of Chinhat fought on 30th of June and revolutionaries, including Sepoys, *Mujahideen* and common people, won a resounding victory. British officials and other European inhabitants were forced to take refuge in the Residency and its compound and Machhee Bhawan numbering about three thousand. Later on, the British were forced to leave Machhee Bhawan as it was destroyed by the revolutionaries. The British troops met a great loss of men and money. Three European officers Colonel Case, Captain Stephen, and Mr. Brackenbury were killed and several wounded. Besides the officers already named, Captain Maclean, 71st N.I., was killed, and Captain James of the Commissariat, who received a ballet in the knee. In artillery, the British lost the 8-inch howitzer, and three field-pieces, two of Bryce's and one of Alexander's battery, with almost all the ammunition- wagons of the Native guns. The loss in European soldiers was very severe, the killed being 112, and the wounded 14, and not a few of the Natives had fallen, while more had deserted. The total number killed and missing was nearly 200.[28]

Gubbins gives the details that the force of the mutineers, which consisted altogether of regiments stationed in the province, could be estimate with great precision. They had the two 9-pounder batteries from Secrora and Faizabad, each of six guns, making twelve pieces of artillery. They possessed besides, three or four small Native guns, which could have been of no service in the field, and which they had obtained in the districts. Gubbins also gives the details of the British forces that they had a total infantry force of 5550 men, 800 cavalry, and 160 artillery.[39]

Now the revolutionaries fully occupied the city of Lucknow, and the siege of the Lucknow Residency and Machhi Bhawan commenced on 1st of July 1857. On the first day, the revolutionaries occupied the Machhi Bhawan, and the British army left the place by destroying 240 barrels of gunpowder and 594,000 rounds of ball and gun ammunition.[30]

About 6000 revolutionaries fought in the siege of Residency by shouting the war cry, "Ali, Ali" and "*Chalo Bahadur*" filled the passion of war among them and attacked upon the British sheltered in the Residency from all its sides. On the first July's success at Machhi Bhawan, the revolutionaries were full of enthusiasm and fought the second day on 2nd July for the siege of Residency. After a full fight in the night at Machhi Bhawan,

Sir Henry returned to the Residency, and being much fatigued, laid down on his bed. Soon after an eight-inch shell from the eight-inch howitzer of the enemy, entered the room at the window, and exploding, a fragment struck the Brigadier-General on the upper part of the right thigh near the hip, inflicting a fearful wound. Captain Wilson, who was standing alongside the bed with one knee on it at the time, reading a memorandum to Sir Henry, was knocked down by falling bricks and slightly wounded in the back by a piece of shell, Sir H. Lawrence's nephew, Mr. Lawrence, had an equally narrow escape, being on another bed close by: he was not hurt; the fourth individual in the room was a Native servant, who lost one of his feet by a fragment of the shell. The heavily wounded Sir Henry was died shortly afterwards on 4th of July 1857. However, before his death Sir Henry had nominated Major Banks as his successor to the Chief Commissionership and Colonel Inglis to the command of the troops.[31]

Like Delhi, the revolutionaries of Lucknow also set up a new Government by proclaiming the end of the East India Company's Government. They recognised the authority of Begam Hazrat Mahal, the former wife who remained their foremost leader throughout the duration of the siege. On 5th July, 1857, representatives of the armed forces, Risaldar Shahabuddin of the 12th Cavalry and Barkat Ahmad installed Begam Hazrat Mahal's minor son (13 or 14 years old) Birjis Qadr on the throne. All orders from Delhi were to be obeyed implicitly. The army was all powerful in the new Government. The Government was not to interfere with the army in regard to the treatment of the English and of their friends. The pay of the troops was doubled. The Prime Minister and the Chancellor of the Exchequer were the ex-officials Sharfuddaula and Maharaja Balkishan, who had held those posts under the late Nawab. The Chief Justice was Mummoo Khan, the Begam's favourite. The War Minister was Raja Jeylal Singh, a Lucknow courtier; while the men put in command of the troops and the charge of the siege, were two Lucknow courtiers, Meer Mehndi and Muzaffar Ali, a nephew of the Prime Minister, and Risaldar Kasim Khan, of the 12th Cavalry.[32]

It was decided that the Emperor at Delhi should be informed. The petition was sent, and an acknowledgement was promptly received: "Dutiful Son, Mirza Birjis Qadr Bahadur, King of Awadh, you deserve felicitations for this big achievement in such a young age. Rest assured that soon the Seal of Title will also be sent to you. You will be granted more territories than what you have traditionally possessed." Emperor Bahadur Shah, later awarded the title of Safeerud Dowlah. And again, the Emperor reiterated: "I do grant him the Crown." After this confirmation, Birjis Qadr was crowned on August 6, 1857. A Military Council, based on the Delhi Court of Administration, was also established in Lucknow to govern the all state of affairs in the Government of Brijis Qadr. His mother Begam Hazrat Mahal played very important role in mobilizing the revolutionaries and controlling the administration.[33]

George Dodd narrates about Begam Hazrat Mahal that, "The prime mover in all the intrigues was his mother, the Begam Hazrat Mahal, who professed to be regent during his minority, and to be assisted by a council of state. She was a woman of much energy of character, and conducted public affairs in an apartment of the Qaiser Bagh. Morally she was tainted in full measure with oriental vices. Like Catherine of Russia she raised one of her paramours, Mummoo Khan, to the office of chief judge, and did not scruple openly to acknowledge her relations towards him."[34]

The new King of Awadh Brijis Qadr rode into the city in the procession in order to prove his closeness with his subjects. The newspaper *Tilism* narrates as follows:[35]

"When the procession of the prince came out, the town's populace came out to see. Whoever came and saw the solemn convoy was relieved of his agony and prayed, "O Lord of the under-privileged, Ruler of rulers, do preserve this ancient House until the Day of Judgment." Even though there was not much arrangement for the royal processions, only those who were on duty at the palace accompanied the son of the monarch. However, there was unique grandeur, which was surprising the people.

One day King Brijis Qadr called all officers, soldiers, and irregulars in the army. He himself rode on horseback. Twenty one canons boomed in salutation. Slowly he began speaking, "Brave soldiers! we are very pleased with you for fighting valiantly. But I am deeply grieved that you are plundering the city. Stop that, otherwise the citizens will curse us." Officers assured the King with folded hands that the city would no more be looted.[36]

Brijis Qadr's position was widely recognized and Emperor Bahadur Shah Zafar not only accorded recognition even to Brijis Qadr's Ambassador, but also sent the Seal of Royal Title. Peshwa Nana Sahib also, firstly, sent a political agent to the court of Birjis Qadr at Lucknow then arrived himself, and received a 17-piece *Khillat* and accepted the same. Firoze Shah, Mirza Kochak Sultan, General Bakht Khan Rohila, Shafiullah Khan (ruler of Najibabad), Walidad Khan (ruler of Balagarh), Mazhar Ali Khan (ruler of Mowana), Enayatullah Khan of Pilibhit, Ghulam Kader Khan (ruler of Shahjahanpur), Nana Sahib and Tatya Tope, the leaders of their respective areas, were potentates who in their turn petitioned Birjis Qadr and were given due recognition according to their ranks. Some Rajas brought their armies to Lucknow, and themselves paid for the upkeep. Some others got rations from the Government. And all these armies of Rajas, talluqdars and zamindars totalled one lakh, fifty thousand, and five hundred. Coins were struck in the name of Brijis Qadr as, "*Sikka zad bar seem-o-zar chun mehr-o-badr, Nayyer-e deen Mirza Birjis Qadr.*"[37]

Many proclamations were issued from Lucknow Muslim theologians inviting the people to join against the British for the sake of religion and nation. The excerpts of some of them are as follows:[38]

".... If all the Mohammedans join and remain firm to their faith, they would no doubt gain victory over the Christians, because victory is due to the faithful.... If the Mohammedans have any shame, they should all join and prepare themselves to kill the Christians without binding anyone who says to the contrary; they should know that no one dies before his time, and when the times, nothing can save them...... To be killed in a war against Christians is a proof of obtaining martyrdom. All good Mohammedans pray for such a death; therefore, everyone should sacrifice his life for such a reward. Everyone is to die assuredly, and those Mohammedans who would spare themselves now will be sorry on their death for their neglect..... As it is the duty of all men and women to oppose, kill, and expel the Europeans for deeds committed by them at Delhi, Jhajjar, Rewari, and the Doab, all the Mohammedans should discharge their duty with a willing heart; if they neglect, and the Europeans overpower them, they will be disarmed, hung, and treated like the inhabitants of other unfortunate countries, and will have nothing but regret and sorrow for their lot. Wherefore this notice is given to warn the public."

Another proclamation issued by Awadh Government, addressed principally to zamindars and Hindus in general, but to Mohammedans also, was couched in the following terms:[39]

"All the Hindus and Mohammedans know that man loves four things most: 1, his religion and caste; 2, his honour; 3, his own and his kinsmen's lives; 4, his property. All these four are well protected under Native rulers; no one interferes with any one's religion; ...... All the respectable people Sayyad, Shaikh, Mughal, and Pathan, among Mohammedans; and Brahmins, Kshatris, Kaisths, among the Hindus are respected according to their castes. ..... The British are quite against these four things they want to spoil every one's caste, and wish both the Mohammedans and Hindus to become Christians. Thousands have turned renegades, and many will become so yet; both the nobles and low caste are equal in their eyes; they disgrace the nobles in the presence of the ignoble; they arrest or summon to their courts the gentry, Nawabs, and Rajas at the instance of a chamar, and disgrace them; wherever they go they hang the respectable people, kill their women and children; .... In some places, they deceive the landholders by promising them remittance of revenue, or lessen the amount of their lease; their object is that when their Government is settled, and everyone becomes their subject, they can readily, according to their wish, hang, disgrace, or Christianise them. ....Therefore, all the Hindus and Mohammedans who wish to save their religion, honour, life, and property, are warned to join the Government forces, and not to be deceived by the British. The passees (low-caste servants) should also know that the chowkidari (office of watchmen) is their hereditary right, but the British appoint barkandazes in their posts, and deprive them of their rights; they should therefore kill and plunder the British and their followers, and annoy them by committing robbery and thefts in their camp."

The independent government at Lucknow sought support of the almost all the revolutionaries of the neighbouring districts and even the Bihar leader Kunwar Singh. The revolutionaries of Lucknow were in close association of Nana Sahib of Kanpur, Maulvi Ahmadullah of Faizabad and most of the rebellious leaders and commanders came from Delhi after its occupation by the British. Raja Jai Lal Singh, the Nazim of

Azamgarh was the right hand of the Birjis Qadr/Hazrat Mahal Government. He was not only the member of the Military Council which took all major decisions, but also acting as commander of the revolutionary army. He was instrumental in mobilising military support from the districts around Lucknow.[40]

Gubbins narrates that the British, hided in the Residency, were continually insulted by the music of the mutineers. At early dawn, their bugles regularly begin sounding the Assembly and a variety of regimental calls; while the shrill horns and drums of the *Rajwara* (a name used to designate the zemindari forces) kept up loud and dissonant screams, which were again renewed every evening. Occasionally, their bands paraded in the English sight and played "God save the Queen," or other tunes which they had learnt in British service.[41]

After the reoccupation of Delhi, it became the matter of 'do or die' for the British to re-conquer Lucknow, the second most important bastion of Indian revolutionaries. The recapture of Lucknow was a matter of urgency; without control over Lucknow British rule could not be re-established in Awadh. They not only occupied the neighbouring areas of Lucknow, but committed the inhuman cruelties without fear of shaming themselves in the civilized world. They threatened the city as well as rural population by their brutal retribution in order to demoralize the revolutionaries. The infamous genocide of notorious General Neill was the worst example of their cruelties.

Charles Raikes mentions that due to the ongoing fight between the British and revolutionary forces, the financial position of the Awadh treasury became miserable. In order to settle the matter Begam Hazrat Mahal held a a Darbar and summoned all the Native commandants of troops and the revolutionary Chiefs, and told them that she was unable to keep them in the pay of the King any longer, and that she desired to pay them up, and discharge them. Then the soldiers and revolutionaries replied that in a day or two they would attack the British force near Alambagh, and either drive the British out of the place, or perish in the attempt.[42]

On 23rd September 1857, the British forces under Havelock and Outram stormed the Alambagh, the summer palace of the Kings of Awadh, eight miles from Lucknow city. On 25th of September, the combined forces attacked on Lucknow. General Havelock's force consisted of three thousand one hundred and seventy-nine men of all arms: European Infantry- 2,388, European Cavalry- 109, European Artillery- 282, Sikh Infantry- 341, Native Irregular Cavalry- 59, totaling- 3,179. General Havelock divided it into three brigades. — two of infantry, the third of artillery. The first brigade consisted of the 5th Fusiliers, the 84th Regiment, and, attached to it, two companies of the 64th, the 1st Madras Fusiliers. It was commanded by Neill. The 2nd Brigade, composed of the 78th Highlanders, the 90th Light Infantry, and the Sikh regiment of Firozpur, was commanded by Brigadier Hamilton, 78th Highlanders. The 3rd Brigade comprehended Captain Maude's battery, Captain Olpherts's battery. Major Eyre's battery of heavy 18-pounders, the whole of the third Brigade was commanded by Major Cooper. Besides these, there were a hundred and nine volunteers, and some fifty-nine of the 12th Irregulars, believed to be faithful, under the command of Captain L. Barrow. Major-General Outram was one of these volunteers. All these combined forces managed to reach the Residency, where the united force had to stay, closely blockaded, for two months more. The infamous General Neill was killed during the fighting in town; Outram received severe wound in arm.[43]

The problem with the British garrison was that the revolutionaries from all parts India were daily crowding at Lucknow. Kaye and Malleson write that the strength of the revolutionaries at Lucknow was about 96,000. This count did not include artillerymen, the number of whom was unknown, nor the armed followers of the tallukdars, estimated at 20,000. Altogether there could not have been less than 120,000 armed men in Lakhnow at the end of January 1858. Kaye and Malleson also estimate that the total strength of troops at the disposal of Colin Campbell was about twenty thousand men (excluding ten thousand Gorkhas under Jang Bahadur, the Prime Minister of Nepal) and a hundred and eighty guns. Malleson quotes the exact computation of revolutionary forces as estimated by Outram on 27th of January 1858:[44]

37 trained regiments of Sepoys 27,550

14 regiments of new levies.... 5,400

106 Najib, or irregular regiments 55,150

26 regiments of cavalry 7,100

Camel corps 800

Totalling....96,000

However, the siege of the Residency continued and again in November 1857 the British forces bitted the dust by the hands of the revolutionaries. Colin Campbell's military action on this occasion was only a partial success. Havelock and Inglis were killed during the siege. The city contained 30,000 revolted Sepoys, 50,000 volunteers or *Mujahideens* and armed retainers of chieftains. The British garrison was also reinforced with many British regiments, including ten thousand Gorkhas under Jang Bahadur. The siege-train also arrived from Agra. Now the British garrison was totaling about 30,000 including 18,000 Europeans. Eventually, a massive offensive was launched in March 1858. Campbell set up his headquarters in the Dilkusha Palace located in the Dilkusha Gardens on the outskirts of the city. His contingents occupied Lucknow on 21st March 1858 after capturing the Moosa Bagh.[45]

The European efforts of Lucknow siege was on its apex in March 1858, and wherever they occupied the area plundered it mercilessly more likely in the case of Delhi. House after house was plundered of its furniture and miscellaneous contents, and swords, in rich scabbards, embroidered cloths, shawls, ornaments, and a most extraordinary and varied assortment of European articles of every kind and description, guns, ctocks, books, etc., were spread about in every direction. After a series of skirmishes, the Residency, Machi Bhawan, and other strong portions of the revolutionaries were taken by the British.

There was a great deal of plundering, beginning with the well-known Begam Kothi, where accursed Hodson of 'Hodson's Horse' lost his life, when he had no military function there whatever. The revolutionaries were forced to fly towards North and North-West in thousands in the number. Until 18th of March almost all the cities were occupied by the British forces except Moosa Bagh, a large Native garden, with a fine house or palace at one end of the enclosure. In the morning of the 19th, the British troops attacked on the revolutionaries at Moosa Bagh and after a strong fight, the revolutionaries left the ground leaving their guns. However, again on 21st of March the revolutionaries dashed into the city, and again a fierce battle took place in which both the parties met a heavy loss, and eventually they fled towards countryside leaving the city on the mercy of the Europeans. According to an estimate, the casualties amounted to only 16 British officers, 3 Native officers, and 108 men killed; 51 British officers, 4 Native officers, and 540 men wounded, while 13 men were missing totaling about 1100. This estimate included 51 killed, and 287 wounded of the Maharaja Jang Bahadur's force under General Kharrak Bahadur as he was also fighting against the revolutionaries with 15000 men of 23 battalions and 24 guns. The loss of the revolutionaries was about 4000.[46]

The total fighting strength left at the end of the siege was 982. Thus, the casualties had been over 30 per cent. A large number of women and children were killed or died. There was a lot of bloodshed in conquering the city of Lucknow. According to the quote of *Naya Daur*, "For practically every inch of land there was heavy fighting, and important places like Begam Kothi, Sikandar Bagh, Moti Mahal, Shah Najaf, Qaisarbagh, etc. could be captured only after stepping on the dead bodies of the soldiers."[47]

Charles Wright quotes the Cooke's description as Follows:[48]

"Had I not seen it myself and known it to be the fact that we had taken it from so strong and numerous an enemy, I should never have believed it. I never saw so strong a place in my life. It was full of fortifications and strongholds. Such beautiful buildings are not to be seen elsewhere, and every street and house was loop-holed. It seemed impossible for English, or any other troops to have taken such a place. Surely God hath fought for England. The city was nothing but one mass of batteries, everywhere loop-holed, from a pig stye to a palace. The position of our troops was pointed out to me, and the ground where their several charges were made. The buildings are most of them greatly damaged by our shot and shell, and the walls covered with the marks of musket balls, showing plainly the desperate struggle that had taken place. A great many houses were altogether destroyed or burnt. Many of the enemy were buried in the ruins, for the soldiers in their fury spared but few of the Sepoys who came in their way. At the time I marched through it after the fall, the stench was suffocating, and dead bodies were lying in heaps in the ditches just covered over slightly with earth. Afterwards, when I was located in the outskirts of the town, many dead bodies of the enemy lay about unburied in the villages and Jangles, and dead camels and bullocks were to be found in every direction."

Edward Gilliat writes that after the fall of Lucknow, the city looked like Delhi after its capture. The dead bodies of Sepoys, carcasses of animals clogged the narrow passages and rendered the air nauseous and unhealthy. Most of the inhabitants had fled; the Residency was a heap of ruins; pillars were broken; rooms were choked by the debris of fallen ceilings and roofs, and the church was leveled to its foundations. It is also said that all around Lucknow for miles the country was covered with dead carcasses, men, horses, camels, bullocks, and donkeys lay about everywhere. Most of the rebels from Lucknow retreated North-west towards Bareilly and Rohilkhand.[49]

Urdu Newspaper *Naya Daur* gives the details of the valour and loyalty of some Rajas of Brijis Qadr. One of his loyalists Maulvi Mohammad who went to the battle of Sandila declared that either he would conquer or would be killed. So he did not turn his back to the battlefield and along with his 5000 fighters, fought valiantly. Another one the Raja Kunwar Singh of Hardoi on being surrounded by the British army, ordered his forces to surrender. However, instead of surrendering himself, he told that these soldiers were under his command, and there is no benefit in getting them killed. Nevertheless, he was under the command and discretion of Birjis Qadr, who was not there to guide him. And alone braved the volley of bullets and instantly got killed. Another Rana Beni Madho Singh of Shankarpur surrendered his fortress without a fight to Sir Hope Grant as he was unable to defend his fort. However, he never surrendered himself as his own person was the property of his King. He asked only those of his companions to accompany him who wished to die. Among 250 men only two chose to leave, and the rest laid their lives fighting along with the Raja.[50]

Begam Hazrat Mahal shifted her base to the fort of Bundi (district Bahraich), where she continued her struggle until she was forced to evacuate the fort in December 1858. When she was at Bundi, Queen Victoria issued her famous proclamation in November 1858. In this proclamation, British Crown directly assumed responsibility for governance of the Indian empire. It was also declared that all inhabitants of the empire became subjects of the crown. By this proclamation, the British monarch was projected as the benevolent protector of her Indian subjects. Freedom of religion was the part of the proclamation.[51]

In response to Queen Victoria's proclamation Hazrat Mahal issued a counter-proclamation by the name of Birjis Qadr in which she exposed the falsehoods of British assurances and the deceit upon which colonial rule was based. Drawing attention to the hypocrisy of British declarations, Hazrat Mahal said, "to eat pigs and drink wine, to bite greased cartridges and to mix pig's fat with sweetmeats, to destroy Hindu and Musalman temples on pretense of making roads, to build churches, to send clergymen into the streets to preach the Christian religion, to institute English schools, and pay people a monthly stipend for learning the English sciences, while the places of worship of Hindus and Musalmans are to this day entirely neglected; with all this, how can people believe that religion will not be interfered with?" In her counter proclamation, Begam Hazrat Mahal also said, "The Company has seized on the whole of Hindusthan, and if this arrangement be accepted, what is there new in it? The Company professed to treat the Chief of

Bharatpur as a son and then took his territory. The chief of Lahore was carried off to London, never to return again. The Nawab Shams-ud-din Khan, on the one hand, they hanged, while, on the other hand, they salaamed to him. The Peshwa they expelled from Poona and Satara and imprisoned for life in Bithur. The Raja of Banaras they imprisoned in Agra. They have left no names or traces of the chiefs of Bihar, Orissa, and Bengal. ....But, even recently, in defiance of oaths and treaties, and notwithstanding that they owed us millions of rupees, without reason and on pretences of misconduct and the discontent of our people, they took our country and property worth millions of rupees. If our people were discontented with our royal predecessor, Wajid Ali Shah, how comes it then, that they are content with us? And no ruler ever experienced such loyalty and devotion of life and goods as we have. What, then, is wanting that they do not restore to us our country?" Further, Begam asked in the counter proclamation, "If the Queen has assumed the Government, why does Her Majesty not restore our country to us when our people wish it?" She also appealed to the people, "Let no subject be deceived by the proclamation!"[52]

Gubbins had quoted a mail which fully describes the condition of Lucknow after its siege by the British. The mail was as follows:[53]

"The tomb of Saadat Ali Khan, in the Kaiser Bagh (the larger of the two in the illustration which forms the frontispiece), has been turned into a Christian Church. The lesser, Imambara, in the Hazrat Gunj, is now the Scotch Kirk. Both these are excellent moves. The Chief Commissioner resides in the house which was Major Banks. The Sikandar Bagh (the scene of fearful slaughter on the 16th of November last) is now a club coffee-house. All the small houses and the high walls of the Kaiser Bagh are being levelled: and the King's Dancing Hall, in the cenfare of the Zanana Garden, has been turned into a theatre royal of the 23rd Welsh Fusiliers. Changes, which certainly must have metamorphosed Lucknow, and which no one will regret."

On the conquest of Bundi, Begam Hazrat Mahal moved to the dense jangles of the Tarai area, and subsequently, she took refuge in Nepal. She lived on until 1879 and was buried in an Imambara in Kathmandu. It is said that now the grave of this brave freedom fighter lady has virtually been obliterated.

Brijis Qadr, despite his minority in 1857, was ever since treated as a rebel against all canons of law and justice. Ultimately, he along with his children was killed by poison in an unholy conspiracy. Those who escaped the assassination were deprived of their ancestral properties, jagir, and Government Promissory Notes worth lakhs of rupees.[54]

After the capture of Lucknow, the capital of Awadh, almost all the surviving revolutionary and troops shifted themselves to other places and continued their fighting against the British. Outram assumed the charge of Chief Commissionership after his victory over Lucknow. Meanwhile, the Governor General Lord Canning created a new crisis by issuing a proclamation in March 1858, which confiscated the estates of the talluqdars. They were two hundred and seventy-two in number, and at the time of the annexation of Awadh; in February 1856, they had possession of two-thirds of the province. The proclamation proceeded to name six men — three of whom were Rajas, two zamindars, and one a talluqdar — who had remained faithful, of whom the Raja of Balrampur was the most prominent, were exempted. This measure of Canning led to a serious crisis. Talluqdars throughout Awadh promptly mobilized themselves against the British. This was a desperate struggle on their part to hold on to their land and feudal privileges. Even fence-sitters now joined the fight. Canning's proclamation prolonged the Revolt in Awadh for several months. There began the sharp differences over the proclamation. These differences almost led to the fall of the minority ministry in Britain headed by Lord Derby. In India, there were differences between Outram and Canning on that question. Canning eventually agreed to a policy of reconciliation, and Outram tried to negotiate with the talluqdars, assuring them that they would not lose their estates if they gave up the path of rebellion. The *Sunnuds* or charters were granted to the tallukdars, that "all holding under them should be secured in the possession of all the subordinate rights they formerly enjoyed." It was obvious that the Awadh countryside could not be won through a military conquest. Consequently, in the post-1858 period the landed elite became the main support of the colonial state.[55]

Undoubtedly the province of Awadh and particularly the Lucknow city was the hard nut for the British. Here the revolutionaries were much organized than Delhi and showed the unforgettable courage and strength. They were lucky enough to kill thousands of the British including the Commander-in-Chief Sir Henry Lawrence, General Havelock, and infamous Hodson and Neill, the Delhi and Kanpur massacre mastermind.

References:

1. Dodd, p-86, see also Savarkar, p. 36
2. *Ibid*, see also Savarkar, p. 36
3. *Ibid*, p-86
4. Martin, R. Montgomery, *The Indian Empire,* Vol. II, London, 1858, p. 71, see also Savarkar, p. 38 (V.D. Savarkar says that this youthful prince introduced strict regulations as to the discipline of the Sepoys and even personally supervised their drill. All the regiments had to undergo the drill every morning before the Nawab, who used to dress in the uniform of the commander- in-chief of the troops. He issued strict orders that every regiment that was late in presenting itself on the parade ground should be liable to a fine of Rs. 2000 (£ 200) and he, at the same time, bound himself to pay the same amount as fine if he himself failed in this duty. The Company, of course, could not bear to see the Nawab develop his strength. The British Resident, therefore, in a short time forced the Nawab to give up these military activities and at the same time suggested that, if he so desired to increase the strength of the army, the Company was quite willing to increase the subsidiary. Savarkar further says that the hot-blooded Nawab was quite indignant. But he was forced to give up his darling scheme of military reform and was reduced to complete inactivity. Savarkar, p. 38)

5. Martin, R. Montgomery, *The Indian Empire,* Vol. II, London, 1858, pp. 71-73, see also Wright, Charles H.H., *Memoire of John Lovering Cooke*, London, 1873, pp. 26-27

6. Martin, R. Montgomery, *The Indian Empire,* Vol. II, London, 1858, p. 74, see also R. W. Frazer, *British India,* New York, 1896, p. 64, (There was also a religious fanaticism and strife in the city of Ayodhya near Faizabad. A Maulvi, named Ameer Ali, had started a story that the Hanuman Garhi, the great Hindu temple, had been built on the site of a Muslim mosque; having then collected a band of followers, he had attacked the temple, but had been repulsed by the Hindus who had flocked in to its defence. The story was groundless, and was proved to be so by reference to the archives at Delhi; and a religious war would have ensued had not General Outram stepped in and insisted on the maintenance of law and order. The Maulvi, however, continued his threatening attitude towards the temple, and eventually, trusting to the secret support of the Nawab, advanced to its attack; but was met by Nawab's troops commanded by English officers, with the result that he was himself killed and his followers dispersed. *Lucknow & Oude in the Mutiny,* pp. 58-59, see also Innes, McLeod, *The Sepoy Revolt: A Critical Narrative,* London, 1897, pp. 32-33, and Martin, R. Montgomery, *The Indian Empire,* Vol. II, London, 1858, p. 77)

7. Argyl, Campbell, George Douglas, Duke of, *India Under Dalhousie and Canning,* London, 1865, p. 17, see also Martin, R. Montgomery, *The Indian Empire,* Vol. II, London, 1858, p. 74

8. Gibbon, p. 233

9. Argyl, Campbell, George Douglas, Duke of, *India Under Dalhousie and Canning,* London, 1865, pp. 20-22

10. Savarkar, pp. 39-40

11. *Ibid,* pp. 41-42

12. Gubbins, pp. 55-56, see also Campbell, George, *Memoirs of My Indian Career,* Vol. II, (edited by Charles E. Bernard), New York, 1893, p. 2

13. *A History of the Indian Mutiny,* Vol. I, London 1904, p. 155

14. Martin, R. Montgomery, *The Indian Empire,* Vol. II, London, 1858, p. 82

15. *People's Democracy, (Lucknow In 1857-58: The Epic Siege*-Amar Farooqui), Vol. XXXI, No. 41, October 14, 2007, (Henry Lawrence wrote to Edwardes, "....Man can but die once, and if I die in Oude, after having saved some poor fellows' hearths, or skins, or *izzut* (reputation), I shall have no reason for discontent....." Gibbon, p. 236)

16. Inglis, Julia Selina Lady, *The Siege of Lucknow: A Diary,* London, 1892, p. 2 (Lady Inglis writes that on the eve of the Uprising, during the dinner, Sir Henry was very grave and silent. He told her that he considered the annexation of Awadh the most unrighteous act that was ever committed. Inglis, Julia Selina Lady, *The Siege of Lucknow: A Diary,* London, 1892, p. 11)

17. Cunningham, Henry Stewart, *Earl Canning,* Oxford, 1891, p. 51

18. Adam and Charles Black, *History of the Siege of Delhi,* Edinburgh, 1861, p. 9, see also *People's Democracy, (Lucknow In 1857-58: The Epic Siege*-Amar Farooqui), Vol. XXXI, No. 41, October 14, 2007

19. Mead, Henry, *The Sepoy Revolt: Its causes and its Consequences,* London, 1858, p. 113, see also Inglis, Julia Selina Lady, *The Siege of Lucknow: A Diary,* London, 1892, p. 2, Malleson, George Bruce, *History of the Indian Mutiny of 1857-58, Commencing from the Close of the Second Volume of Sir John Kaye's History of the Sepoy War,* Vol. III, (Contemporaneous with Sir John Kay's Third Volume), London, 1878, pp. 56-57, *Lucknow & Oude in the Mutiny,* p. 16, and *A Sketch of the Principal Military Events,* p. 78

20. Gibbon, pp. 245-246, see also *A Sketch of the Principal Military Events,* p. 78

21. Dodd, p. 88, see also *Lucknow & Oude in the Mutiny,* p. 63

22. *Ibid*, p. 88

23. Gibbon, pp. 248-250

24. Evelyn Wood, *The Revolt in Hindustan 1857-59,* London, 1908, pp. 129-131, see also *People's Democracy, (Lucknow In 1857-58: The Epic Siege*-Amar Farooqui), Vol. XXXI, No. 41, October 14, 2007, and Gubbins, pp. 120, 128 &131, (Although the revolutionaries were defeated but caused heavy loss to the European force. Lady Inglis narrates that Brigadier Handscomb was shot dead when imprudently venturing down the lines. Mr. Grant, 71st N.I., was murdered at the quarter guard of his regiment Mr. Chambers, adjutant, 13th N.I., was badly wounded, but saved by some of his own men, and escorted to the Residency. Cornet Raleigh, a young officer in the 7th Cavalry, was murdered. Mrs. Bruere, wife of the colonel of the 13th N.I., had a narrow escape. Inglis, Julia Selina Lady, *The Siege of Lucknow: A Diary,* London, 1892, pp. 22-23)

25. Savarkar, pp. 66-67, (Savarkar quotes the letters of the Sepoys of Barrackpur which were mentioned by Kaye. "The second grenadier said that the whole regiment is ready to join the Nawab of Awadh." "Subedars said that they would join the Nawab of Awadh." "Subedar Madar Khan, Sardar Khan, and Ram Shahi Lal said, "that in treachery no one could come up to the level of the 'Beti-chod' Firangis." Savarkar, p. 68)

26. John William Kaye, *A History of the Sepoy War in India, 1857-58,* Vol. III, London 1876, pp. 38-42

27. Duff, Alexander, *The Indian Rebellion: Its Causes and Results, in a Series of Letters,* New York, 1858, p. 33

28. Gubbins, pp. 212-213, see also Inglis, Julia Selina Lady, *The Siege of Lucknow: A Diary,* London, 1892, p. 51, and Gibbon, p. 291

29. Gubbins, p. 213-214 (John William Kaye quotes Brigadier Havelock, "This morning, we went out eight miles to meet the enemy, and we were defeated and lost five guns, through the misconduct chiefly of our Native artillerymen, many of whom have deserted. The enemy have followed us up, and we have now been besieged for four hours, and shall probably to night be surrounded. The enemy are very bold, and our Europeans are very low. I look upon our position as ten times as bad as it was yesterday. Indeed, it is now critical. We shall be obliged to concentrate, if we are able. We shall have to abandon much supplies, and to blow up much powder. Unless we are relieved quickly, say in fifteen or twenty days, we shall hardly be able to maintain our position." John

William Kaye, *A History of the Sepoy War in India, 1857-58,* Vol. III, London 1876, p. 512)

30. Wilson, T.F., *The Defence of Lucknow: A Diary,* London, 1858, pp. 44-45
31. *Ibid,* pp. 45-46, see also Gibbon, p. 294, and Gubbins, pp. 227-228 & 244, and *People's Democracy, (Lucknow In 1857-58: The Epic Siege*-Amar Farooqui), Vol. XXXI, No. 41, October 14, 2007
32. *Lucknow & Oude in the Mutiny,* p. 117
33. *Naya Daur, (Brijis Qadr: The Last King of Awadh*- Mirza Qaukab Qadr) Awadh Number, a Monthly Urdu Journal published by the Information & Public Relations Department of the Government of Uttar Pradesh, Lucknow, February-March 1994, see also *People's Democracy, (Lucknow In 1857-58: The Epic Siege*-Amar Farooqui), Vol. XXXI, No. 41, October 14, 2007
34. Dodd, p. 413
35. *Tilism,* Lucknow, December 19, 1856
36. *Naya Daur,* Lucknow, February-March 1994
37. *Ibid*
38. Dodd, p. 427
39. *Ibid,* pp. 427-428
40. *People's Democracy, (Lucknow In 1857-58: The Epic Siege*-Amar Farooqui), Vol. XXXI, No. 41, October 14, 2007
41. Gubbins, p. 246
42. Raikes, Charles, *Notes on the Revolt in the North-Western Provinces of India,* London, 1858, p. 105
43. Malleson, George Bruce, *History of the Indian Mutiny of 1857-58, Commencing from the Close of the Second Volume of Sir John Kaye's History of the Sepoy War,* Vol. III, (Contemporaneous with Sir John Kay's Third Volume), London, 1878, pp. 526 & 545-546, see also Marx, Karl, *Notes on the Indian History (664-1858),* Russian Edition, Moscow, 1947, p. 153
44. Malleson, George Bruce, *Kay's and Malleson's History of the Indian Mutiny of 1857-8,* Vol. IV, London, 1911, pp. 251& 254, see also Forrest, Volume III, Calcutta, 1902, p. 454, (Sedgwick quotes the account of Forrest with a little difference. He says that the rebels had collected the following troops at Lucknow to oppose Sir Colin Campbell: 37 Regiments of Sepoys- 27,550; 14, new levies- 5,400; 106, Najibs- 55,150; 26, Cavalry- 7,100; Camel Corps-300; Total- 95,500, but this does not include the armed retainers of the landowners of Awadh. *A Sketch of the Principal Military Events,* p. 111
45. Dodd, pp. 413&415, see also *People's Democracy, (Lucknow In 1857-58: The Epic Siege*-Amar Farooqui), Vol. XXXI, No. 41, October 14, 2007, and *A History of the Indian Mutiny,* Vol. II, London 1904, p. 368 (To attack it Sir Colin Campbell had collected a force of rather more than 30,000 men and 164 guns, distributed as follows:
Cavalry Division- Hope Grant

1st Brigade:

9th Lancers 2nd Battalion Military- 454

Train- 210

Wale's Horse (Sikhs)- 466

2nd Punjab Cavalry- 520

Detachments- 160

2nd Brigade:

2nd Dragoon Guards- 471

7th Hussars- 422

Volunteer Cavalry- 59

1st Punjab Cavalry- 106

Hodson's Horse- 743

Total- 3,613

Artillery Division- Wilson

Naval Brigade- 431

Field Artillery Brigade- 800

Siege- 382

Total- 1,613

Engineer Brigade: Napier.

Royal Engineers- 217

Bengal Engineers- 247

Punjab Pioneers- 782

Delhi Pioneers (unarmed)- 754

Total- 2,002

1st Infantry (or Outranks Division)- Outram

1st Brigade:

5th Regiment- 534

84th Regiment- 665

1st Madras Europeans- 498

2nd Brigade:

78th Regiment- 519

90th Regiment- 736

Firuzpur Regiment- 323

Total 3,275

2nd Infantry Division- Lugard

3rd Brigade:

34th Regiment- 572

38th Regiment- 986

53rd Regiment- 811

4th Brigade:

42nd Regiment- 879
93rd Regiment- 936
4th Punjab Rifles- 470
Total- 4,654

3rd Infantry Division- Walpole

5th Brigade:
23rd Regiment- 879
79th Regiment- 908
1st Bengal Europeans- 576
6th Brigade:
 2nd Battalion Rifle Brigade- 793
3rd Battalion Rifle Brigade 877
2nd Punjab Infantry- 590
Total- 4,623

Frank's Division

Artillery: Four Batteries- 344
Cavalry: Banaras Horse- 70
Lahore Light Horse- 133
Pathan Horse- 109
3rd Sikh Irregulars- 216
Total- 872

British Infantry

10th Regiment- 698
20th Regiment - 676
97th Regiment- 613
Total- 1,987

This makes a total of 22,654 men and about 5,500 horses. It excludes 6 Battalions of Gorkha Infantry and Artillery 3,019 and Jang Bahadur's Force about 6,000. The approximate total of this force was about 9,000. *A Sketch of the Principal Military Events,* pp. 115-117)

46. Julius George Medley, *A Years Campaigning in India from March 1857 to March 1858,* London 1858, pp. 182-186, see also Dodd, p. 426, Gilliat Edward, *Heroes of the Indian Mutiny; Stories of Heroic Deeds,* London 1914, p. 252, Campbell, George, *Memoirs of My Indian Career,* Vol. II, (edited by Charles E. Bernard), New York, 1893, p. 4, and Forrest, Volume III, Calcutta, 1902, p. 490

47. *A Sketch of the Principal Military Events,* p. 81, see also *Naya Daur,* Lucknow, February-March 1994

48. Wright, Charles H.H., *Memoire of John Lovering Cooke,* London, 1873, pp. 95-96

49. Gilliat Edward, *Heroes of the Indian Mutiny; Stories of Heroic Deeds,* London 1914, pp. 118-119

50. *Naya Daur*, Lucknow, February-March 1994
51. William Dalrymple, *The last Mughal: The fall of a Dynasty: Delhi, 1857*, New Delhi 2006, p. 69, see also *People's Democracy, (Lucknow In 1857-58: The Epic Siege*-Amar Farooqui), Vol. XXXI, No. 41, October 14, 2007
52. *People's Democracy, (Lucknow In 1857-58: The Epic Siege*-Amar Farooqui), Vol. XXXI, No. 41, October 14, 2007, see also Savarkar, pp. 421-422
53. Gubbins, p. XV (Preface)
54. *Naya Daur*,Lucknow, February-March 1994
55. Malleson, George Bruce, *Kay's and Malleson's History of the Indian Mutiny of 1857-8,* Vol. V, London, 1911, pp. 184-186, see also, *People's Democracy, (Lucknow In 1857-58: The Epic Siege*-Amar Farooqui), Vol. XXXI, No. 41, October 14, 2007, and Argyl, Campbell, George Douglas, Duke of, *India Under Dalhousie and Canning*, London, 1865, p. 113

Chapter 5

Jhansi and Rani Luxmi Bai

The fortress of Jhansi in Bundelkhand area was built by the Bundela Chief of Orchha, Bir Singh Deo. It stands on a great rock rising out of the plain, and is solidly and skillfully constructed of blocks of granite; except on the west it is surrounded by the town of Jhansi, a walled city of some 4 miles circumference. The origin of the name of Jhansi as explained by the people of Orchha that once the Raja of Jaitpur was on a visit to Bir Singh Deo, and when one day both were sitting on the roof of the palace at Orchha, the latter, pointing in the direction of his new fort, in the distance (about six miles off), asked his guest if he could see it. Shading his eyes with his hand, and looking intently in the direction indicated, the Jaitpur Raja replied, "Jhan-si," meaning "shadow-like," by which he intended that he could see it indistinctly; and through this incident, the city which afterwards grew up around the fort came to be named Jhansi.[1]

After the fall of the Mughal Empire Maratha stormed the area and one of their free-lances seized the State of Jhansi and had his claim by conquest confirmed by a *Sunnad* from his Master, the Peshwa. He and his successors governed it, under the title of Subedar, as a vassal of the Peshwa. Under the Marathas, Jhansi was continued to be ruled by governors appointed from time to time by the Peshwa. Nevertheless, when the Peshwa's power began to wane, as was the case toward the end of the eighteenth century, the governors at Jhansi ruled more like independent chiefs than as viceroys. The British succeeded in getting the whole Bundelkhand, including Jhansi from the Peshwa by a treaty held on 18th November 1817. However, due to the valuable services of the current Prince Ram Chandra Rao, he was allowed to rule over Jhansi with the title of Subedar, under the protection of the British. He was also agreed to pay an annual tribute of seventy-four thousand rupees of the currency of his State. In return, the British Government declared him hereditary ruler of the country.[2]

The administration of Ram Chandra was carried on so satisfactorily, that, in 1832, the title of Maharaja was publicly conferred on him, in lieu of that of Subedar, by Governor-General Lord William Bentinck, who was returning by Jhansi to Calcutta, from a tour of inspection in the Upper Provinces. Raja Ram Chandra Rao enjoyed his new dignity for three years and then died without issue in 1835.[3]

As the Ram Chandra Rao was guaranteed that the State would be hereditary to his family; his uncle Raghunath Rao was given the chance to rule over Jhansi. Raghunath Rao was incapable and a leper. After three years of unpopular rule, he died in 1838, and the throne became again vacant. There were several claimants to succeed him. Their pretensions were examined by a commission appointed by the Governor-General of India, and after a long interregnum all but one were pronounced invalid. The expected claim was that of Gangadhar Rao, brother of the deceased. He, therefore, was nominated as Raja. Raja Gangadhar Rao ruled Jhansi for eleven years and maintained good relations with the British. He died in November 1854 without heirs.[4]

Raja Gangadhar Rao left no child but on the day before he died, very unexpectedly, he adopted a child named Damodar Rao. The day before his death, he wrote to the political assistant of Bundelkhand, Mr. Ellis, and the officer in command Captain Martin, "(After compliments.) The manner in which my ancestors were faithful to the British Government, previous to the establishment of its authority (in Bundelkhand), has become known even in Europe; and it is well known to the several agents here, that I also have always acted in obedience to the same authority. I am now very ill; and it is a source of great grief to me, that notwithstanding all my fidelity, ... such a powerful Government, the name of my father will end with me; and I have therefore, with reference to the second article of the treaty concluded with the British Government, adopted Damodar Gangadhar Rao, commonly called Anand Rao, a boy of five years old, my grandson through my grandfather........... Should I not survive, I trust that, in consideration of the fidelity I have evinced towards Government, favour may be shown to this child, and that my widow, during her lifetime, may be considered the regent of the state (Malika) and mother of this child, and that she may not be molested in any way."[5]

Major Malcolm, the political agent for Gwalior, Bundelkhand, and Rewa forwarded the claim of Rani, the widow of the late Gangadhar Rao, in whose hands he has expressed a wish that the Government should be placed during her lifetime, was a woman highly respected and esteemed, and according to his belief, fully capable of doing justice to such a charge. In case of the annexation of the state, Malcolm urged that in compliance with her husband's last request, all the state jewels, and private funds, and any balance remaining in the public treasury, after closing the accounts of the state, should also be considered as her private property.[6]

However, unfortunately, the Governor-General Lord Dahousie didn't recognize the hier, and by refuting the entire plaint, stated clearly, "there is no need of, and no room for, argument. The historical facts on record negative the Rani's assertion conclusively; for the previous Raja did adopt a boy, but the British Government did not acknowledge the boy as successor, and it nominated another person to be Raja." The annexation of Jhansi was almost final in the absence of any near blood relative. Mallesan writes very sympathetically regarding Rani Luxmi Bai, the widow of Gangadhar Rao, "Under Hindu law she possessed the right to adopt an heir to her husband when he died childless in 1854. Lord Dalhousie refused to her the exercise of that right, and declared that Jhansi had lapsed to the paramount power. .... With a stroke of his pen he deprived this high-spirited woman of the rights which she believed, and which all the Natives of India believed, to be hereditary. That stroke of the pen converted the lady, of so high a character and so much respected, into a veritable tigress so far as the English were concerned. For them, thereafter, she would have no mercy. There is reason to believe that she, too, had entered into negotiations with the Maulvi and Nana Sahib before the explosion of 1857 took place."[7]

Colonel Low, one of the Members of Council, clearly pointed out in a Minute the distinction between Sovereign Native States and Dependent Native States. "The Native rulers of Jhansi," he wrote, "were never Sovereigns, they were only subjects of a sovereign, first of the Peshwa, and latterly of the Company; the Government now had a full right to annex the lands of Jhansi to the British administration." Lord Dalhousie declared in an official paper that "as the Raja had left no heir of his body, and there was no male heir of any Chief or Raja who had ruled the principality for half a century, the right of the British Government to refuse to acknowledge the present adoption was unquestionable."[8]

The Jhansi State was confiscation and annexed, and the British Government granted to the widowed Rani Luxmi Bai a pension of £6000 a year. The Rani felt exceedingly indignant on account of the smallness of the annuity, 6,000 pounds which had been assigned to her by the British authorities, which at first she refused but later on accepted. She was still further aggrieved as she was ordered to make the payment of her husband's debts around 30 lakhs of rupees from her personal annual allowances. Against this the Rani earnestly protested and repeatedly pleaded, very reasonably, that as the debts were not her debts, she was not answerable for their payment out of her personal allowance.[9]

Rani Luxmi Bai, the great heroine of 1857 Uprising, was born to Moropant Tambe and Bhagirathi Bai in 1835 at Varanasi. Her childhood name was Manu Bai, which later changed as Luxmi Bai. When Manu was hardly three or four years old, the whole family left Varanasi and went to the court of Baji Rao at Bithur. There she was so much liked by all the people that they called her "Chhabeli." Prince Nana Sahib and the Chhabeli played together in the armoury and learned their lessons for the defence of their country and religion. At that time Nana was eighteen years old and Luxmi Bai was seven. In 1842, at the age of seven, the Chhabeli was given in marriage to Maharaja Gangadhar Rao of Jhansi, and thus became Maharani Luxmi Bai of Jhansi. Only nine years of her married life and at the age of sixteen, she was unfortunately widowed in 1851. After being deprived of power and property she rose against the British and also united and provided the leadership to the revolutionaries of Indian Uprising.[10]

She united the martial spirit of the Maratha soldier with the subtlety of the Deccan Brahman, demanded the succession for the boy. She strongly objected the refusal of the adoption and pleaded that the child was the legal hier as he was adopted by the late Raja in his lifetime and that very child had performed the funeral ritual over his body according to the Hindu law. Continuing to brood over the injury and the disgrace of annexation, she hated the English with the deadliest hatred. Somehow her claim to the Governor General was considered, and she was allowed to act as Regent until the boy

75

chosen by the Raja to be his successor should become of age, and even after the installation of the new Raja she would have remained in a position of commanding influence. However, fate of the dominion was not decided, and the administration was carried on by the British magistrate and other officers. Her influence was confined to the fort only, and she was almost deposed excepting the annual pension amounting six thousand pounds, titles and the Palace, which was in her possession.[11]

Rani's animosity with the British grew stronger as her plead bore no fruit. The insult was further added to injury by the slaughter of kine (sacred in the estimation of Hindus), which was as a matter of course introduced by the British into their newly acquired territory.[12]

At the time of Uprising she was a well-favoured woman of twenty-nine or thirty years of age, having of masculine energy and feminine vindictiveness. She boldly discussed her affairs with Commissioners and Governor but unfortunately considered by them a mere child under the influence of others, and that she was much given to intemperance. Nevertheless, when she heard the news of Uprising, she also began to cunningly persuaded Captain Skene, the Political Agent, to sanction her enlisting some troops for her own safety against the Sepoys, with whom she at once secretly negotiated. After obtaining the permission, she rapidly invited the old soldiers of the State to rally around her, at the same time that she secretly caused to be unearthed heavy guns, which had been buried at the time of her husband's death. The British contingent at Jhansi was not enough to guard its capital. There was a detachment of foot artillery, the left wing of the 12th Regiment of Garrison Native Infantry, the headquarters and the right wing of the 14th Irregular Cavalry. Captain Dunlop of the 12th commanded the garrison, and Captain Alexander Skene was the Political Agent.[13]

The Sepoys of 12th Bengal Infantry stationed at Jhansi, suddenly started firing on 5th of June. The mutiny commenced in Jhansi and the European by leaving their women and children in the Town Fort remained themselves in the cantonment. The commanding officer, Captain Dunlop, arranged to attack the mutineers next day; but, with other officers, he was shot dead by his men. The mutineers breaking up into bands proceeded to set fire to the bungalows and to release the convicts from the jail. A party consisting of 350 Sepoys then approached the town, with two guns and a number of police personnel. They opened the gate Rani's palace (Orchha) with a thundering roar of "*Deen Ki Jai.*" The Rani placed guards at her gate and shut herself up in her palace. Captain Gordon sent an urgent message soliciting her assistance at this crisis, but this was refused, as the mutineers threatened to put her to death and to set fire to her palace in case of her compliance with Captain Gordon's request. The Rani's guards then joined the mutineers. Risaldar Kala Khan and Tahsildar Mohammad Hussain of Jhansi and other valiant soldiers led the attack on the British, and the flag of revolution was hoisted on the fort of Jhansi. The revolutionaries occupied the town except Town Fort where the Europeans were galloped. On the night of the 6th June a meeting was held between the mutineers and deligates of the Rani to settle this momentous question of the future government of the country. The Sepoys were in favour of Sadashiv Rao as their ruler who the kinsman of the late Raja and living at that time at Unao village about twelve miles from Jhansi. They invited him to Jhansi, and a proclamation went forth, declaring that "The People are God's; the country is the Padshah's; and the two Religions govern."[14]

On 7th of June, the British held a council of war and decided to send three of the garrison to the Rani to ask her to use her influence to enable them to proceed unmolested to some place of refuge within British territory. Political Agent Captain Skene was confident about Rani as she had secretly negotiated with him when the Meerut news was received. The following morning Messrs. Andrews, Purcell, and Scott issued from the fort, disguised as Muslims, with the intention of seeing the Queen and obtaining her aid, but the feint being discovered the gentlemen were taken to her palace. She did not even condescend to honour them with an interview, but ordered them to be carried before the mutinous Risaldar for orders. Her words were to the effect "she had no concern with the English swine." This was a signal of death. So the three gentlemen were then dragged out of the palace. Mr. Andrews was killed before the very gate of the Rani's residence and the other two were dispatched beyond the walls of the town."[15]

The revolutionaries threatened the Rani with instant death if she refused to throw in her lot with them. She accordingly consented, and supplied them with a reinforcement of 1000 men, and two heavy guns which she had ordered to be dug out of the earth which had been buried three years ago. After that a fierce battle started in which Captain Gordon was killed. Rani also supplied the arms to the revolutionaries who were busy in the siege of the fort. When the revolutionaries of Jhansi not became successful in crushing the walls of the Town Fort, they hatched a treachery.[16]

According to the conspiracy, Rani sent messengers to the fort under a flag of truce, demanding a parley. Hakim Salay Mohammad, a prominent citizen of Jhansi, promised to spare the lives of the English, if they surrendered unconditionally. Captain Skene responded. The Native messengers then declared that the Rani wanted only the fort; that if the Europeans laid down their arms and surrender the position they held they would be escorted to some other station. These terms were affirmed by the most solemn oaths. Captain Skene, on behalf of the garrison, acceded to them. The members of the garrison then laid down their arms, and walked out of the fort in the evening of 8th June. However, when the English came out of the gates, the soldiers shouted, "*Maro Firangi Ko*." They were made to march in the procession as prisoners of war. As they were approaching Johan Bagh the Sepoys asked the general, "Risaldar Sahib, what further orders?" The Risaldar ordered that the Firangis who were guilty of treason in having dared to dethrone the Rani and annex the country should not be spared. So the Firangi procession was forced to range in three lines, the first containing the adult males, the second the adult females, the third of the children. Then, suddenly, the head Native official of the jail raised his sword and cut down Captain Skene. This was the signal. The captives numbering about 66 were pitilessly hewn down. Not a man, woman, or child, survived that afternoon's butchery.[17]

After cleaning the Jhansi from the Europeans the question of leadership again arose. Rani Luxmi Bai cunningly bribed the mutineers who were supporting Sadashiv Rao and lastly, the Rani was made the ruler with a consensus. A Proclamation went forth: "The people are God's; the country is the Padshah's; and the Raj is Rani Luxmi Bai's." John William Kaye states that she threw all her energy and activity into the work of firmly establishing the Raj. She raised fresh troops; she strengthened her fortified places; she established a mint; and she sent delegates to Dhondu Pant, Nana Sahib, with whom she had previously been in communication.[18]

It is said that after firmly establishing herself at Jhansi, she tried to make cordial relations with the British. She wrote to several high officials, lamenting the massacre which had taken place in Jhansi, with which she disavowed having had any connection whatever. She asserted that she was only holding the Jhansi district until the British could make arrangements for reoccupying it. The Rani remained in power until April 1858, when by the advent of a British army and its operations against the doomed city, the situation was again changed.[19]

Major-General Sir Hugh Rose launched an attack on Jhansi on 25th of March. On the same day, the battle was started. Rani was having a garrison of eleven thousand five hundred men, including fifteen hundred Sepoys who had been trained in the British army. The Rani herself was in command. Even ladies and children provided their services according to their capability. The British force under Hugh Rose was seemed to be more powerful with a 7000 fighting force.[20]

At the same time when the battle at Jhansi was going on, very surprisingly Tatya Tope[21] joined the forces of Rani, their number increased vehemently about thirty three thousand in total. However, Tatya's forces were fighting outside the fort while Rani's force was defending from inside of the fort. It was unfortunate that the combined forces could not fight at a time with the British force. In a pitched battle, the revolutionary forces under Tatya Tope met a crushing defeat with a loss of fifteen hundred dead and wounded along with several guns. The remaining force of the revolutionaries under Tatya Tope fled towards Kalpi, the stronghold of Nana Sahib. In the first week of April, the British could not besiege the Fort. For them, turmoil added when the masses flocked upon them and a street fight started. Even the faqirs and gosains left their holy places and jumped into the Uprising. The houses were burnt by the British, and the street was full of dead bodies. On the bravery of Rani, Hugh Rose described about her, "The best and bravest military leader of the rebels".[22]

At last, the fort was besieged by the British with loss of three hundred forty three dead and wounded of whom thirty six were officers. The total loss of the revolutionaries was about five thousand. Sardar Khuda Baksh, and Ghulam Ghose Khan, the chief gunner of the artillery, have both been shot down by the Enghsh! Rani fled from Jhansi along with some of his soldiers numbering about five hundred and rode straight to Kalpi, which was about ninety five miles away. Both the armies of Rani and Tatya Tope joined at Kalpi, where Nana's nephew Rao Sahib was stationed with a number of revolutionaries.[23]

At Kalpi, Rao Sahib ordered the Tatya Tope to command the revolutionaries, including Rani's troops on the attack of the British forces which was early expected. Rani herself joined the army which encouraged the enthusiasm of the revolutionaries. They stationed at the town Koonchh, which was forty miles from Kalpi and waited for the British. A battle took place on 6th of May with the severe defeat and loss of five hundred men killed and wounded while the victorious British lost three officers and fifty-nine men dead and wounded. Tatya fled towards his home village while Rani retreated towards Kalpi for another encounter.[24]

Nawab of Banda along with two thousand soldiers and personal followers joined the company of Rani and Rao Sahib at Kalpi. Hugh Rose was also reinforced by the assistance send by the Commander-in-Chief Collin Campbell. On 22nd May, battle started and again, the victory sided with the British. The revolutionaries fled towards Gwalior and stationed at Gopalpur town, forty six miles south-west of Gwalior. From that very station, the revolutionary tried to oust the ruler Jiyaji Rao Sindhia from Gwalior. A battle was fought between Sindhia and the revolutionaries on 1st of June in which Sindhia was defeated badly and fled away towards Agra, along with his minister Dinkar Rao. The revolutionaries formed their Government at Gwalior. Nana Sahib was declared as Peshwa, Rao Sahib, the representative of Nana Sahib was appointed as Governor of Gwalior and held darbar as Peshwa, Ram Rao Govind as Chief Minister, Rani Luxmi Bai was made commander of the forces outside of the city, and Tatya Tope was the commander of the forces inside of the city. Amar Chand Bhatia, the Finance Minister of the old government joined the new regime and surrendered the whole Sindhia treasury. Twenty lakh of rupees were distributed in the army.[25]

On 17th June 1858, the final battle was held at Morar near Gwalior, between British and the revolutionaries, in which the British became victorious. By the 19th of June, Gwalior was captured by Lieutenants Rose and Waller. Rani fought gallantly, but she too was bound to flee after her defeat. However, her horse in crossing the canal near the cantonment stumbled and fell. Then a Cavalry soldier, ignorant of her sex and her rank, cut her down. That night, her devoted followers burned her body, determined that the English should not boast that they had captured her though dead. Tatya Tope fled towards Awadh, and later on was captured by Captain Richard Meade on 7th April, and executed at Sipri on the 18th of April, 1859.[26]

In 1861, the British Government gave the Jhansi Fort and Jhansi city to Jiyaji Rao Sindhia of Gwalior as a reward of loyalty during the Uprising of 1857. In 1886, the British Government again took back Jhansi from Gwalior State and annexed into Indian Empire.

References:

1. James F. Holcomb, and Helen H. Holcomb, *In the Heart of India: or, Beginning of the Missionary Work in Bundela Land, with a short chapter on the Characteristics of Bundelkhand and its People, and four Chapters of Jhansi History*, Philadelphia 1905, p. 26, (Hereafter quoted as *In The Heart of India*)

2. Malleson, George Bruce, *History of the Indian Mutiny of 1857-58, Commencing from the Close of the Second Volume of Sir John Kaye's History of the Sepoy War*, Vol. III, (Contemporaneous with Sir John Kay's Third Volume), London, 1878, pp. 179-180, see also *In The Heart of India*, pp. 31-36

3. Martin, R. Montgomery, *The Indian Empire,* Vol. II, London, 1858, p. 56

4. Malleson, George Bruce, *History of the Indian Mutiny of 1857-58, Commencing from the Close of the Second Volume of Sir John Kaye's History of the Sepoy War*, Vol. III, (Contemporaneous with Sir John Kay's Third Volume), London, 1878, pp. 180-181

5. Martin, R. Montgomery, *The Indian Empire,* Vol. II, London, 1858, pp. 56-57

6. *Ibid*, p. 57

7. Argyl, Campbell, George Douglas, Duke of, *India Under Dalhousie and Canning*, London, 1865, pp. 31-32, see also, Malleson, George Bruce, *The Indian Mutiny of 1857*, New York, 1891, pp. 32-33

8. *A History of the Indian Mutiny,* Vol. III, London 1904, p. 3

9. Malleson, George Bruce, *History of the Indian Mutiny of 1857-58, Commencing from the Close of the Second Volume of Sir John Kaye's History of the Sepoy War*, Vol. III, (Contemporaneous with Sir John Kay's Third Volume), London, 1878, p. 182, see also, *A History of the Indian Mutiny,* Vol. III, London 1904, p. 4 and Argyl, Campbell, George Douglas, Duke of, *India Under Dalhousie and Canning*, London, 1865, p. 33

10. Savarkar, pp. 24-26

11. *A History of the Indian Mutiny,* Vol. III, London 1904, p. 4

12. Kaye, John William, *A History of the Sepoy War in India, 1857-58,* Vol. III, London 1876, pp. 360-361, see also *In The Heart of India*, pp. 37-40

13. *A History of the Indian Mutiny,* Vol. III, London 1904, pp. 4-5, see also Malleson, George Bruce, *History of the Indian Mutiny of 1857-58, Commencing from the Close of the Second Volume of Sir John Kaye's History of the Sepoy War*, Vol. III, (Contemporaneous with Sir John Kay's Third Volume), London, 1878, p. 184

14. Kaye, John William, *A History of the Sepoy War in India, 1857-58,* Vol. III, London 1876, pp. 364-369, see also *A History of the Indian Mutiny,* Vol. III, London 1904, pp. 6-9, and *In The Heart of India*, pp. 47-49

15. Malleson, George Bruce, *History of the Indian Mutiny of 1857-58, Commencing from the Close of the Second Volume of Sir John Kaye's History of the Sepoy*

War, Vol. III, (Contemporaneous with Sir John Kay's Third Volume), London, 1878, pp. 187-188, see also *A History of the Indian Mutiny*, Vol. III, London 1904, pp. 6-9

16. *Ibid*, p. 189

17. *Ibid*, p. 190, see also Savarkar, p. 195, (Regiment Subedar wrote to Captain Skene to come out of the fort saying, 'we will not kill any of you, we will send you all to your own country'; so Captain Skene wrote to the Rani to tell the Sepoys to take their oath and to sign her name on the letter, all the Hindus took their oath: 'if any of us touch your people just as we eat beef; and those Muslims took their oath 'if any of us touch you just as we eat pork.' And the Rani signed her name on the top of the letter and it was given to Captain Skene. As soon as he read the note everyone was agreed to it. *A History of the Indian Mutiny*, Vol. III, London 1904, pp. 9-12)

18. John William Kaye quotes the report of a most trusted authority that she, "endeavoured to keep terms with our Government, by writing to the Commissioner of Jabalpure and to others, lamenting the massacre of our countrymen; stating that she was in no way concerned in it; and declaring that she only held the Jhansi district till our Government could make arrangements to reoccupy it." (John William Kaye, *A History of the Sepoy War in India, 1857-58*, Vol. III, London 1876, p. 370)

19. *In The Heart of India*, pp. 53&55

20. *Ibid*, p. 57, see also *A Sketch of the Principal Military Events*, p. 130

21. Tatya Tope, whose original name was Ramchandra Pandurang also known as Raghunath and Pandurang Rao Tope, was born in about 1814. His father's name was Pandurang Bhat. Pandurang Bhat had eight sons and of them, the second was called Raghunath. It is this Raghunath who shines as the brilliant star of liberty in the galaxy of the heroes of Hindustan. Pandurang Rao Tope was a Deshasth Brahmin and was the head of the charity department under the late Baji Rao Peshwa at Bithur. So, it was Bithur, where the three heroes of 1857, Nana Sahib, Luxmi Bai and Tatya Tope played together the games of their childhood. The friendship of Nana Sahib and Tatya Tope was continued until the Uprising broke out in 1857. Savarkar, p. 170

22. *A Sketch of the Principal Military Events*, p. 130, see also *In The Heart of India*, pp. 57,62,65&70

23. *In The Heart of India*, pp. 72,76&78, see also Gilliat Edward, *Heroes of the Indian Mutiny; Stories of Heroic Deeds*, London 1914, p. 343

24. *Ibid*, pp. 80-82

25. *Ibid*, pp. 83-85&89-90, see also Savarkar, p. 396

26. Malleson, George Bruce, *Kay's and Malleson's History of the Indian Mutiny of 1857-8*, Vol. V, London, 1911, p. 154, see also *In The Heart of India*, p. 92, and *A Sketch of the Principal Military Events*, p. 138

Chapter 6

Affairs of Kanpur

The city of Kanpur, a revolutionary abode of Nana Sahib and his followers, lies 250 miles South-East of Dehli, with a population of 60,000 Natives. By the treaty of Faizabad, in 1775, the East India Company engaged to maintain a brigade for the defence of Awadh. Kanpur was made the military station and the revenue of extensive tract of country adjoining the city was fixed for the maintenance of this force. In 1801, Lord Wellesley closed the mortgage, and the territory lapsed to the Company.[1]

In May 1857, the Europeans in Kanpur, including civil and military, were consisted of combatants numbered about 465, including 80 officers of all arms, 60 men of the 84th Regiment; 74 men of the 32nd Regiment (mostly invalids or sick), who were invalided (sick); 15 men of the Madras Fusiliers, and 59 men of the Bengal Artillery. The civilians such as railway engineers, merchants, shopkeepers, soldiers' wives were 200 and the children were also numbering 200. The total number of Europeans at Kanpur including the combatants and civilians was amounting to more or less 800. The Native troops consisted of the 2nd Regiment, Light Cavalry, the 1st, 53rd, and 56th Regiments Infantry, and the Golundaz, or Native gunners attached to the battery. Including all the total Native soldiers about 3000 were stationed at Kanpur. They were all commanded by Major-General Sir Hugh Wheeler. He was an officer of fifty years' distinguished service with seventy-five years of age. Mr. Hillersden was the magistrate of the Kanpur district.[2]

At the distance of 12 miles from the city of Kanpur, there was the famous town of Bithur, the original abode of Nana Sahib. There were several Hindu temples and Ghats which gave access to the sacred stream. Brahma was specially reverenced here. It is said that after completing the act of creation, Brahma had offered an *Aswamedha* (Hecatomb) at the principal Ghat, in token that his great work was good. On that occasion, the pin of his slipper was left behind him, fastened into one of the steps of the Ghat, which later on became the object of worship. There was an annual gathering to that spot at the full moon of November, prodigious numbers of devotees assemble from all parts of India to celebrate the present god with frankincense, and flowers, and barbarous music, and drunken frenzy. It contributes quite as much to the prosperity of the town as it does to the piety of the pilgrims.[3]

Bartlett describes the beauty of the Bithur palace that it was spacious, and though not remarkable for any architectural beauty, was exquisitely furnished in European style. He further says, "All the reception-rooms were decorated with immense mirrors and massive chandeliers in variegated glass, and of the most recent manufacture. There were saddles of silver for both horses and camels, guns of every possible construction, shields inlaid with gold, carriages for camel-driving, and the newest turn-outs from Long Acre; plate, gems, and curiosities in ivory and metal; while without in the compound might be seen the fleetest horses, the finest dogs, and rare specimens of deer, antelopes, and other animals from all parts of India. It would be quite impossible to lift the veil that must rest on the private life of this man. There were apartments in the Bithur palace horribly unfit for any human eye; in which both European and Native artists had done their utmost to gratify the corrupt master, from whom they could command any price."[4]

During the Uprising of 1857, Kanpur became the rallying point of the revolutionaries and Nana Sahib of Bithur led them. The Maratha leader Dhondu Pant popularly known as Nana Sahib was the adopted son of Peshwa Baji Rao II. He ruled from Kanpur and the adjoining territory under the Emperor Bahadur Shah Zafar following the other revolutionary leaders of India. He proclaimed himself as the Peshwa of the Maratha Empire during the days of Uprising.

About the origin of Nana, it is said that he was the offspring of a poor Konkanee Brahmin of Venn, a miserable little village about thirty miles east of Bombay, where he was born in 1824 to Madhav Rao (also called Narayan Bhatt), and Ganga Bai. When Baji Rao II was sent to Bithur, many Mahratha families had followed him as the last Peshwa was generous enough to support them in good state on his pension. Many new families were also migrated to Bithur. Among the latter was the family of Madhav Rao, who went to Bithur in 1827 to seek the generosity of Baji Rao. There, the little son of Madhavarao captivated the heart of Baji Rao, and little Nana Sahib became a great favourite of the whole Palace. On the 7th of June 1827, Baji Rao placed him on his lap, formally adopted him as his son and declared him the heir-presumptive to the throne.[5]

Peshwa, once the ruler of mighty Maratha Empire, was defeated in the year 1818 by the English, and surrendered to them. He was deprived of his throne and Kingdom, but he was given the annual pension of eight lakhs of rupees, and within the limits of the small estate assigned to him at Bithur, near Kanpur, he was allowed to exercise sovereign rights; he was also allowed to retain his title. Before his death, he had adopted Dhondu Pant, as his son, and had besought the English Government to let this adoption make Dhondu Pant heir to his title, pension, as well as to his private estate. In his will he had named Dhondu Pant "sole master of the throne and the dominions of the Peshwa." The Home Government refused absolutely the title of Peshwa to his adopted son, and the question of the pension was reserved for future consideration that until the seat of the ex-Peshwa should be vacant.[6]

However, after the death of Peshwa Baji Rao II in 1851, the East India Company declined to continue to the Nana Sahib, the title and the pensions, though it allowed him to retain the rent-free estate of Bithur. The excuse was made that the allowance made to Baji Rao II was purely in the form of an annuity and there was no reason to continue to his adopted son Dhondu Pant. Although Nana Sahib had performed all the religious rituals, as a son, at the time of the death of Baji Rao II, which was considered necessary for every single Hindu by religion.[7]

A slight relaxation of the hard-and-fast policy characteristic of Lord Dalhousie's rule might have saved the British from many future troubles. The anti-adoption policy of Lord Dalhousie not only affected the Hindu Princes of India but injured the Hindu religion as a well. The Nana Sahib contended that to withhold the title and pension was to invalidate the act of adoption, which is against the Hindu sacred code and interdict the practice of the Hindu religion.

At the time of Uprising Nana Sahib was about thirty-six years old, was exceedingly corpulent, of sallow complexion, of middle height, with thoroughly marked features, and like all Marathas, clean shaven on both head and face. He was living at Bithur with two brothers, Baba Bhatt or Baba Sahib, Bala Sahib or Bala Rao and one nephew Rao Sahib. He does not speak a word of English, though well educated in Sanskrit, and was known for his deep religious nature. Despite his lack of western education, he subscribed to all the leading Anglo-Indian journals, which were translated to him daily. He was fond of hosting parties in the European style at his mansion, inviting British merchants and officials, all of whom praised his generosity and hospitality; although he got none of their hospitality in return, because no salute was permitted in his honour. His palace was furnished expensively; his stables contained well-bred Arabs, elephants and camels; his ladies were tricked out with costly jewels; his little army, horse and foot, paid four rupees each man a month. Due to his religious feelings, he never went abroad and sent his Vakil Azimullah Khan to London in 1854, to press his demand to the Court of Directors.[8]

Azimullah Khan, a good-looking young Indian, once was a waiter, or Butler, in the house of an Anglo-Indian from where he learnt to speak English and French fluently and write accurately in them both. He afterwards became a pupil, and subsequently, a teacher in the Kanpur Government school, and from the teacher's position, he was selected to become the Vakil or prime agent of the Nana Sahib at Bithur. V.D. Savarkar has praised the personality of Azimullah, "Of the important characters in the Revolutionary War of 1857, the name of Azimullah Khan is one of the most memorable. Among the keen intellects and grand minds that first conceived the idea of the War of Independence, Azimullah must be given a prominent place. And among the many plans by which the various phases of the Revolution were developed, the plans of Azimullah deserve special notice."[9]

In 1854, Nana Sahib appealed to the Court of Directors through his Vakil Azimullah Khan at Leadenhall Street, against the decision of the Governor General of India and for the continuance of Baji Rao's pension to him. His appeal was couched in logical, temperate, and convincing language. He asked why the heir to the Peshwa should be treated differently from other Native princes who had fallen before the Company. He instanced the case of Delhi and of Mysore. However, they directed the Governor General to inform the plaintiff that the pension of his adoptive father was not hereditary, that he has no claim whatever to it, and that his application is wholly inadmissible. The justifications were as follows:[10]

"The Nana's claims were unquestionably invalidated by a fallacy. He seemed to think that Baji Rao's pension was the result of a contract; he to give up his territories, and the Company, in consideration of the fact, to make him a grant. Nothing could be less true. The Peshwa took the field against the forces of the Company, was completely defeated, and had his territories taken from him. Then the Company, in pity for his fallen fortunes, made him a most munificent provision for life."

However, Azimullah Khan could not induce the Company to grant his master the pension. On his way back to India via France, Azimullah Khan stayed at Constantinople and crossed over to the Crimea in order to see those great soldiers, the Russians, who had beaten French and English together. After his return to Bithur, he told his master that the power of England was about to shatter and advised Nana Sahib for revolt. The non-acceptance of his appeal turned Nana Sahib's heart black with hatred against the British. Outwardly, however, he was all smiles and fair words. Nana Sahib treated the English officers with generous hospitality, for he never allowed any suspicion of his loyalty to arise from look or word or deed.[11]

Nevertheless, the hatred was maintained in Nana Sahib's chest, and he had full intention to wage war against the British at any time. Only for that reason, Nana Sahib, who was seldom seen beyond the limits of his own estate, visited Kalpi, made a journey to Delhi, and a little later paid a visit to Lucknow on the 18th of April, 1857. John William Kaye writes that on Nana's journey, Henry Lawrence wrote a long letter to the Governor-General, telling him that he had discerned signs of dangerous coalitions between the regular Sepoy regiments, the Irregulars taken into our service from the old Awadh Army, and the men of the Police battalions; symptoms also of intrigues on foot among some of the chief people of the city. There were many elements of trouble; and now they were beginning to develop themselves in a manner significant of a general outburst of popular discontent. However, due to some treacherous reasons he declared his loyalty to the British, earning their trust, in the early periods of the Uprising. He along with 300 Maratha soldiers and two guns occupied the treasury of Kanpur in order to assist the British. He went to Kanpur and entered into the Native Infantry under the pretense of being loyal to the British Empire. Once inside, however, Nana Sahib declared that he was a participant in the Uprising and a vassal to Bahadur Shah Zafar.[12]

Keene, Henry George writes that the cause of the mischief was Azimullah Khan who, on returning from Europe and becoming aware of the discontents of Queen Zeenat Mahal at Delhi, thought he saw his way to fame and fortune as a political creator. Azimullah Khan had not only watched the Crimean collapse, but also had been in correspondence with foes of England on the Continent as the letters and drafts were found at Bithur and fell into the hands of an officer of Bengal Artillery. The Persian war seemed to him a part of the advance of Russia, and he had just enough knowledge of the cause and consequences of the political drama. There are a lot of evidences that Azimullah Khan negotiated with some agents or leaders of the Sepoys before they mutinied, though their subsequent march towards Delhi renders it doubtful how far these negotiations had been ratified by the men in general.[13]

British military also had smelt the uneasiness of the Natives and made the arrangements for their safety. They told their wives and children to leave the station and retreat to Calcutta for safety, but they unanimously declined to remove so long as General Wheeler retained his family with him. Sir Hugh Wheeler made arrangements for the protection of the women and children. A mud wall, four feet high, was thrown up around the old dragoon hospital. The buildings thus entrenched were two brick structures, one thatched, the other roofed with masonry. On the 21st of May, the women and children were all ordered into these barracks, the officers still sleeping at the quarter guards in the lines with their respective corps. The general gave orders to lay in supplies for twenty-five days. Ghee, salt, rice, pulses, tea, sugar, rum, malt liquor, and hermetically sealed provisions were ordered; but peas and flour formed the bulk of the food obtained. Ammunition was plentiful, there being in the field magazines two thousand pounds of powder, with ball cartridge and round shot in abundance. General Wheeler visited the lines daily, chatted with the Sepoys, and encouraged their confidence, but could get no certain intelligence of anything like plotting in their midst. All the fear was based on the rumour and self-assessment.[14]

Nana Sahib was although annoyed with the British, however, maintained very cordial relations. The district magistrate of Kanpur, Mr. Hillersdon, and Nana Sahib had considerable official intercourse, and he had been pleased by the friendly and courteous manner and conversation with Nana. At this time of suspicion and insecurity, Mr. Hillersdon being greatly concerned for the safety of the large amount of treasure under his charge, more than a hundred thousand pounds, after consultation with Sir Hugh Wheeler, sent over to Bithur requesting the presence and aid of Nana Sahib. Nana Sahib came instantly, attended by his body guard, and engaged to send a force of two hundred cavalry, four hundred infantry, and two guns to protect the revenue. Consequently, the treasury was placed under the custody of the detachment from Bithur, together with a company of the 53rd Native Infantry. Nana Sahib himself resided in the civil lines of the cantonment.[15]

There were secret societies consisting of both civil and military people who held regular meetings to uproot the British Empire. Savarkar mentions regarding one of such meetings that the meeting place of secret societies were the houses of Subedar Tika Singh and Sepoy leader Shams-ud-din Khan at Kanpur. At these secret meetings, two faithful servants of the Bithur palace household, Jwala Prasad and Mohammad Ali, used to attend on behalf of Nana Sahib. Both Subedar Tika Singh and Jwala Prasad were bold, freedom-loving, and passionately sincere patriots. They soon got a hold on the assembly, and the whole army had unanimously sworn to obey their orders. So, the voice of Subedar Tika Singh was the voice of the whole army.[16]

At Kanpur, the Sepoys mutinied in the morning of 5th of June 1857 about 3 am, when the 2nd Native Cavalry broke out. They first set fire to the riding-master's bungalow, and then fled, carrying off with them horses, arms, colours, and the regimental treasure-chest. An hour or two after the flight of the cavalry, the 1st Native Infantry also revolted, leaving their officers untouched upon the parade ground. The 56th Native Infantry followed the next morning or 6th June. The 53rd mutinied in the last, most probably on the same day or in the morning of 7th June. The revolutionaries made their way to Delhi. Mowbray Thomson narrates that when they reached Nawabgunj, the Nana came out to meet them, and at their head proceeded to the treasury, where he had all the Government elephants laden with the public money, and distributed a vast amount of it among the Sepoys, whose command he forthwith assumed.[17]

George W. Forrest narrates that at the time of Uprising a deputation of the Native officers from the 2nd Cavalry and 1st Native Infantry went to the Nana's place and said to him: "Maharaja, a Kingdom awaits you if you join our cause, but death if you side with our enemies." The ready reply was, "What have I to do with the British? I am altogether yours." He then laid his hands on the heads of the Native officers and swore to join them. The deputation, quite satisfied, departed to join their comrades at Kalyanpur. When the deputation left Nana, he made consultation with his brothers and Azimullah Khan on the offer of the Sepoys. Azimullah advised him that at the imperial city, they would be overshadowed by the Mughal Court and lose their individual power and influence. It would be far wiser for the Nana to seize Kanpur and extend his power to the sea.[18]

The above arguments of Azimullah convinced them as to the proper course to be pursued, and the Nana, with his brother Baba Sahib and Azimullah, at once hastened to Kalyanpur. By the offer of unlimited plunder and a gold bangle to each Sepoy, they gained the ready consent of the troops to their plans. By the name of the Nana Sahib, promotions and appointments were made in the army of the Peshwa. The Subedar, Tika Singh, who had been from the commencement the most active promoter of revolt, became chief of the 2nd Cavalry with the title of General; Jamadar Dalganjan Singh became Colonel of the 53rd Native Infantry, and Subedar Ganga Din was appointed as Colonel of the 56th Native Infantry. It followed a large-scale loot and plunder in the city. A detachment of cavalry was sent into the cantonment, who, galloping hither and thither, some shouting "Victory to Raja Ram Chand!" others calling out "Shout, ye faithful army, Allah has routed the Kafirs!" set fire to the houses.[19]

Tatya Tope in his evidence narrates that, "Two days afterwards the three regiments of infantry and the 2nd Light Cavalry surrounded us, and imprisoned the Nana and myself in the treasury, and plundered the magazines and treasury of everything they contained, leaving nothing in either. Of the treasure, the Sepoys made over two lakhs and eleven thousand rupees to the Nana, keeping their own sentries over it. The Nana was also under the charge of these sentries, and the Sepoys which were with us also joined the rebels. After this, the whole army marched from that place, and the rebels took the Nana Sahib and myself and all our attendants along with them, and said, 'Come along to Delhi.' Having gone three *kos* (six miles) from Kanpur, the Nana said that as the day was far spent it was far better to halt there then and march on the following day. They agreed to this and halted. In the morning, the whole army told him (Nana Sahib) to go with them towards Delhi. The Nana refused, and the army then said, 'Come with us to Kanpur and fight there.' The Nana objected to this, but they would not attend to him. And so taking him with them as a prisoner, they went towards Kanpur, and fighting commenced there."[20]

Nirput, the opium contractor of Kanpur, in his diary states, "When the Nana saw that all the regiments were anxious to leave for Delhi, he called the officers and Sepoys and told them it was not proper to go to Delhi until all Europeans, men, women, and children, were destroyed; they agreed to return; and the whole rebel army returned on June 6th and encamped near subedar's tank." Another Native writer, who appears by his narrative of the movements of the rebel force to have been in close proximity with it doing the siege, confirms Nirput's statement. He writes, "When Nana Dhondu Pant saw that the three Native regiments, and the 2nd Light Cavalry had completely thrown off their allegiance to the Company, and were thinking of going to Delhi, he, with joined hands, represented to the Native officers that it would not be correct to proceed towards Delhi until they had entirely destroyed the officers and European soldiers and women and children of the Christian religion; and that they should, if possible by deceiving the officers, accomplish this grand object, or that they should be good for nothing. The Native officers and Sepoys approved this speech, and took counsel to kill all the Christians; and, plundering as they went, on Saturday, the 6th June, they returned to the Subedar's tank."[21]

Gilliat Edward narrates that on 5th June 1857, the Sepoys mutinied and wounded and killed their senior Native officer, who defended the regimental treasure. The mutineers plundered the treasury and travelled on the Delhi road as far as Kalyanpur when they were overtaken by the Nana, his two brothers, Bala and Baba Bhut, and Azimullah. Nana spoke to them, "Return to Kanpur, destroy all the Europeans, and I will give every man a gold anklet and license to pillage." The Sepoys agreed, saluted the Nana as their Raja.[22]

The story narrates by Tatya Tope, seems to be told in his defence, and in order to prove himself innocent. Nirpat's account bears a lot of reality in the light of the events happened at Kanpur. By analyzing the matter it could rightly be concluded that Nana was much eager to join the Uprising right from the beginning, furthermore, from the time of arrival of Azimullah Khan from Europe. Nana fully engaged himself in the fighting against the British, either they were Wheeler or Havelock.

In the story of Kanpur, another character made the entry at the right time. The new character was Nanhe Nawab who sat on a throne in a corner of Kanpur city with his green flag. When the rising began, his house and property were ordered to be confiscated.

Nevertheless, soon a compromise took place and his name was praised everywhere in that holy war of freedom.[23]

In the forenoon of the 7th June, Nana and his associates like Tatya Tope, Azimullah along with their forces opened their heaviest batteries on the rude parapets of the entrenchments. Hillersdon was killed by a round shot; his chief subordinate, McKillop, was shot as he was drawing water for the women from an unprotected well; Hillersdon's brother, wife, and two children perished in the fatal enceinte. The Europeans suffered a lot from thirst, especially the women and children. For three dreadful weeks, the wretched Europeans were sapped, bombarded, starved, and eventually lost the battle. The revolutionaries became successful to siege the Europeans of Kanpur cantonment on June 23, 1857, proposed to mark the centenary of Plassey by an assault. However, the Europeans still not surrendered.[24]

After twenty-one days full fight, on 25th June, Wheeler received an unsigned letter in the writing of Azimullah Khan. It was offered to the subjects of Her Most Gracious Majesty Queen Victoria, "All soldiers and others unconnected with the acts of Lord Dalhousie, who will lay down their arms and give themselves up, shall be spared and sent to Allahabad." Over this matter, Wheeler consented to evacuate the scene of horror. He sent Mr. Todd to take the document across to the Sevadah Kothi, the Nana's residence, and after about an absence of half an hour, he returned with the treaty of capitulation signed by the Nana. Mr. Todd said that he was courteously received, and that no hesitation was made in giving the signature, which, in point of fact, left the covenant as worthless as it possibly could be.[25]

Wheeler and the remaining Europeans, about 450 in the number, in order of evacuating the position, moved down on 27th of June, to the river at Satichaura Ghat where boats were ready to embark. Nana and his associates arranged 40 boats for the escape of the Europeans. However, when the Europeans reached in the mid-stream and sailed towards Allahabad, Nana's forces started firing. The boatmen jumped from the boats and came to the bank. As soon as anyone took up his head above water, he was shot by a bullet; if he kept it under water, he would be suffocated. General Wheeler was killed in the first rush. Most of the Europeans were killed, and some of them surrendered and send back as captives. However, some of them still sailed their boats and faced the firings in the streams and killed with the exception of one boat's crew, of whom, only four finally escaped, two, at least, of whom were alive until 1883. The surviving Europeans, who were in captivity, were separated from their women and children and killed on the evening of 1st July. Only 5 men and 206 women and children totaling 211 (Frazer records the number as 118 women and 92 children) were lodged in a small house named Bibighar. Here they were very misering position and severely suffered from cholera, diarrhea, and dysentery and died about 26 women and children. After Nana's defeat by General Havelock, the captives of Bibighar were massacred and their bodies were thrown into the nearby dry well.[26]

The four Europeans, who were saved in a boat from the curse of the Nana's forces, were fought under Havelock at the time of recapture of Kanpur. During the days of crisis, they sailed a little long and took refuse and enjoyed the hospitality to Maharaja Digvijay Singh, the Raja of Moora Mhow (Baiswarah). Mowbray Thomson, the author of *The Story of Cawnpore* was also one of the four who were somehow saved. The Raja refused to surrender these four Europeans on the request of Nana's agents or Sepoys and told them that he was a tributary to the King of Awadh, and knew nothing of the Nana's raj.[27]

John William Kaye quotes the account of an eye witness, on the same episode, "...the General sent the Nana something over one lac of rupees, and authorised him to keep the amount. The following day I went and got ready forty boats, and having caused all the gentlemen, ladies, and children to get into the boats, I started them off to Allahabad. In the mean while, the whole army, artillery included, having got ready, arrived at the river Ganges. The Sipahis jumped into the water, and commenced a massacre of all the men, women, and children, and set the boats on fire. They destroyed thirty-nine boats; one, however, escaped as far as Kala Kankar, but was there caught, and brought back to Kanpur, and all on board of it destroyed. Four days after this the Nana said he was going to Bithur, to keep the anniversary of his mother's death." According to another statement "in my presence and hearing Tatya Tope sent for Tika Singh, Subedar of 2nd Cavalry, known as a General, and gave him orders to rush into the water and spare none." Another said, "I was standing concealed in a corner, close to where Tatya Tope was seated, and I heard him tell Tika Singh, a Subedar of the 2nd Cavalry, who was known as the General, to order the Sawars to go into the water and put an end to the Europeans, and accordingly, they rushed into the river and murdered them." Another witness spoke distinctly to the same effect, "All orders regarding the massacre, issued by the Nana, were carried into execution by Tatya Tope."[28]

The British authorities of that time while giving Nana, the full responsibility of the massacre, consider him as the second rate and irresponsible activist. They told that at sunset, a consultation was held in the Nana's tent, when it was decided that the British should be massacred at the Satichaura Ghat. Baba Bhut, the Nana's brother, Azimullah, Brigadier Jwala Prashad, Tatya Tope, Shah Ali, and Ahmad Ali, etc. were present in the meeting. They were the most active in controlling the rebellious administration and organized the fight against the British. Nana was happy to sit on the throne of Peshwa and getting the glory of 100 guns fired in his honour.[29]

Apart from controlling the administration by the Generals of Nana Sahib, he was surely an instrumental in boosting the rebellion. On 1st of July, 1857, Nana Sahib wrote to the Chief Magistrate or Kotwal of Kanpur, Holas Singh, "Whereas, by the grace of God and fortune of the King, all the English at Puna and in Panna have been slain and sent to hell, and five thousand English who were at Dehli have been put to the sword by the Royal troops. The Government is now everywhere victorious; you are, therefore, ordered to proclaim these glad tidings in all cities and villages by beat of drum, that all may rejoice on hearing them. All cause for apprehension is now removed."[30]

Nana Sahib again writes to Holas Singh Kotwal on 5th of July 1857, in order to remove the fear of his subject, "Whereas sundry persons of the town, on hearing the report of European troops having marched from Allahabad, are abandoning their homes and seeking shelter in villages, you are hereby ordered to have proclaimed throughout the town that infantry, cavalry, and artillery have marched to repel the English. Wherever they may be met, at Fatehpur, Allahabad, or wherever they may be, the revenging force will thoroughly punish them. Let all remain without fear in their homes, and pursue their usual avocations."[31]

While boosting the courage of his soldiers, Nana Sahib wrote on 7th July 1857, "I have been greatly pleased with your zeal, valour, and loyalty. Your labours are deserving of the highest praise. The organisation and scale of pay and rewards established here will have, likewise, to be established for you. Let your minds be at rest, all promises made will be fulfilled. Troops of all arms have this day crossed the Ganges en route to Lacknow; you will be aided in every possible way to slay the unbelieving Nazarenes, and dispatch them to hell. The greatest reliance is placed on your readiness and bravery to secure victory. On receipt of this order, certify to me, under your hand and seal, that you have learned its contents, and are ready to cooperate in the destruction of the infidels. Have no fears as regards ordnance stores. Any amount of ammunition and heavy guns is available. Sharfuddaula and Ali Reza Beg, Kotwal of Lacknow, have been ordered to supply provisions. They will do so; but should they fail in this duty inform me, and a conspicuous example will be made of them. All of you display valour and fortitude. May victory speedily crown your efforts, thus shall I myself be at liberty to proceed towards Allahabad. There can be no hesitation on your part or on mine. After this rapid success, march to Allahabad and conquer there."[32]

Nana continued to rule on Kanpur and the adjacent areas until 13th of July, when Havelock encountered the Nana's troops at Fatehpur, under Tika Singh, a Risaldar of the 2nd Cavalry. The revolutionaries were totally routed out and returned back to Kanpur. On the 15th of July, the revolutionaries again engaged with General Havelock at river Pandu, but met the same defeat. In utter confusion of that day, the Nana put all his captives to death. On the 16th, another fight took place in which Nana and his ten thousand revolutionaries defeated after a few hours battle. In the morning of the 17th, General Havelock along with his forces entered the city, and the Native populace fled in every direction to the villages' adjacent.[33]

After Nana's defeat at Kanpur on 16th July, he left Kanpur and by spending a night, sailed to Fatchpur in Lucknow Province, along with his family and spent some time in the hospitality of Chaudhary Bhopal Singh. After a few days Tatya Tope along with the army joined him at Fatehpur. He sent Bala Sahib to occupy the Fort of Kalpi and reorganize the revolutionary force. Later on, Tatya also joined Bala Sahib at Kalpi.[34]

After fully occupying the Kanpur city, General Havelock turned towards the Bithur Palace, the residence of Nana Sahib. In the way General Neill joined him with 220 men on 20th of July. Subsequently, on 25th, General Havelock left Kanpur leaving Neill in command. Havelock's retirement was severely criticized; Neill, in particular, criticised him in the most insubordinate language. Later on, Havelock returned to Kanpur in the lack of re-enforcement. On the 29th of July, a battle with the Nana's force at Baseerat Ganj took place in which the revolutionaries lost the ground. The Palace of Bithur was occupied by the British and destroyed afterwards. The infamous order of General Neill, to clean the blood of the slained Europeans by the tongues of the Indian captives, was carried on after his arrival. A reward of 100,000 rupees was offered for the Nana Sahib's head.[35]

After settling the matter of Kanpur, there was the need for the British to advance towards Lucknow, the most important centre of the Uprising after Delhi. After receiving the re-enforcement under General Outram, Havelock commenced to cross the Ganges to proceed to the relief of Lucknow on 19th of September.[36]

Nana continued to reside at Fatehpur and along with his associates like Kunwar Singh, Maulvi Ahmadullah, etc. fought with the British in many important battles. After fall of the Lucknow in mid of March 1858, Nana along with other revolutionaries fled towards Rohelkand to join the Government of Maulvi Ahmadullah Shah at Mohammadi. However, after fall of the Mohammadi, Nana rode away to an unknown destination in the border area of Nepal in 1859, and died in the forests of Terai.[37]

About the Nana Sahib and his brother Bala Sahib's death Charles Edward Stewat narrates that at the end of the June 1859; he was posted in Sidhonia Ghat of river Rapti; it was reported that Nana, his brother Bala and his followers were hiding some twenty miles away from them. The British force, 5th Punjab Infantry was continuously chasing the revolutionaries. The commander of the British force Colonel Vaughan's spy informed that the Nana was very ill with fever. The daily bulletins of his state and the medicines he had taken were brought in, and finally, a well-authenticated account of his death and that of his brother from fever, and of the cremation of their bodies by their followers. The report of the death of the Nana from fever in the Terai was confirmed and reported to the Government.[38]

All hopes of the revolutionaries and the Indian people were shattered by the defeat and flight of the Nana and his forces. When Nana was alive, the people and his associates had thought that he had sent an envoy to Russia for help. They believe that the Russians are all Muslims and that the armies of the Czar were to liberate the faithful and their land from the yoke of the British. However, all the rumours elapsed when the British occupied the city and started severe retribution.

References:

1. Mowbray Thomson, *The Story of Cawnpore*, London 1859, pp. 23,
2. *A Sketch of the Principal Military Events*, pp. 30-31, see also Forrest, Volume III, Calcutta, 1902, p. Appendix-II, Evelyn Wood, *The Revolt in Hindustan 1857-59*, London, 1908, pp. 59-60, George Trevelyan, *Cawnpore*, London, 1910, pp. 1-2, and R. W. Frazer, *British India*, New York 1896, p. 291
3. Mowbray Thomson, *The Story of Cawnpore*, London 1859, pp. 46-47, see also Bartlett, D.W., *The Heroes of the Indian Rebellion*, Columbus, 1859, p. 196, and George Trevelyan, *Cawnpore*, London, 1910, p. 43
4. Bartlett, D.W., *The Heroes of the Indian Rebellion*, Columbus, 1859, p. 196
5. Savarkar, pp. 22-23, see also *A History of the Indian Mutiny*, Vol. I, London 1904, pp. 403-404, Mowbray Thomson, *The Story of Cawnpore*, London 1859, p. 45, and Bartlett, D.W., *The Heroes of the Indian Rebellion*, Columbus, 1859, p. 195
6. Malleson, George Bruce, *The Indian Mutiny of 1857*, New York, 1891, p. 28
7. Bartlett, D.W., *The Heroes of the Indian Rebellion*, Columbus, 1859, p. 195, see also, *Eight Days*, p. 85
8. Mowbray Thomson, *The Story of Cawnpore*, London 1859, p. 46, see also Forrest, Volume III, Calcutta, 1902, p. Appendix-XXII, Evelyn Wood, *The Revolt in Hindustan 1857-59*, London, 1908, pp. 2-3, and Gilliat Edward, *Heroes of the Indian Mutiny; Stories of Heroic Deeds*, London 1914, p. 256
9. Savarkar, p. 28 (V.D. Savarkar says that his face was noble, his speech sweet and silvery. Knowing very well the customs and manners of contemporary English life, he soon became very popular among Londoners. Attracted by his pleasant and silvery voice, his spirited mien, and Oriental magnificence, several young English women fell in love with Azimullah. There used to be a crowd, in those days, in the parks of London and on the beach at Brighton, to see this jewelled Indian "Raja." Some English women of respectable families were so much infatuated with him that, even after his return to India, they would send him letters couched in the most affectionate terms. When, later, Havelock's army captured Bithur, he saw there the original letters written by some English ladies to their "Darling Azimullah!" Savarkar, pp. 28 29
10. Malleson, George Bruce, *The Indian Mutiny of 1857*, New York, 1891, p. 29, see also, Sherer, John Walter, *Havelock's March on Cawnpore, 1857*, London 1910, p. 168, and Sherer, John Walter, *Daily Life During the Indian Mutiny: Personal Experiences of 1857*, Allahabad, 1910, p. 86
11. Bartlett, D.W., *The Heroes of the Indian Rebellion*, Columbus, 1859, p. 201
12. John William Kaye, *A History of the Sepoy War in India, 1857-58*, Vol. I, London 1875, pp. 574&577 see also Evelyn Wood, *The Revolt in Hindustan 1857-59*, London, 1908, pp. 21&60, *Eight Days*, pp. 83-84 and Gilliat Edward, *Heroes of the Indian Mutiny; Stories of Heroic Deeds*, London 1914, p. 257
13. Keene, Henry George, *Fifty-Seven: Some Account of the Administration of Indian Districts during the Revolt of the Bengal Army*, London, 1883, pp. 72-73
14. Mowbray Thomson, *The Story of Cawnpore*, London 1859, pp. 29-32&38

15. *Ibid*, pp. 32-33

16. Savarkar, p. 175

17. Forrest, Volume III, Calcutta, 1902, p. Appendix- IX, see also Mowbray Thomson, *The Story of Cawnpore*, London 1859, pp. 38-41

18. *A History of the Indian Mutiny*, Vol. I, London 1904, pp. 420-421

19. *Ibid*, pp. 421-422, see also Kaye, John William, *Kay's and Malleson's History of the Indian Mutiny of 1857-8*, Vol. II, London, 1910, p. 238

20. *Ibid*, p. 420

21. *Ibid*, pp. 420-421

22. Gilliat Edward, *Heroes of the Indian Mutiny; Stories of Heroic Deeds*, London 1914, p. 257

23. Savarkar, p. 184

24. Keene, Henry George, *Fifty-Seven: Some Account of the Administration of Indian Districts during the Revolt of the Bengal Army*, London, 1883, p. 73, see also Evelyn Wood, *The Revolt in Hindustan 1857-59*, London, 1908, pp. 21& 61-62 and Gilliat Edward, *Heroes of the Indian Mutiny; Stories of Heroic Deeds*, London 1914, p. 262

25. Mowbray Thomson, *The Story of Cawnpore*, London 1859, pp. 149-154, see also Bartlett, D.W., *The Heroes of the Indian Rebellion*, Columbus, 1859, p. 229, and Forrest, Volume III, Calcutta, 1902, p. Appendix-VII

26. Keene, Henry George, *Fifty-Seven: Some Account of the Administration of Indian Districts during the Revolt of the Bengal Army*, London, 1883, pp. 73-74, see also Evelyn Wood, *The Revolt in Hindustan 1857-59*, London, 1908, pp. 64-66, R. W. Frazer, *British India*, New York 1896, p. 298, and *A History of the Indian Mutiny*, Vol. I, London 1904, p. 451 (George Dodd writes that their number was 900 and further says that it might be possible that the number who took their departure in this mournful procession from the entrenchment was four hundred and fifty, then one half of the original number of nine hundred must have fallen victims to three weeks of privation and suffering. See Dodd, p. 137, Bartlett writes that The wretched company of women and children now consisted of 210; namely, 163 survivors from the Kanpur garrison, and 47 refugees from Fatehgarh, of whom that Bithur butcher had murdered all the males except three officers, whose lives he spared for some purpose, but for what it is impossible to say. Bartlett, D.W., *The Heroes of the Indian Rebellion*, Columbus, 1859, p. 260)

27. Mowbray Thomson, *The Story of Cawnpore*, London 1859, p. 195, see also Forrest, Volume III, Calcutta, 1902, p. Appendix-VIII

28. Kaye, John William, *Kay's and Malleson's History of the Indian Mutiny of 1857-8*, Vol. II, London, 1910, p. 257

29. Sherer, John Walter, *Havelock's March on Cawnpore, 1857*, London 1910, pp. 170-171, see also Sherer, John Walter, *Daily Life During the Indian Mutiny: Personal Experiences of 1857*, Allahabad, 1910, p. 88, and *A History of the Indian Mutiny*, Vol. I, London 1904, p. 453

30. Kaye, John William, *Kay's and Malleson's History of the Indian Mutiny of 1857-8,* Vol. II, London, 1910, p. 501

31. Kaye, John William, *Kay's and Malleson's History of the Indian Mutiny of 1857-8,* Vol. II, London, 1910, p. 502

32. *Ibid*

33. Mowbray Thomson, *The Story of Cawnpore,* London 1859, pp. 213-214, see also Sherer, John Walter, *Havelock's March on Cawnpore, 1857,* London 1910, p. 172, and Wright, Charles H.H., *Memoire of John Lovering Cooke,* London, 1873, p. 51

34. Savarkar, pp. 307-308

35. *A Sketch of the Principal Military Events,* p. 43, see also Bartlett, D.W., *The Heroes of the Indian Rebellion,* Columbus, 1859, p. 65, and Julia Selina Lady, *The Siege of Lucknow: A Diary,* London, 1892, p. 39

36. Bartlett, D.W., *The Heroes of the Indian Rebellion,* Columbus, 1859, p. 67

37. *A History of the Indian Mutiny,* Vol. I, London 1904, pp. 502-505

38. Stewart, Charles Edward, (Edited by Basil Stewart), *Through Persia in Disguise with Reminiscences of the Indian Mutiny,* London, 1911, pp. 41-42

Chapter 7

Arrah and Jagdishpur

Arrah, the headquarter of Bhojpur district in Bihar, is situated in thirty-five miles west of Patna. It has been carved out from Shahbad district in 1992. Its most famous town Jagdishpur is about 20 miles South-West of Arrah near river Son. In June 1857, it was under the control of the Commissioner Mr. William Tayler. The other stations under him were Gaya, fifty miles to the south, and Chhapra, forty miles to the North of Patna. The places like Arrah and Jagdishpur are famous in the annals of history because of the Kunwar Singh, the chief whose lionourable and straightforward character stood high even among the Europeans. He was the foremost freedom fighter of the 1857 Uprising in Bihar.

Kunwar Singh of Jagdishpur was the eldest son of Sahabzada Singh and was born probably in 1777. Kunwar Singh succeeded to the gaddi (ancestral estate) sometime in 1826. He owned a large, valuable landed estate included a vast tract of land comprising of 900 villages in Shahabad district. The total annual income of his estate was about rupees six lakh. However, extravagant living, generosity beyond his means, put the estate under ruinous debts, which amounted to rupees twenty lakh on the eve of the Uprising of 1857.[1]

In order to get the arrears of the debt, the British Government appointed an Agent on the estate of Kunwar Singh in 1854-55, to administer the estate and collect the revenue. After paying the British Government's rent and defraying the collection charges, he was to repay the debts by installments. However, this arrangement made helpless to Kunwar Singh and rather annoyed him against the British, to whom he was always in terms of fidelity. Perhaps this decision of the British Government compelled the Kunwar Singh to join the Uprising.[2]

Malleson describes the reason of his association with the revolutionaries. He says, "Kunwar Singh, a Rajput chieftain of ancient lineage, had been made an enemy of the English rule by the action of our revenue system. The action of this system, which he imperfectly understood, had reduced his means so considerably that some short time before the outbreak of the mutiny his estates had been placed in liquidation."[3]

Another chronicler Sedgwick writes about Kunwar Singh that this leader was a man of eighty, but he proved a bold and resolute soldier. He had been treated harshly by the Government, and undoubtedly had a grievance against the British.[4]

On hearing some seditious activities of aged chief Kunwar Singh, Mr. Tayler sent an agent to his palace at Jagdishpur, near Arrah. This was to intimate the suspicions entertained of his loyalty, and to bid him repair in person to Patna, to give an account of himself. Kunwar Sing intentionally received him lying on a bed, and pleaded age and infirmity in reply to the commissioner's summons, but pledged to repair to Patna as soon as his health permitted.[5]

The military station of Dinapur, ten miles to the westward of Patna, was garrisoned by Her Majesty's 10th Foot, the 7th, 8th, and 40th Native Infantry, one company of European, and one of Native artillery. Major-General Lloyd was the officer in command of the station. The Sepoys of all the three regiments 7th, 8th, and 40th Native Infantry at Dinapur mutinied on 25th July 1857. There was only one Her Majesty's 10th Foot to guard over there. Finding the right opportunity, Kunwar Singh also gathered a large number of followers, who included his brothers Amar Singh and Ritnarain Singh, Dayal Singh; his nephews Nishan Singh and Jai Krishna Singh; and other relatives like Bisheswar Singh. The revolutionaries of Dinapur, Chhotanagpur, Manbhum, Singhbhum, and Palamau wanted to carry on the struggle together under the common leadership of Kunwar Singh. Almost all Bihar was united under him. Jadunath Sahi (the son-in-law of Kunwar Singh's brother Dayal Singh) who had taken a leading part in the rebellion in Ranchi was located as a follower of Kunwar Singh. Raja Arjun Singh of Singhbhum as well as Arjun Singh's brother, along with many local leaders, were keen on fight under Kunwar Singh's leadership. Many of them sought to help Kunwar Singh by sending their forces to join him.[6]

On 26th July 1857, the troops reached the district headquarter, Shahabad in order to plunder the treasury and kill the Europeans. They had also an intension to organise themselves under the leadership of Kunwar Singh, the Raja of Jagdishpur, who had already launched a movement against the British. Hearing the news of Sepoys' revolt, Kunwar Singh also marched along with his men. They all joined at Arrah and in the morning of 27th of July, they broke open the jail, released 400 prisoners, and looted the treasury of 85,000 rupees. They were further joined by the jail guards, prisoners, and hundreds of revolutionaries from the neighbouring villages. After which they charged the bungalow, where Mr. Boyle, Mr. Wake (the Magistrate), and his assistant, Mr. Colvin, Mr. Littledale, the judge, and some sub-officials and railway men, including a few Muslims, 16 Eurasians with fifty Sikhs, had taken up their position. The revolutionaries besieged the European officials and civilians of Arrah and Shahabad.[7]

George Trevelyan writes that Kunwar Singh brought with him a mighty following, and recruits poured in by hundreds and thousands daily. The Sepoy veterans, who were living on pensions in their Native villages, came forward to share the fortunes of their ancient regiments in greater numbers. George Trevelyan quotes the Calcutta papers, "That old fool, Coer Sing,' have held a review of eight thousand armed men, besides the three regular battalions. There was one cry throughout the province — that now or never was the time to shake off the oppression of the stranger."[8]

The British sent an expedition from Patna under Captain Dunbar to defeat the Kunwar Singh. The force was consisting of nearly three hundred and fifty men of the 37th

Queen's regiment, sixty Sikhs, and some young civilians who volunteered to accompany the party. Captain Dunbar was quite unfit for such a duty, his military experience having been gained in a paymaster's bureau. Due to weak command of Dunbar and strong revolutionary force under experienced Kunwar Singh, the British met the defeat with heavy losses in this battle near Arrah. Captain Dunbar and several officers were shot dead to the first discharge.[9]

About the battle James Halls writes, "Out of the 400 fine fellows that started for Arrah, nearly 200 were killed, and of the remainder I do not think more than fifty to sixty were not wounded; out of seven volunteers, five were knocked over, four killed and one wounded. This has been the most disastrous affair that has happened out here."[10]

Hearing the news of the defeat of the British force under Dunbar, Major Vincent Eyre marched with his force consisted of hundred and fifty and four English bayonets, twelve mounted volunteers, and three field-pieces, with their complement of artillerymen. George Trevelyan writes that Kunwar Singh's whole forces; two thousand five hundred mutineers, and the posse comitatus of the province, estimated at eight thousand men. The rebels, whom their recent success had inspired with unwonted confidence, did not wait to be attacked. The battle was started at Bibiganj on 3rd of August. George Trevelyan mentions that initially the revolutionaries disheartened the English but finally Kunwar Sing retreated, leaving on the ground six hundred of his followers, most of whom had been killed in the attack upon the battery. Malleson also mentions that the Sepoys, after their crushing defeat, had hastily abandoned their position in Mr. Boyle's larger house, and packing up their spoils, had fled precipitately to the forest stronghold of their leader, Kunwar Singh, at Jagdishpur.[11]

After the occupation of Arrah, Major Vincent Eyre combed and arrested the revolutionaries. He held a drumhead court-martial, at which he, as President, took precedence of the Judge and magistrates, who sat under him. Many of the townspeople testified against these captive revolutionaries, and they were promptly hanged, or in effect strangled, in the gardens of Arrah house. The request made in most instances simply was that they might be allowed to adjust the rope themselves; 'and all met the death with dignity.' It testifies strongly to the point of view with which the Indian regards death. Death to them was no great matter; the only question which did really matter was whether they had been true to their religious traditions.[12]

Sieveking quotes, Sir Evelyn Wood, alluding to that drumhead court-martial at Arrah, says that an old man, while awaiting his turn on the gallows, and witnessing the painful struggles of a man dying in the air, opening his Kummerbund, took out all his property three rupees and said calmly, "This is my will! I give one rupee for prayers for my soul, one I leave for charitable purposes, and the third I bequeath to the man who hangs me."[13]

After completing the punishment of the revolutionaries and even innocents, Major Vincent Eyre decided to take an expedition to Jagdishpur, to track out the escaped Raja and his army. He only waited until he was reinforced by Her Majesty's 10th Foot, and by 100 of Rattray's Sikhs from Dinapur, and then he started from Arrah on 11th of August. Here at Jagdishpur, Kunwar Singh had in the field altogether about five thousand two hundred men, of whom twelve hundred were Sepoys. But the fight was almost one-sided; Eyre had taken Jagdishpur, the abode of the King, after only about two-and-a-half hours' fighting. The total loss in Kunwar Singh's army was about 200 or 300 men, whilst in the English camp, there was no loss of life, only six men wounded. Kunwar Sing had another palace at Jutowrali, some little distance from Jagdishpur; which was destroyed by a detachment sent by Eyre for the purpose; as were also the residences of Amar Sing and Dayal Singh, the two brothers of the old chief.[14]

James Halls writes, ".... afterwards found that they had at once rapidly decamped in the direction of Sasseram. We remained several days at Jugdeespore, principally, I fancy, for the sake of the wounded, some of whom were seriously injured indeed, two or three afterwards died perhaps also to give the major time to communicate with the authorities at Dinapore. We then, after hanging a few more rebels, blew up and destroyed Koowar Singh's palace, and a new Hindoo temple in its vicinity; set fire to the village in several parts and departed, following the route of the rebels towards Sasseram."[15]

For the British, the campaign terminated with the victory at Jagdishpur but this did not mark the end of Kunwar Singh's struggle. He shifted out of Bihar, moving to Mirzapur, Rewa, Banda, Kalpi, Lucknow, and Kanpur, along with his comrade-in-arms Nishan Singh. Passing through Mirzapur and Rewa, he arrived at Banda in September with a view to joining Tatya Tope. He was joined by the Gwalior forces at Kalpi, and fought in the battle of Kanpur in December 1857.[16]

Subsequently, he arrived in Lucknow, where the King of Awadh awarded him a robe of honour and a *Farman* for the area comprising the Azamgarh district. The Governor-General ordered the re-occupation of Azamgarh as Kunwar Singh had already taken it, which forced the latter to march towards Ghazipur. From Ghazipur, Kunwar singh eventually decided to return to his home district and re-entered Jagdishpur on 23rd of April 1858. He was grievously injured during the retreat and lost his right hand but his determination to fight the English had not weakened. The next day a force under Captian Le Grand proceeded to attack the old, injured veteran, but it was repulsed. Three days later, Kunwar Singh died of injuries.[17]

In a rare tribute to Kunwar Singh, George Trevelyan, a prominent British politician who had served in India during the 1860s, wrote.[18]
"For long past Coer Singh had been watching the course of events with keen interest and a definite purpose. This remarkable man came in for an abundant share of the abuse so indiscriminately dealt out to all those who took part against us at the crisis. Coer Singh was described in the contemporary journals as a devil whose villainy could be accounted for only on the theory that he was not of "human flesh and blood." The time for shrieking and scolding has gone by and we can afford to own that he was not a devil at all but the

high-souled chief of a warlike tribe who had been reduced to a non-entity by the yoke of a foreign invader. ... Surely a people whose favourite heroes are Lochiel and Rob Roy Macgregor may spare a little sympathy for the chieftain, who at eighty years old bade fill up his brass lotah, saddle his elephants and call out his men ... ; who inflicted on us a disaster complete and tragical; who exacted from the unruly mutineers an obedience which they paid to none other; who led his force in person to Lucknow and took a leading part in the struggle which decided the destinies of India; who after no hope was left for the cause North of the Ganges did not lose heart but kept up his men together during a long and arduous retreat in the face of a victorious enemy; and as the closing act of his life by a masterly manoeuvre, baffled his pursuers and placed his troops in safety on their own side of the great river, when friend and foe alike believed their destruction to be inevitable. On that occasion a round shot from an English gun smashed his arm as he was directing the passage of the last boat full of his followers.... It was uncommonly lucky for us that Coer Singh was not forty years younger."

After the death of Kunwar Singh, his brother Amar Singh led his followers, who held out bravely in different parts of Bihar. Their activities continued to be a cause of serious concern for the East India Company's administration. The forest area of Jagdishpur was the base of Amar Singh's military campaign. The struggle between Amar Singh and the British force under Sir E Lugard in the first half of 1858, assumed epic dimensions.[19]

Engels writes about him in the *New York Daily Tribune*, that these impenetrable forests (in Jagdishpur) of bamboo and underwood are held by a party of insurgents under Ummer (Amar) Singh, who shows rather more activity and knowledge of guerrilla warfare; at all events, he attacks the British wherever he can, instead of quietly waiting for them. If, as it is feared, part of the Oude insurgents should join him before he can be expelled from his stronghold, the British may expect rather harder work they have had of late. These Jangles have now for nearly eight months served as a retreat to insurgent parties, who have been able to render very insecure the Grand Trunk Road from Calcutta to Allahabad, the main communication of the British.[20]

Amar Singh had full support of the revolutionaries to continue the revolt and he himself had determined to fight the British until his last breath. His hope strengthened when he heard the Nana Sahib's retreat towards Nepal border. Amar Singh went over to the Terai region to assume the leadership of Nana's troops, but was captured in December 1859. He was imprisoned by the British at Gorakhpur, but died of illness at Gorakhpur on January 3, 1860 before he could be placed on trial.[21]

References:

1. *The Pioneer*, 6th May, 2007
2. Halls, John James, *Two Months in Arrah in 1857*, London, 1860, p. 86

3. Malleson, George Bruce, *History of the Indian Mutiny of 1857-58, Commencing from the Close of the Second Volume of Sir John Kaye's History of the Sepoy War*, Vol. III, (Contemporaneous with Sir John Kay's Third Volume), London, 1878, p. 76

4. *A Sketch of the Principal Military Events*, p. 48

5. Martin, R. Montgomery, *The Indian Empire,* Vol. II, London, 1858, p. 400

6. *Ibid*, p. 398, see also *People's Democracy*, (Ram Swaroop- *Some Aspects of the 1857 Rebellion in Bihar*), Vol. XXXI, No. 18, May 6, 2007

7. Halls, John James, *Two Months in Arrah in 1857*, London, 1860, p. 39, see also Martin, R. Montgomery, *The Indian Empire,* Vol. II, London, 1858, p. 404

8. George Trevelyan, *The Competition Wallah*, London, 1864, p. 92

9. Ibid, pp. 93-96, see also Malleson, George Bruce, *History of the Indian Mutiny of 1857-58, Commencing from the Close of the Second Volume of Sir John Kaye's History of the Sepoy War*, Vol. III, (Contemporaneous with Sir John Kay's Third Volume), London, 1878, p. 85

10. Halls, John James, *Two Months in Arrah in 1857*, London, 1860, p. 94

11. George Trevelyan, *The Competition Wallah*, London, 1864, pp. 105-109, see also Malleson, George Bruce, *History of the Indian Mutiny of 1857-58, Commencing from the Close of the Second Volume of Sir John Kaye's History of the Sepoy War*, Vol. III, (Contemporaneous with Sir John Kay's Third Volume), London, 1878, p. 102

12. Isabel Giberne Sieveking, *A Turning Point in the Indian Mutiny*, London, 1910, pp. 105-106

13. *Ibid*, pp. 107

14. *Ibid*, pp. 110-112, see also Malleson, George Bruce, *History of the Indian Mutiny of 1857-58, Commencing from the Close of the Second Volume of Sir John Kaye's History of the Sepoy War*, Vol. III, (Contemporaneous with Sir John Kay's Third Volume), London, 1878, p. 129, and Martin, R. Montgomery, *The Indian Empire,* Vol. II, London, 1858, pp. 405-6

15. John James Halls, *Two Months in Arrah in 1857*, London, 1860, p. 61

16. *People's Democracy*, (Ram Swaroop *Some Aspects of the 1857 Rebellion in Bihar*), Vol. XXXI, No. 18, May 6, 2007

17. *Ibid,* see also John James Halls, *Two Months in Arrah in 1857*, London, 1860, p. 87

18. George Trevelyan, *The Competition Wallah*, London, 1864, pp. 89-92

19. *People's Democracy*, (Ram Swaroop- *Some Aspects of the 1857 Rebellion in Bihar*), Vol. XXXI, No. 18, May 6, 2007

20. *New York Daily Tribune*, October 1, 1858

21. *People's Democracy*, (Ram Swaroop- *Some Aspects of the 1857 Rebellion in Bihar*), Vol. XXXI, No. 18, May 6, 2007

Chapter 8

National Perspective or War of Independence

From the beginning of the Uprising until the current times, there was a rustling sound of national character of the Uprising. During the Uprising, the British House of Commons opposition leader Benjamin Disraeli and Karl Marx characterized the Uprising as the national revolt. Immediately, after this war, Sir Syed Ahmad Khan boldly challenged the Company's Government by declaring that whatever happened during the Uprising of 1857 was due to the British policies, and the discontented people raised their arms against the British irrespective of their race and religion. After Sir Syed Ahmad Khan, this controversy stopped as the Company's rule was taken over by British Crown and assured the Indians to protect their rights and honour. However, the Uprising episode again gained a momentum when it completed fifty years, and the British people celebrated the golden jubilee of their victory in 1907.

In the first decade of the twentieth-century V.D. Savarkar in his book, *The Indian War of Independence of 1857*, propagated the fifty years old idea of Benjamin Disraeli and described this revolt as "a national struggle." To V.D. Savarkar, the revolt was a national war, it stood for two principles, namely, Swadharma and Swaraj, which were the basic objectives of any national movement. Later on, Ashok Mehta also followed V.D. Savarkar. Jawaharlal Nehru in his book, *The Discovery of India*, described it as the feudal revolt of 1857 and added that it was much more than a military mutiny, and it rapidly spread and assumed the character of a popular rebellion and a war of Indian independence. This school of historical thought describes this revolt as First War of Independence.

The book of V. D. Savarkar left a far-reaching effect, and the gap between the Indian people, and the British Government was again widened and the nationalists of both the moderates and extremists thrown their full energy into the first anti-British movement of Swadeshi. Even after the Surat split of the Indian National Congress, the nationalists of extremist mentality proved themselves as a hard nut against the British in and outside India. At that time, the new generation of radical nationalists began to challenge the decrees of colonial historiography and started writing their own version of the past on national point of view. Although V.D. Savarkar based his work on colonial historians, but turned the Uprising into a national war, and the rebels into nationalist heroes. He inaugurated a potent swadeshi historiography of the rebellion, which tells us perhaps as much about the choices that Indian nationalism faced in the first decade of the twentieth century, as about the Uprising itself. After the Indian independence, the scholars conducted a full-fledged and independent research over the topic of Uprising and by their research, the Uprising speedily changed its character and became a national insurrection.

V.D. Savarkar refuted the rakings of the cartridge episode and the theory of Mutiny of the colonialist historians. In support of his theory of War of Independence, he says, "If the Revolution had been due only to the cartridges, why did Nana Sahib, the Emperor of Delhi, the Queen of Jhansi, and Khan Bahadur Khan of Rohelkhand join it? These were not surely going to serve in the English army, nor were they compelled to break the cartridges with their teeth! If the rising were due wholly or chiefly to the cartridges, it would have stopped suddenly as soon as the English Governor General issued a proclamation that they should not be used anymore! He gave them permission to make cartridges with their own hands. But instead of doing so, or ending the whole by leaving the Company's service altogether, the Sepoys rose to fight in battle. Not only the Sepoys but thousands of peaceful citizens and Rajas and Maharajas also rose, who had no direct or indirect connection with the army. It is therefore clear that it was not these accidental things that roused the spirit of Sepoy and civilian, King and pauper, Hindu and Mohammedan."[1]

In support of his theory, V.D. Savarkar quotes the proclamation of the Mughal Emperor Bahadur Shah Zafar which says, "Oh, you sons of Hindusthan, if we make up our mind we can destroy the enemy in no time! We will destroy the enemy and will release from dread our religion and our country, dearer to us than life itself!"[2]

There was one category of many civilian classes who had no direct or indirect connection with the British army, participated in the revolt due to their personal grievances, but later on assumed the national character. The first and foremost of this category were the aristocracy or feudal nobility followed by general masses; all actively took part in the Uprising. The Native nobility offered their leadership to regain their power and prestige. The other class which participated in the Uprising was of the upholder of the revenue-free lands which were lost by regulation VI of 1819. There were the zamindars other than the *Maafi* land holders were also unsatisfied as their land was sold on the flimsy pretexts of non-paying the revenue. The third unsatisfied group was of the farmers and peasants whose land revenue was hiked beyond their paying capacity. Another was the class of educated people, which was totally depended on the Government service, was also unsatisfied with their unemployment. Although there were the personal grievances of each class abovementioned but when all the people united against the British, it surely assumed the national character. The participation of the *Ghazis* or religious heroes in the Uprising was purely having national motifs through the religious emotions. The people of different classes united with a common goal to overthrow the British with national enthusiasm. This process of overthrowing the British and getting independence from foreign yoke was considered as War of Independence.

The feudal nobility lost the titles and domains under the annexation policy of British Government. The subsidiary alliance of Lord Wellesley curtailed the power of the Native rulers. Lord Dalhousie's doctrine of lapse took control of the several states causing considerable resentment in the Indian elites. That's why in the Uprising, the men who were most irritated and dismayed at such a step, were the noblemen, and independent princes of India. These all saw that sooner or later such a policy must lead to the overthrow of their independence and confiscation of their own lands. The feudal lords found themselves unemployed and humiliated, and their powers were steadily eroded. According to the Doctrine of Lapse, the domain belonging to a feudal ruler were annexed by the Company, wheather on his death, the ruler did not leave a male heir of his own. Through this infamous annexation policy of Dalhousie, several states were annexed and in many cases affected. These were Satara in 1848, Jaitpur and Sambhalpur in 1849, Baghat in 1850, Udaipur in 1852, Jhansi in 1853, Nagpur in 1854, Tanjore 1855, Awadh 1856, Carnatic 1853, Bithur 1853 and arrangement for the abolition of Mughal Emperor's title at Delhi.[3]

The anti-adoption policy of the Government was also an attack on the Hindu religion. It had long been the tradition for a childless landowner to adopt an heir. To every Hindu, it is necessary that there should be a son, real or adoptive, to carry out the funeral rites enjoined by his religion as obligatory for the salvation of his soul after death. The adopted son, whether nominated by the deceased or appointed with his consent by his widow, has an undoubted right under Hindu law to succeed to the private property of his father by adoption. However, Lord Dalhousie's infamous anti-adoption policy never cared the Hindu law and deliberately ignored this custom with a plea that previous Indian rulers had also practiced the same in the medieval times.

The company even didn't spare the nominal Mughal Emperor Bahadur Shah Zafar and announced that his successors would not use the title of 'Emperor'. It was also decided that in all probability Mughal Emperor Bahadur Shah Zafar might be persuaded to vacate the Red Fort and should be settled at Qutub complex, some twelve miles to the south of Dehli, and that as the place was held in great veneration, generally and particularly, as the burial-place of a noted Muslim Saint and of some of the ancestors of Bahadur Shah Zafar. It was presumed that His Majesty, and the Royal family were not likely to object to their removal, and if they did object, it was to be considered whether pressure might not be put upon them, and their consent obtained by the extreme measure of withholding the royal stipend. Such discourtesies were resented by the deposed Indian rulers, and the effects were seen during the Uprising as Lucknow and Delhi emerged as its most important centres.[4]

By quoting the letter of the Governor General of 1856, related to the fate of the Mughal dynasty, John William Kaye states, "... On the King's demise, Prince Mirza Muhammad Korash should be informed that government recognise him as the head of the family upon the same conditions as those accorded to Prince Mirza Fakhruddin, excepting that, instead of the title of King, he should be designated and have the title of Shahzada, and that this communication should be made to him not in the way of writing, negotiation, or bargaining, which it is not the intention of the Governor General in Council to admit, but as the declaration of the mature and fixed determination of the Government of India. .... The sum of fifteen thousand rupees per mensem, from the family stipend, to be fixed as the future assignment of the heir of the family."[5]

The stoppage of Nana Sahib's pension and title was a big mistake on the part of the British as he was emotionally representing almost entire Hindu community and also having enough sympathy of Muslim population. Nana Sahib sent emissary to England, and getting failed in his efforts, fomented intrigues far and wide. The Sepoys and civilians of Northern India greatly infuriated due to the withdrawal of the British financial support of Nana Sahib.

The annexation of Awadh, on the baseless excuse of mal-administration, left a deep impact on the minds of the people of Northern India. It was the general perception that British were merely the revenue collectors of Bengal and illegally exceeding their authority, and since the Nawab of Awadh, Wajid Ali Shah, was the Wazir, or guardian, of the Mughal Empire, the seizure of his kingdom was an attack on Mughal sovereignty itself. The annexation of Awadh was much profitable to the British Government as the revenue of Awadh Kingdom was five million Sterling. Besides the annexation of the Indian principalities, the intention of the Company was also to humiliate the Indian princes. Rev. Mr. Allen who had completed twenty-five years service in India remarked, "The pension and ammunities to these fallen Princes have commonly been on a princely scale, but generally accompanied by conditions of a humiliating nature, though regarded by the English as necessary for the public safety or the stability of their own power."[6]

The regulation VI of 1819 was most obnoxious and Sir T. Munro, and the Duke of Wellington said truly enough that to resume lands granted revenue-free was to set the whole people against them, and to make beggars of the masses. Sir Syed wrote, "I cannot describe the odium and the hatred which this act brought on Government, or the extent to which it beggared the people. Many lands which had been held revenue-free for centuries were suddenly resumed on the flimsiest pretexts. The people said that Government not only did nothing for them itself, but undid what former Governments had done. This measure altogether lost for the government the confidence of its subjects."[7]

The rebels in their proclamations mentioned the two things: the one, interference in matters of religion; the other, the resumption of revenue-free lands. So this was one of the two chief causes of the public discontent, and Muslims suffered a lot, by this Act, than their Hindu brethren and enormously profited the British Government. Mr. Disraeli in his speech to the House of Commons computed that the resumption of estates from their proprietors is not less than £500,000 a year in the Presidency of Bengal; £370,000 in the Presidency of Bombay; £200,000 in the Punjab. Not content with this one method of seizing upon the property of the Natives, the British Government discontinued the pensions to the Native grandees, to pay which it was bound by treaty.[8]

The landlords of UP, Bihar and Bengal, under the permanent settlement, unable to pay the arrears of revenue, were compelled to sell their zamindari rights. These zamindars were the head of their overall estate, and the peoples were deeply attached with them. Sir Syed pointed that whether this system of sales was the result of necessity or of ignorance, it has at all events had a hand in bringing on the rebellion.[9]

The assessments imposed by the British Government through land revenue settlements were much heavy and in the course of time it became beyond the paying capacity of the landlords and the cultivators alike. From being cultivated to the same extent year after year, land becomes weak and unfruitful, and does not yield an equal amount. It ceases to have the same value as was put upon it at the time of the Settlement. The cultivators were obliged to borrow money in order to pay the revenue. The landlords also suffered a lot as they could no longer extort rent illegally or make the illicit profit. They rose in the revolt as the heavy land revenue assessment resulted in many landowning families either losing their land or going into great debt with money lenders.[10]

The class which was totally based on the Government jobs was poorer and in more in distress. They had no champion to stand up for their rights and to see justice done to them, and they were constrained to weep in silence. The army, which was composed of Sepoys, was the only service obtainable by Indian Natives. According to Sir Syed Ahmad Khan, "The consequence of this was that when the mutineers wanted recruits, thousands flocked in, just as in a famine hungry men rush upon food. Many took service upon one anna or one anna and a half per day and many, instead of cash, received a couple or perhaps three pounds of grain daily. It is evident; therefore, that however much they might desire service, the Natives of India were unable to obtain it, the number wanting service being greatly in excess of the number of posts to be filled up."[11]

Under the British Government, this serving class reduced to the poverty as a result they inclined for the change of the rulers. Gubbins narrates the same matter but in the defending mood. He says, "again, the Native gentry, especially the Mohammedan portion of it in India, look chiefly to the service of the State for a means of subsistence. But as all the chief offices in British India are monopolized by Europeans, the minor ones only are open to them. In fixing the remuneration of those, we have too much followed the scale of pay we found to prevail in the Native Governments which we succeeded; forgetting that with them bribes and pecuniary gratifications were not forbidden. Under our system they could not openly be received: and in consequence several departments of the public service have been grossly underpaid. In the police service this was so particularly the case, that it has been found difficult to induce Natives of good family to enter it at all. Our revenue service was better paid, and a Native officer, responsible for collecting 20,000/. Per annum, might receive a salary of 20/. per month. The Natives complained, and with some justice, that in the earlier years of our Government we had shown more liberality; and that a Native collector had then been used to receive a commission of 10 per cent, on his collections, which would give him ten times the salary which has been latterly allowed."[12]

It was the time when almost all the Europeans claimed the Uprising as Sepoy Mutiny; very strangely Benjamin Disraeli has called it a national revolt. On the topic of revolt in India, a heated discussion was followed in the House of Commons in England in which Mr. Benjamin Disraeli, the Opposition Leader of the Conservative Party of England, stated his views. Karl Marx in the *New York Daily Tribune* has quoted Disraeli's speech in which he asked in the House of Commons, "does the disturbance in India indicate a military mutiny, or is it a national revolt? Is the conduct of the troops the consequence of a sudden impulse, or is it the result of an organised conspiracy?"[13]

Mr. Benjamin Disraeli further asserted that from the late years a new principle was adopted in the Government of India, it was the principle of destroying nationality. The principle was realized by the forcible destruction of Native princes, the disturbance of the settlement of property, and the tampering with the religion of the people. Mr. Benjamin Disraeli finally concluded that Indian disturbance was not a military mutiny, but a national revolt, of which the Sepoys were the acting instruments only. He ended his harangue by advising the Government to turn their attention to the internal improvement of India, instead of pursuing its present course of aggression.[14]

The Sepoys entered Delhi were received with great national enthusiasm by both the communities, particularly Muslims. John William Kaye writes that the great national cause was swelling into portentous external dimensions under the inflations of the King and princes, and others of stronger lungs than their own. Everywhere it had been noised about from early morning that the King was on the side of the mutineers, and that to fight against the English was to fight for the King; to fight for the restoration of the Mughal throne; to fight for the religion of the Prophet.[15]

John William Kaye, although not fully supporting the theory of national revolt, characterizes this Uprising as all India level against the British domination. He says, "But whether designed or not designed by man, God's mercy forbade its accomplishment; and in a few hours after this first great explosion, the Electric Telegraph was carrying the evil tidings to all parts of the country. The note of warning was sounded across the whole length and breadth of the land; and wherever an Englishman was stationed there was the stem preparation of defence."[16]

Kanpur, which was the third most important centre of Uprising after Delhi and Lucknow, had been full of national feelings and enthusiasm. The revolutionaries were having an intention of occupying not only the Northern India but the South as well, which was untouched by the Uprising. G. W. Forrest quotes that one of the two women who survived the Kanpur massacre told him that when she was brought before Azeemullah he said to her, "Why are you crying? The Mughal Emperor has taken Delhi and driven the

English from Northern India; when we take Kanpur and Lucknow we will march to Calcutta and be masters of Southern India, and your husband (the sowar who captured her), who has now been made a Colonel, will then be a great man and you a great woman."[17]

How it could be possible that without national feeling, such the large people of North and Central India unified against the foreign domination. Even the British who profoundly called this Uprising as mutiny perhaps smelt the national consciousness of the Indian people and invested Delhi with so much importance and considered storming it such a priority, even though from a military point of view, it did not deserve that significance. V.D. Savarkar in his book *Indian War of Independence of 1857* mentioned the quotes of the *Red Pamphlet*, according to which, "Not only the regular troops but 60 thousand men of the army of the ex-King, the Zamindars and their retainers, the 250 forts, most of them heavily armed with guns, had been working against us. They have balanced the rule of the Company with the Sovereignty of their own Kings and have pronounced, almost unanimously, in favour of the latter. The very pensioners who have served in the army have declared against us and to a man joined in the insurrection".[18]

V.D Savarkar again quotes Justin McCarthy, who says, "The fact was that throughout the greater part of the Northern and North-Western provinces of the Indian peninsula, there was a rebellion of the Native races against the English power. It was not alone the Sepoy who rose in revolt; it was not by any means a merely military mutiny. It was a combination of military grievance, national hatred, and religious fanaticism against the English occupation of India. The Native princes and the Native soldiers were in it. The Mohammedan and the Hindu forgot their old religious anti-pathies to join against the Christian. Hatred and panic were the stimulants of that great rebellious movement. The quarrel about the greased cartridges was but the chance spark flung in among all the combustible material. If that spark had not lighted it, some other would have done the work .... The Meerut Sepoys found, in a moment, a leader, a flag, and a cause, and the mutiny was transformed into a revolutionary war. When they reached the Jumna, glittering in the morning light, they had all unconsciously seized one of the great critical moments of history and converted a military mutiny into a national and religious war!"[19]

The Europeans scholars generally condemn the elite class of India due to their involvement in the Uprising. They complain that they obtained the Jagirs on the mercy of the British Government but during the Uprising, they forgot the aid and assistance and jumped in the insurrection. Broadly speaking it was definitely the national feeling which forced the local chiefs to forfeit the loyalty of the foreign rule and unite in favour their own Mughal ruler who was the only symbol of national unity. Gubbins' complaint regarding this matter needs to be quoted here. He says, "Since Delhi was taken, the Newab of Jhajjar has been hanged for treason. .... His ancestor had commanded a body of Irregular Horse under Lord Lake, and had been rewarded by a jagir, ... Several successions had taken place in the family, and the next of kin had regularly succeeded to this valuable inheritance in virtue of the British grant. Yet no sooner did our Native army mutiny and the puppet King raise his standard at Delhi, than our Jhajjar vassal forgot his faith and joined our enemies. The very similar is the story of the Raja of Ballabhgarh, who has also lately paid the penalty of his treason at Delhi. He, however, belonged to an old family, anciently settled at Ballabhgarh, but had ever been treated by us with kindness and consideration. Another instance of treason, not inferior in complexion to that of the chief of Jhajjar, is found in his neighbour, the Newab of Farrukh Nagar, who also owed his estate to us. This jagir also had come to him through more than one succession, the original grant being British. It seems, however, to have excited no loyalty in his breast; and he, too, early joined the rebels, and has paid for his treason with his life. Many other cases of like miserable defection might be instanced."[20]

The same person Gubbins, who once criticized the Rajas and Nawabs for their faithless attitude during the Uprising, eventually admits the sufferings of the elite class which was prosperous in its Native Government. He states, "But, perhaps, the class most entitled to sympathy was the nobility itself; and the numberless relatives and friends who hung upon it. The nobles had received large pensions from the Native Government, the payment of which, never regular, ceased with the introduction of our rule. Government had made liberal provision for their support; but before this could be obtained, it was necessary to prepare careful lists of the grantees, and to investigate their claims. It must be admitted that in effecting this there was undue delay; and that for want of common means of support the gentry and nobility of the city were brought to great straits and suffering. We were informed that families which had never before been outside the zanana, used to go out at night and beg their bread."[21]

It is also stated that although the British Government abolished innumerable taxes of the Native Government, but the new taxes which it introduced were totally unfamiliar to the Indian population and Government faced a tough resistance during the Uprising. As for Awadh, British introduced a new tax which was highly unpopular, viz. that on the consumption of opium. This drug was very largely consumed in the dissipated capital; and the tax upon it, which obtained in every other part of the British dominions, and then which a juster source of revenue could scarcely be named, was highly obnoxious to the citizens of Lucknow.[22]

All the sufferings mentioned above was not the local but nationwide in India, which created unity among its people irrespective of their religion and race. They all jumped into the fire of Uprising against the colonial rule and tried to set up their own government under their respective rulers or feudal nobility. It is therefore, clear that it was not these accidental things that roused the spirit of Sepoy and civilian, King and pauper, Hindu and Muslim but only and only goal of independence or deliverance from the foreign yoke. They all considered the nominal Emperor Bahadur Shah Zafar as the rightful descendant of Akbar, the great Mughal. Emperor Bahadur Shah Zafar, a crowned descendant of the Mughal dynasty was strongly followed and supported by a well-trained and powerful army rose in revolt against the foreign rule. He was looked upon by the Indian feudal chiefs, as well as the masses, as the national symbol and traditional sovereign of India.

Gaining full control over Red Fort in Delhi, and proclaiming Bahadur Shah Zafar as the Emperor of Hindustan, was a clear-cut message that the Mughal King was the legitimate ruler of India and a symbol of authority, while the British were usurpers who had to be defeated and expelled from the country. Librating Delhi from British rule and enthroning Bahadur Shah Zafar in the Red Fort became a potent war cry for an independent Indian national state. It is clear from the above that those who participated in the 1857 revolt were motivated chiefly by a desire to oust the hated rule of the Company and replace it by a national sovereign state of their own and restored the Mughal Emperor, the Maratha Peshwa, and the Nawab of Awadh, as their rulers. However, it could rightly be concluded that whatever happened in 1857 was not a mutiny but a War of Independence or National Revolt.

References:

1. Savarkar, p. 6
2. *Ibid*, p. 8
3. Roberts, P.E., *A Historical Geography of the British Dependencies: India*, Vol. VII, London, 1914, pp. 352-355
4. Kaye, John William, *Kay's and Malleson's History of the Indian Mutiny of 1857-8*, Vol. II, London, 1910, p. 13, see also Anderson, Clare, *The Indian Uprising of 1857-8: Prisons, Prisoners and Rebellion*, London, 2007, p-8 and *The Living Age*, Volume 0055, Issue 702, New York, November 7, 1857, p. 328 (When Bahadur Shah Zafar succeeded to Shah Akbar in 1837, an attempt was made, under instructions from the Governor General, to obtain a formal renunciation of all claims upon the East India Company. The King, who was an old man when he succeeded, refused to comply. Another proposal to remove the King to the Qutub was also indignantly rejected. This matter was raised from time to time. The English newspapers pressed the necessity of removing the titular Mughal Emperor Bahadur Shah Zafar. On January 13, 1849, the Delhi Gazette, reported, "On Thursday morning departed this life Prince Dara Bakht, heir-apparent to the throne of Delhi, leaving Shahzada Fakhruddin as heir, and with him we have some reason to believe that all the right of the Royal House to the succession dies out, such having been guaranteed to him individually and to no other member of the family. We sincerely trust that such is really the case, and that our Government will now be in a position to adopt steps for making efficient arrangements for the dispersion, with a suitable provision, of the family on the death of the King." *Two Native Narratives*, pp. 17-18)

5. Kaye, John William, *A History of the Sepoy War in India, 1857-58,* Vol. II, London 1874, p. 32

6. *The   United States Democratic Review,* Volume 0040, Issue 5, New York, November 1857, p. 407

7. *Asbab-e-Baghawat-e-Hind,* p. 26

8. *New York Daily Tribune,* August 14, 1857

9. *Ibid,* p. 27

10. *Ibid,* pp. 29-30 see also *New York Daily Tribune,* August 14, 1857

11. *Ibid,* p. 36

12. Gubbins, p. 62

13. *New York Daily Tribune,* August 14, 1857

14. *Ibid*

15. Kaye, John William, *Kay's and Malleson's History of the Indian Mutiny of 1857-8,* Vol. II, London, 1910, p. 70

16. John William Kaye, *A History of the Sepoy War in India, 1857-58,* Vol. II, London 1874, p. 110

17. *A History of the Indian Mutiny,* Vol. I, London 1904, p. 421

18. Savarkar, p. 211

19. *Ibid,* p. 11

20. Gubbins, p. 63

21. *Ibid,* p. 78

22. *Ibid,* pp. 78-79

Chapter 9

Mutiny or Military Perspective

The East India Company established its rule over India through its huge and powerful Indian army. The company was staffed by military men holding military titles and positioned its cantonments to overawe the principal towns and cities. As the Company's rule was a military regime, the state itself was imperiled as soon as the military mutinied in 1857. The British scholars generally called the Uprising as the mutiny in which some of their own Sepoys mutinied due to their personal grievances. Sir Marshman, John Lawrence, P.E. Roberts, Malleson, Holmes, Seelay, Sambhu Chandra Mukhopadhaya, Haris Chandra Mukharjee, Sir Syed Ahmed Khan, Raj Narain Basu, Godsay Bhattji, etc. have described this great event as 'Mutiny of the Sepoys'.

It was the military which played the pivotal role for establishing the rule of the East India Company. However, the same military proved fatal to the Company when it ignored their customs, traditions and religions. 1857 was the year when the military all over Northern and Central India mutinied and tried to free their dominion with the aristocratic and popular support. The most powerful wing of the army; cavalry and infantry rose with their arms. The cavalry regiments were composed chiefly of Muslims, as the infantry regiments were of Hindus. In Bengal Army about four-fifths of the Bengal Native Infantry were Hindus, mainly of the Brahmin and Rajput castes; and the remainder Muslims. On the other hand, three-fourths of the Bengal Native Cavalry were Muslims, the Hindus being generally not equal to them as troopers.[1]

The Uprising of 1857 was heralded by many minor outbreaks, the most notable of which occurred on 10th July 1806, in Madras Presidency, in which two battalions of Sepoys stationed at Vellore near Madras, mutinied. They surrounded four European companies of 69th Regiment. The mutineers were attacked and dispersed by the 19th Light Dragoons from Arcot, under Colonel Gillespie. Over Six hundred of them were cut down in the fight that ensued, and two hundred were afterwards shot who had been dragged from their hiding places. Of the four European companies 164 men, besides officers, perished, and many British officers of the Sepoys were murdered.[2]

The Vellore mutiny may rightly be considered the dress rehearsal of the Uprising of 1857. The reasons assigned for the mutiny were the introduction of a leather stock, a new head-dress, and regulations respecting, shaving and wearing earrings or marks of caste on the forehead, in the Madras Army. Every single point of which affected strongly the religious prejudices of the Natives. The Sepoys considered it an attack on their caste and religion. In addition, they were also much annoyed with the intentions of the British commanders who were openly preaching the Christianity among them.

Eighteen years after the Vellore Mutiny, on the occasion of the first Burmese War in 1824, the 47th Bengal Native Infantry, was ordered to march for Burma. The Sepoys declared that they would not violate their religion by crossing the "black water," or sea, and that they would not proceed by land, unless they were guaranteed increased allowances. The Sepoys of that regiment broke out into mutiny were warned of the grave consequences of disobedience. Eventually, the poor offender Sepoys met a harsh treatment and gunned down. The surviving Sepoys were hanged, and the name of the guilty regiment disappeared from the Army List.[3]

In 1844, at the time of conquest of Sindh, the 34th Regiment had refused to march beyond Firozpur, unless they were granted the additional allowances usually given to soldiers beyond the Indus at the time of war. Consequently, the offending regiment, 34th Bengal Native Infantry was disbanded, and its number was erased from the Army List. In 1849-50, the 22nd, 13th, and 66th Bengal Native Infantry mutinied on a question of pay. As a result various punishments were inflicted on individuals, and the 66th Regiment was disbanded, and; like the 34th, its number was struck out of the Army List.[4]

Before discussing the further details of the military perspective of the Uprising, it is necessary to analyse the army strength and proportions and structure. Before the Uprising, the British army of the entire three Presidencies of Bombay, Madras and Bengal, consisted of 232,224 Natives of all ranks. The Native forces of all the Presidencies were divided into the following regiments and companies:[5]

Madras Army:
7 Regiments of Cavalry,
52 Regiments of Infantry,
4 Companies of Artillery,
10 Companies of Engineers.
Bombay Army:
3 Regiments of Cavalry,
29 Regiments of Infantry,
10 Companies of Artillery,
2 Companies of Engineers.
Bengal Army:
34 Regiments of Cavalry (Regular and Irregular),
119 Regiments of Infantry (Regular and Irregular),
32 Companies of Artillery,
6 Companies of Engineers.

The whole European force was about 60,000, belonging both the Queen's troops and the Company. Out of these 60, 000 about 5000 were the officers commanding both the Native and European forces. Adding to them the Companies Native Regulars about

160,000, the Company's Irregular Corps of Horse about 60,000, the contingents supplied by Native Princes about 40,000, the armies of the independent and semi-independent princes, more or less available by treaty was about 380,000. The total force available in India at the time of Uprising was swelled to 700,000, men.[6]

The whole army of the Company in India was divided into Regiments, which was headed by a Commander, generally a Lieutenant-Colonel; below him was an Adjutant, who attended to the drill and the daily reports; below him was a Quarter-Master and interpreter, whose double duties were to look after the clothes and huts of the men, and to interpret or translate. Besides these three, there were ten subordinate officers for the ten companies, each expected to make a morning scrutiny into the condition and conduct of his men.[7]

Only Bengal Army was consisting of 139,807 Sepoys and out of it, about 60,000 Sepoys were from Awadh alone. Out of the above mentioned number of the Bengal Army Sepoys, only about 7000 Sepoys remained loyal to the British Government during the Uprising.[8]

As the Uprising was closely associated to the Bengal Regular and Irregular Army, it is needed to be mentioned in details. A Regular Regiment was formed and administered in much the same way as a British Regiment. An Irregular Regiment was commanded by British Officers, but the interior administration was to a great extent in the hands of the Native officers. The details are as follows:[9]

1. Queen's Royal Troops- two regiments of Light Cavalry, fifteen regiments of Infantry, one battalion of 60th Rifles.
2. Company's Regular Troops- three brigades of Horse-Artillery (European and Native), six battalions of European Foot-Artillery, three battalions of Native Foot-Artillery, Corps of Royal Engineers, ten regiments of Native Light Cavalry, two regiments of European Fusiliers, seventy-four regiments of Native Infantry, one regiment of Sappers and Miners.
3. Company's Irregular and Contingent Troops- twenty-three regiments of Irregular Native Cavalry, twelve regiments of Irregular Native Infantry, one corps of Guides, one regiment of Camel Corps, sixteen regiments of Local Militia, Shekhawati Brigade, Contingent of Gwalior, Contingent of Jodhpur, Contingent of Malwa, Contingent of Bhopal, Contingent of Kota.

Julius George Medley remarks that the enlistment of so large an army from almost entirely one class of men was disastrous for the Company. The *Purbeas* of Awadh and Hindustan in general constituted three-fourths of the Bengal Regular Army. And though divided into Hindus and Musalmans, and subdivided into two or three castes or classes, there was yet a strong feeling of a union among them all, until at length the army became quite a close service, open only to the few favoured classes. The strength of this feeling was not known, until the attempt of the Government to introduce 200 Sikhs into each regiment of the line. However, the unfortunate Sikhs who were introduced were so bullied, and led such a life of annoyance among the combined *Purbeas*. At the beginning of the Uprising several of the regiments have openly declared that they will remain faithful and support the British authority, but slowly they changed their stand and decided to assist their "*bhaies*" (brothers). In other words the Native regiments remained passive for a time; but, as soon as they fancied themselves strong enough, they mutinied. In the year of July-August 1857 around one lakh mutinous Sepoys were guarding the revolutionary capital Delhi. Thousands of Sepoys of various races and religion were fighting in various parts of Northern and Central India with their chieftains against the British. Almost all the Cavalry and Artillery and 70 regiments of Infantry rose their arms against their commanders. The majority of the Infantry were Brahmins or high caste Hindus while the Cavalrymen were mostly Muslim or Pathans.[10]

The Sepoys mutinied at Meerut and other parts of India due to the dissatisfaction rankling among them due to various reasons in addition to the greased cartridge episode. These reasons were the British military policies which were totally contrast to the interests of the Native troops. The opening up of service recruitment from nontraditional regions or castes, limited prospects of promotions, grumblings over discriminatory pay, General Service Enlistment Act of 1856, etc. were the policies of the Company which infuriated to the Native troops and made them disloyal to their masters. It was also observed that another reason of discontent among the Sepoys that the British had enlisted the Sepoys under a special promise that their hair and beard shall not be interfered with but after the lapse of some years, they forgot their promise.

No doubt the Bengal troops had indeed carried the British standards into China, into Burma, and had assisted in the conquest of the yet more distant Islands of Java and the Isle of France. However, these were not the Regular regiments of the line, but volunteer corps, raised on the especial condition of foreign services. There were six such among the seventy-four regiments which compose the Bengal army. Viewing over the above problems, the British Government declared its intention of altering radically the constitution of its army, and directed that all the enlistments for local service should cease and from the year 1856, every Sepoy was ordered to be enlisted for general service, wherever the State might require it. The General Service Enlistment Act of 1856 committed the Sepoys to sign a declaration that they would be willing to fight overseas if necessary in the service of the East India Company, and this was resented by the majority who had no desire to travel so far.[11]

Here it is needed a short discussion that how the religion of the Hindu soldiers could be polluted by travelling overseas? It is a fact that in the Bengal Army many high caste persons were enlisted to serve only in India. The Hindu Sepoys were attached to their homes, and service beyond the seas was most distasteful. No increase of pay could compensate for the homesickness, and the loss of caste involved by crossing the "black water." Brahmins, or Kshatriyas were debarred by the tenets of their religion from cooking food on shipboard because they could not bake the cakes of flour, which form his simple food, without clearing for himself a separate plot of ground sacred from the intrusion of others. These ceremonies could not be performed on board ship, and therefore, there the Hindu must fast, or subsist on another substitute, which his tenets permit him to eat when so circumstanced. The Sepoys, therefore, rejected very strongly the idea of going out of India. It is also said that the Bengal soldiers faced difficulties of revisiting their homes, and it was rather impossible to get the leave for any purpose as the distance of some of the cantonments was so great.

Another matter of discontent was the demand of extra allowances by Sepoys for foreign services. As the Wellesley, Hastings, and Dalhousie had enlarged the area in which the Sepoy was bound to serve without the extra allowance which increased bitterness and ill feelings between the Sepoys and the British. Sometimes it assumed a dangerous form. At the time of the conquest of Sindh, and Punjab, the Sepoys raised the question of the extra allowance for foreign services, and ultimately, the concerned regiments were struck out of the Army List.

Under the old regulations of the Native army, they were generally retired after fifteen years' service, and went to their home on a monthly pension of four rupees. This system was changed, and the government granted an increase of pay for length of service, allowing the Sepoy the addition of one rupee after fifteen, and two rupees after twenty years' service. An allowance, also, called hutting money, was granted to them by Lord Hardinge which they had not previously received. By the new regulation of General Enlistment Act, it was directed that a Sepoy that was declared unfit for foreign services, would no longer be permitted to retire to his home on pension, but would be retained with the colours, and employed in ordinary cantonment duty. This order was as usual, read out to each regiment on parade, and it followed an excited murmur of general dissatisfaction throughout the ranks. By these orders, the retired Sepoys were transformed into a local militiaman, and the former militia became general service soldiers.[12]

The other factor of military dissatisfaction was that the Sepoys were badly treated, racially abused, religiously insulted, denied all dignity as human beings, paid only a fraction of the salaries of British soldiers, and stood absolutely no chance of promotion. The promotion at the lower level was strict and slow based on the seniority. The promotion of Sepoy or private soldier was becoming a Naik or Corporal, the Naik being promoted to be Havaldar or Sergeant, the Havaldar in time assuming the rank of Jamadar or Lieutenant, and the Jamadar becoming a Subedar or Captain and there after Subedar Major. According to Irfan Habib, one out of twenty, or it could be thirty, could become a Jamadar. Then from such Jamadars, one out of thirty, perhaps, could become a Subedar; from those, just a few could become a Subedar Major; and that was the end in the promotion ladder. They had hardly any dignity as men left to them in the army. They were paid, but constantly humiliated by their officers as people of an inferior race.[13]

The difference of salaries was another cause of discontent among the Sepoys of British Army. Under Native Governments, such as that of Ranjeet Singh in Punjab, or those of Nagpur and Awadh, Natives, be it remembered, held the highest civil and military offices, and enjoyed emoluments not inferior to those received under European regime. As Gubbins stated, the father may have received 1000 rupees per mensem, as commandant of Cavalry under Ranjeet Singh; the son draws a pay of eighty rupees as sub-commander in the service of the British Government. The difference probably thought by themselves was too great. Gubbins quotes an example of Sikh Naib Risaldar Sher Singh, who said that his father was getting 500 rupees a month in command of a party of Ranjeet Singh's horse, and he himself use to receive only fifty rupees per month under the British Government.[14]

Another military factor was the pride of the Sepoys due to their numerical strength and services to the Company. They were puffed up with pride and thought that there were none like them in the world. They looked upon the European portion of the army as a myth, and thought that the many victories which the Company had gained were entirely by their own prowess. A common saying of theirs was that they enabled the British to conquer India from Burma to Kabul and wanted to show their power and superiority before English. It was the same month of April, the Sepoys disobeyed at Meerut, when the Sepoys defeated the Persian army and captured Mohammera and forced the Persians back from Heart and Afghanistan. A British army officer General Nicolson observed about the cause of the Uprising by saying, "Neither greased cartridges, annexation of Awadh, nor the paucity of the European officers were the causes. For years, I have watched the army and felt sure; they only wanted their opportunity to try their strength with us."[15]

The military rules and regulations also very much hurt the sentiments of the Sepoys. The Sepoys in the British army were clothed, accoutered, and drilled after the European model. They were compelled to wear a head dress abominated by Muslims and Hindus alike; the Brahmins were forbidden to wear the cherished caste-mark on their foreheads; the ear-rings, which were regarded as charms against evil spirits, were no longer permitted; the Muslims were deprived of the beards of which they had been so proud; and in other ways Native sentiments had been impatiently ignored by the British, who could not understand the customs, which to them appeared most childish, could be so dear to the hearts of the Sepoys.

One more factor which was equally fundamental like others was the heavy taxation by the British Government. Under the British Government, the area, the bulk of its Sepoys came from, had been turned into the highest taxed area of the country. The peasantry as well as the 'village zamindars' here had been made subject to an ever rising burden of tax under their different land revenue systems. The heavy taxation reduced both the peasantry and zamindars as the pauper. The Sepoys in general also affected by the land tax policies of the British as they belonged the same area where the taxation was hiked. The wide-range cholera epidemic of 1856 added more filth to the dissatisfaction to both peasants and the zamindars.[16]

Adding the further dissatisfaction in the army, the Company introduced in its force a new Enfield rifle of more than the double range, in place of old two-grooved Brown Bess rifle. The new Enfield rifle's cartridges were wrapped with tallow paper. The user was required to bite open this paper cartridge to expose the powder. Due to an incidental rumour both Hindu and Muslim users were horrified as the tallow had been made of a swine and kine fat. The tidings flashed from cantonment to cantonment in that mysterious fashion peculiar to India.

Allen Charle's quotes from the book *Red Pamphlet* that the new Enfield rifle required a particular species of cartridge, and this cartridge in England was greased with lard made from the fat either of the hog or the ox. Without reflecting, or if reflecting, ignoring the consequences of his act, Colonel Birch ordered that the cartridges for use in India should be made up similarly to the cartridges in use in England, and should be used by the Native troops, that is to say, that Hindu Sepoys should handle cartridges besmeared with the fat of their sacred animal, the cow. Allen Charles again quotes the *Red Pamphlet* that the excited state of the minds of the Sepoys, consequent upon the discovery of the nature of the grease, was reported to them, not a single explanation was offered, not an attempt made to soothe them. After the interval of almost a month, an order was issued to serve out no more greased cartridges.[17]

However, Allen Charles who quoted the words of *Red Pamphlet* says that Colonel Birch had nothing to do and justified about the cartridges that some were greased in England, and others prepared with grease composed of tallow and bees-wax, and made up in the Indian arsenal, had been served out in the ordinary course by the Ordnance authorities. Immediately, on its being reported to Government that the men objected to them, Colonel Birch, under date 26th January, 1857, wrote to the Inspector General of Ordnance to allow the Sepoys to apply whatever grease was required themselves and on 27th January, 1857, he sent a telegram to the Adjutant General of the army, directing that all cartridges were to be thence forward issued ungreased. Allen Charles also alleged the author of the *Red Pamphlet* that he had exaggerated the matter by misquote. He says that the interval of one day, the writer of the Pamphlet calls almost a month. Moreover, General Hearsey paraded all the troops at Barrackpur on the 9th of February, and fully explained the matter to them but the writer of the Pamphlet says there was no explanation.[18]

At Barrackpur Colonel Hearsey endeavoured to allay the excitement of his troops, the 34th Native Infantry. He assured them that they may grease their own cartridges with bee wax or ghee or any materials suitable to the purpose, that it was childish to suppose the Government had any desire to interfere with their caste or religion. A change was introduced into the system of Rifle drill, by which the process of pinching off by the hand was substituted for biting off by the teeth. However, the damage had already been done, and the new orders strengthened the suspicion of the Sepoys. Battalion after battalion refused to use the new cartridges. "We have at Barrackpore," wrote General Hearsey in

February, "been dwelling upon a mine ready for explosion. I have been watching the feeling of the Sepoys here for some tune. Their minds have been misled by some designing scoundrels, who have managed to make them believe that their religious prejudices, their caste, are to be interfered with by Government that they are to be forced to become Christians."[19]

The Sepoys also had the feelings that they had shed their blood in its cause and conquered many countries for it that in return, it wished to take away their caste and had dismissed those who had justly stood out for their rights. Due to their fear of losing the caste and still more by reason of their pride, arrogance, and vanity, the whole army was determined, comes what might, not to bite the cartridges.

The absence of the European army from many stations in Northern India encouraged the disgruntled Sepoys to raise their arms and murder their European commanders without fear of suppression. From Meerut in the North-west to Dinapur in the south-east, two weak English regiments only were to be found. These were the 3rd Bengal Artiliers at Agra and the 32nd Foot at Lucknow. All the principal cities were without European troops. There were none at Delhi, or at Bareilly; none at Faizabad, at Mirzapur, or at Banaras. Even the important fortress of Allahabad, the key of the North-Western Provinces, was not having European garrison. At the important station of Kanpur, there was only the depot of the 32nd Foot, and a weak Reserve Company of Artillery. Throughout the entire province of Awadh, there was only one English battery of artillery and all the rest were Natives.[20]

The Sepoy resistance arose from the beginning of the year 1857. It, firstly, began in Damdam, 8 miles North of Calcutta, in January 1857; then 27th February in Barhampur. On 27th February, Barhampur Sepoys refused to use the cartridges. In Barrackpur, the Sepoys were also in suspicion and unsatisfactory position. Cunningham writes in his book, *Earl Canning* that at Barrackpur, there was an outburst of incendiarism in the Native quarters, midnight meetings, excited talk, dispatching of letters to other regiments, every symptom of alarm and agitation. At Calcutta, meanwhile, prompt measures were taken to allay the excitement. An order was promulgated, informing the troops at Barrackpur that they would be allowed to purchase for themselves the ingredients for greasing their cartridges. Cunningham again explains that meanwhile, at Ambala, an incident had occurred in the Commander-in-Chief's camp which showed how widely the alarm about the new cartridges had spread. Then General Anson, the Commander-in-Chief, attempted to allay their anxiety. Summoning the Native officers before him, he assured them that the Government harboured no design against their caste, and that their fears were baseless. The Native officers, respectful, but unconvinced, pointed out in reply that, however, groundless it might be; the story was universally believed in the country, and that, though they were ready to obey any order to use the new cartridge, its use would render them outcasts.[21]

Besides the greased cartridge factor, another rumour emerged at Kanpur, Lucknow and other neighbouring areas. One alarming rumour followed another. Here in Kanpur, some consignments of flour, forwarded in Government boats, were offered to the troops. The proffered boon was refused, and the sale was at once arrested by the report that the grain had been ground in European mills, and that the dust of cow or bullock bones had been mixed with it for polluting it. Not a Sepoy even touched the suspected supply.[22]

Mangal Panday of 34th Native Infantry was the first who turned into an open revolt on March 29th at Barrackpur, 16 miles west of Cacutta. He was captured and hanged on 8th of April in front of the regiment, along with his sympathizer Ishwari Panday. From that day, the word 'Panday' became the term of abuse to the mutineers by the British. It was also thought advisable to get rid of the 34th Native Infantry which had been present in the lines on the 29th of March when Lieutenant Baugh was attacked. So the regiment was paid up, marched across the river without arms, and dismissed. The disbanded Sepoys carried the seeds of mutiny to their homes or wherever they scattered in their fury and wild treason.[23]

The disobedience over the issue of greased cartridges started from Damdam in January, Berhampur in February, and Barrackpur in March, reached to Meerut in April 1857, where the mutiny gained its final shape by the Sepoys in May 1857. Very surprisingly, Meerut from where the revolt started was almost the largest Cantonment of Northern India. Meerut division was commanded by General Hewitt, an officer of fifty-eight years' service; the station of Meerut by Brigadier Archdale Wilson, of the Bengal Artillery. There were the 60th (Rifle) regiment, 1000 strong; the 6th Dragoon Guards or Carabineers, 600 strong; a troop of Horse-Artillery; and 500 Field Artillery recruits altogether about 2200 men, with a full complement of officers. The Native troops were but little more numerous, comprising the 3rd Light Cavalry and the 11th and 20th Native Infantry.[24]

Here at Meerut too the cartridge issue gained enough momentum and the troopers, both Hindu and Muslim, bound themselves by an oath not to use the cartridges when called out for exercise. It was decided by the British that Colonel Smyth, commander of the 3rd Light Cavalry should hold a parade in order to explain to the men, the new mode by which they might load their carbines without biting their cartridges, and accordingly, the parade was held on 24th of April. In the parade, there were ninety men present, fifteen furnished from each troop. The colonel explained to them the reason for ordering the parade, and commanded the Havildar-Major to show them the new way of loading, which he did, and fired off his carbine. Colonel Smyth then ordered the cartridges to be served out; five men accepted them, eighty-five (forty-nine of whom were Muslims and thirty-six Hindus) refused, saying "they would get a bad name if they took them, but that if all the regiment would take their cartridges they would do so." The Colonel explained to them that they were not new cartridges, but the very same they had always been using, and once more called on them to receive the cartridges but result remained the same. As a result of this disobedience, a court of inquiry was held to investigate the matter, and decided that they should be tried by a Native general court-martial. On 8th May, the Court comprising the 15 Native officers found the 85 Sepoys guilty of refusing to obey the order and sentenced to imprisonment with hard labour for ten years. On 9th May, there was a parade of the whole garrison, and the sentence of the court was read out to the men. They were all sentenced for five and ten year's imprisonment.[25]

Eventually, on 10th May, a full-scale mutiny erupted at Meerut where the Sepoys of 11th Bengal Native Infantry killed their Lieutenant John Finnis. The Sepoys mutinied and along with the civilian rioter released their 85 fellows and other prisoners from jail of Meerut. It followed the loot and plunders and massacred the British men, women, and children.

In May 1857, the risings were attempted at Ferozepur, Lahore, and Peshawar, but by the quick initiative of Montgomery and Sir John Lawrence, the Sepoys were disarmed and the Punjab could not rise against the British in the future. Sir John Lawrence not only restored order in Punjab but could able to send a strong force of Sikhs to aid the British in the siege of Delhi.[26]

A good portion of the Bengal Army mutinied, except nineteen Regular Native Infantry and six Light Cavalry, who remained loyal to the British. The detailed list of military action in different parts of the country in this Uprising needs to be quoted here:[27]

Date	Place	Military Action
3rd April	Barrackpur:	10th Native Infantry (NI) disbanded
5th May	Barrackpur:	35th NI (Seven Companies) disbanded
10th May	Meerut:	3rd Light Cavalry (LC), 11th NI, and 20th NI mutinied
12th May	Delhi:	38th, 54th, 74th NI and 3rd Company, 7th Battalion Artillary mutinied
13th May	Meerut:	Sappers and Miners mutinied
13th May	Firozpur:	45th and 57th NI mutinied
14th May	Mian Meer (Punjab):	16th, 24th, 49th NI and 8th LC disarmed
18th May	Roorkee:	S. and M. (300) mutinied
22nd May	Peshawar:	21st, 24th, 51st NI and 5th LC disarmed
22nd May	Aligarh and Mainpuri:	9th NI mutinied opened the jail and left for Delhi
23rd May	Ambala:	5th NI mutinied
25th May	Murduan:	55th NI mutinied
29th May	Naseerabad (Ajmer):	15th, 30th NI, a company of Gwalior Artillary mutinied
31st May	Agra:	44th, 67th NI disarmed (two companies having mutinied)
31st May	Lucknow:	30th, 31st, 7th LC (two troops), 13th (part), 48th (half), 71st (half) NI mutinied
31st May	Barreilly:	18th, 68th NI and 8th Irreg. Cav. 6th Comp. of Artillary mutinied
31st May	Muradabad.	29th NI and deatails of foot Artillary mutinied
3rd June	Neemuch:	72nd NI, 7th Gwalior I, 1st Gwalior C, 4th Comp. Gwalior Art. mutinied
3rd June	Azamgarh:	17th NI mutinied
3rd June	Abuzai:	64th NI disarmed

4th June Banaras: 37th NI, Ludhiana Regiment, 18th Irreg. Caval., Hariyana LI Mutinied

4th June   Allahabad: 6th NI mutinied

4th June   Hansi: 4th Irregular Cavalry., Haryana Light Infantry mutinied

5th June   Jhansi: 12th NI (left wing), 14th Irregular Cavalry mutinied

5th June   Kanpur: 1st, 53rd, 56th NI and 2nd Light Cavalry mutinied

5th June   Multan: 62nd, 69th NI disarmed after mutiny

7th June Faizabad: 22nd NI, 6th Awadh Irreg. Inf. 5th Comp. 7th Battalion Artil. mutinied

8th June   Jallandhar: 36th, 61st NI and 6th DC mutinied

8th June   Shahjahanpur: 28th NI mutinied

13th June   Delhi: 60th NI mutinied

14th June   Banda: 50th NI and Nawab's troops mutinied

14th June   Gwalior, Augar, Sipri, and Lulluspur: All Gwalior Contingent mutinied

14th June Calcutta, Barrackpur: 2nd Grenadier, 25th, 43rd, 50th, 51st, and 70th NI mutinied

19th June   Jabalpur: 52nd NI threaten to mutiny if ordered to disarm

23rd June   Nagpur: Irregular Cavalry disarmed

23rd June   Jaunpur: 2nd Regiment Irregular mutinied

23rd June   Sitapur: 41st NI and 9th Awadh Irregular Infantry mutinied

23rd June   Sangor: 31st 42nd NI and 3rd Irregular Cavalry mutinied

23rd June   Naugaon: 12th NI (right wing) and 14th Irregular Cavalry mutinied

23rd June   Fatehgurh: 10th NI mutinied

1st July   Indore: Holker's two regiments mutinied and went to Delhi

5th July   Mahu: 23rd NI mutinied

5th July   Naushera (Peshawar): 10th Irregular Cavalry disarmed

The involvement of such a huge Bengal Army in the Uprising with their arms and ammunition, killing their officers and even to the British civilians, definitely characterize this movement into a Mutiny. In the Parliamentary debate in House of Commons Lord Granville said, "…..We agree at once with the Government and the journals that it is a military mutiny, not a national revolt which threatens us...........The great continent to which we assign that application contains (exclusively of its Mohammedan invaders) a good score of Native population far more distinct from each other in language, customs and religion than the nations of Europe……….. the population of India not only never formed a nation nor even a confederacy but they nothing national within themselves."[28]

When Delhi was overpowered by the British on 20th September, 1857, they began to change their strategy and began to enhance the number of European forces in the Indian army. About 35599 troops were sent to Indian stations like Calcutta, Bombay, Ceylon, Karachi, and Madras from September 20, 1857 to January 20, 1858.[29]

After the suppression of the Uprising, it was decided to enhance the European forces and reduce the Indian Sepoys. Before 1857, there were over 2,00,000, Indian Sepoys in the three Presidency Armies. This number had been reduced to 1,21,000 by 1862-63, while the number of European soldiers in India was increased from 38,000 to 76,000 — so that there was one European soldier to watch over every two Indian Sepoys! Moreover, Indians were excluded from the Artillery branch.[30]

It must not be avoided that in many cases, the role of the Sepoys was not so sounded as they were expected. They concerned themselves more for their pay rather fighting against the British. The Emperor Bahadur Shah Zafar was more annoyed and irritated with the behavior and demand of the Sepoys. Emperor was also afraid of not being conquered the Ridge where the enemy's force was stationed in a meager amount in comparison of the revolutionaries. On the 2nd of August by hearing the hopeless answer of General Bakht Khan due to the rain, Emperor became very angry and said: "You will never capture the Ridge." The same day the Emperor summoned all his officers to the Hall of Public Audience in the evening, and addressed them "All the treasure that you brought me, you have expended; the Royal Treasury is empty and without a 'pice.' I hear that day by day the soldiers are leaving for their homes. I have no hopes of becoming victorious. My desire is that you all leave the city and go to some other central point. If you do not, I will take such steps as seem to me most advisable."[31]

The demand of pay was the regular feature of the army officers. The monthly pay of the army was five lakhs and seventy three thousand rupees, which were beyond paying capacity of the Emperor. The officers repeatedly urged upon the Emperor to make some arrangement about the pay, threatening to plunder the city. The Emperor replied: "There is no necessity to plunder. I will sell my horses, elephants, silver and gold ornaments of state, and pay the Army. If I do not do so, you can all leave and abandon the city, the more so as I never summoned you. If you intend to plunder the city, kill me first. Afterwards, you can do as you please."[32]

The grievance of the greased cartridges was also not having much ground because the Sepoys, who had objected to the greased cartridges when issued by their British officers, were using and biting the very same cartridge when they were fighting against the British during the Uprising. However, that was done by them at their own free will, not under coercion. They all were filled anti-European feelings and wanted to overthrow them from India. The *Jihadis* and the common people were also having the same feelings. If anybody calls it a mutiny, then certainly the mutineer was the East India Company not the Sepoys. The Sepoys were not only the military men but the peasants in itself as they belonged to the rural agricultural areas. The Sepoys were merely peasants in uniform and represented the discontent of the peasantry, which supplied the bulk of the soldiers.[33]

These Sepoys, belonging to the class of peasantry, became only an instrument in the hands of the Native chiefs or the old rulers of the Indian territories. The places where there were no local chiefs, they raised the slogan by beating drum, "*Khalq-i-Khuda, Mulk-i-Badshah, Hukm-i-Sipah*" (The World is God's; the Empire the King's; the Army is in command). It is worth mentioning that the same Sepoys who were faithful to the British rattled the same phrase with a slight change, *Khalq-i-Khuda, Mulk-i-Company*

Bahadur, Hukm-i-Sahiban alishan. No Sepoy ever declared them as a ruler of any principality, and rather they acted according to the instructions of the chieftains and rulers and became helpful to convert the mutiny into the War of Independence on the religious and national grounds.[34]

The use of the word mutiny in the colonial historical writings was a willful obfuscation of the constitutional basis of British power in India. This theory was aided by a propaganda machine run by the historians and publicists of the Company based on the fictitious history of India. Undoubtedly, there was a fixed intention rather flimsy cartridge rumour or mutiny motives. V. D. Sararkar has rightly observed, "Could that vast tidal wave from Peshawar to Calcutta have risen in flood without a fixed intention of drowning something by means of its force? Could it be possible that the sieges of Delhi, the massacres of Cawnpore, the banner of the Empire, heroes dying for it, could it ever be possible that such noble and inspiring deeds have happened without a noble and inspiring end? Even a small village market does not take place without an end, a motive; how, then, can we believe that that great market opened and closed without any purpose — the great market whose shops were on every battle field from Peshawar to Calcutta, where Kingdoms and empires were being exchanged, and where the only current coin was blood? No, no."[35]

That very fixed intention was to establish the independent national Government by uprooting the British Empire. By concluding all the remarks of the scholars and event that took place during the Uprising, it's dead sure that it was a mutiny from its start, but it took the form of a popular movement as the time passed and subsequently transformed into a national struggle or the War of Independence in which the Indian people fought against the British to save their nation and religion. No doubt in this popular upsurge or war, the Bengal Army Sepoys played the most active role and certainly they deserve every tribute the Indian can offer them. The memory of their staunchness in resistance and suffering would hopefully live forever in the heart of the Indian people.

References:

1. Dodd, p. 27
2. Kofoid, Charles Alwood, *The Story of the Indian Mutiny, 1857-58,* Edinburgh, 1898, pp. 17-18
3. Cunningham, Henry Stewart, *Earl Canning*, Oxford, 1891, pp. 69-70, see also, Hope Grant, *Incidents in the Sepoy War 1857-58*, Edinburgh, 1873, pp. 2-4
4. *Ibid*, pp. 4-5, see also Gubbins, pp. 108-109
5. *A Sketch of the Principal Military Events*, p. 14
6. Dodd, pp. 25-26, see also, Roberts, P.E., *A Historical Geography of the British Dependencies: India,* Vol. VII, London, 1914, p. 365

7. *Ibid*, p. 27

8. Evelyn Wood, *The Revolt in Hindustan 1857-59*, London, 1908, p. 7, see also *Social Scientist*, Vol-26, No. 1-4, January-April 1998, p. 12 and *Peoples Democracy*, *(Remembering 1857-* Irfan Habib) Vol. XXXI, No. 4, January 28, 2007 (Frazer says that when Lord Canning reached India he found there were 45,332 European troops to 233,000 Sepoys, and 12,000 Native gunners to 6,500 European. R. W. Frazer, *British India*, New York 1896, p. 275)

9. Dodd, pp. 25-26

10. Julius George Medley, *A Years Campaigning in India from March 1857 to March 1858*, London 1858, p. 202 see also Clare Anderson, *The Indian Uprising of 1857-8: Prisons, Prisoners and Rebellion*, London, 2007, pp. 3-4 and and *New York Daily Tribune*, July 15, 1857

11. *Asbab-e-Baghawat-e-Hind*, p. 51

12. Cunningham, Henry Stewart, *Earl Canning*, Oxford, 1891, pp. 69-70

13. Dodd, p. 27, see also *Peoples Democracy*, *(Remembering 1857-* Irfan Habib) Vol. XXXI, No. 4, January 28, 2007

14. Gubbins, pp. 113-114

15. Marx, Karl, *Notes on the Indian History (664-1858)*, Russian Edition, Moscow, 1947, p. 150, see also George Browcher, *Eight Month's Campaign Against the Bengal Sepoy Army, During the Mutiny of 1857*, London, 1858, p. 2

16. *Peoples Democracy*, *(Remembering 1857-* Irfan Habib) Vol. XXXI, No. 4, January 28, 2007, see also *Asbab-e-Baghawat-e-Hind*, p. 3

17. Allen Charles, *A few words anent the Red' Pamphlet. By one who has served under the Marquis of Dalhousie*, London, 1858, pp. 23-24 (It is worth mentioning that the greased cartridges for the arm known as the Mini rifle have been used for years by Native troops without objection.)

18. *Ibid*, p. 24-25, (About the order related to the cartridges, the *Red Pamphlet* gives the instance of the apathy of the Government at this momentous period, it will suffice to state that, although disaffection had been manifested in the most marked manner by the Sepoys at Barrackpur and Damdam, on account of the greased cartridges, towards the end of January, it was not before the middle of the following month that Colonel Birch telegraphed to the schools of musketry at Sialkot and Ambala to prohibit the use by the Sepoys at these stations of the greased cartridge. But Allen Charles refutes the *Red Pamphlet* that the telegram was sent on the 27th of January, not the middle of February.)

19. Kaye, John William, *A History of the Sepoy War in India, 1857-58*, Vol. I, London 1875, pp. 521&522, see also Evelyn Wood, *The Revolt in Hindustan 1857-59*, London, 1908, p. 8, and Gibbon, p. 244

20. Gubbins, pp. 114-115

21. Cunningham, Henry Stewart, *Earl Canning*, Oxford, 1891, pp. 83-86

22. *Ibid*, p. 87, see also Gibbon, p. 245

23. Gilliat Edward, *Heroes of the Indian Mutiny; Stories of Heroic Deeds*, London 1914, pp. 36-37

24. Dodd, p. 50, see also Gilliat Edward, *Heroes of the Indian Mutiny; Stories of Heroic Deeds*, London 1914, p.130

25. *A History of the Indian Mutiny*, Vol. I, London 1904, pp. 31-33, see also John William Kaye, *A History of the Sepoy War in India, 1857-58*, Vol. II, London 1874, pp. 58

26. Gilliat Edward, *Heroes of the Indian Mutiny; Stories of Heroic Deeds*, London 1914, p. 26

27. *The Living Age*, Volume 0055, Issue 702, New York, November 7, 1857, pp. 331-332

28. *Ibid*, p. 322-323

29. *New York Daily Tribune*, November 14, 1857

30. *Ibid*

31. *Two Native Narratives*, pp. 177-178 (At one time when the demands were made for pay by deputations of officers, Emperor went into his private apartments, and brought out jewelry and gave them to the officers, saying, "Take this and forget your hunger", but the officers refused, saying: "We cannot accept of your Crown jewels, but we are satisfied that you are willing to give your life and property to sustain us." p. 207)

32. Charles Theophilus Metcalfe, *Two Native Narratives of the Mutiny in Delhi*, (Eng. Trans. of *Roznamcha Mainudin Hasan Khan* and *Munshi Jeewan Lal*), London, 1898, p. 216

33. *Peoples Democracy*, (*Remembering 1857*- Irfan Habib) Vol. XXXI, No. 4, January 28, 2007

34. Gubbins, pp. 66-67, (The Sepoy class in Bengal Army was from the peasantry of Awadh, which was long governed by Muslim sovereigns. Awadh was essentially a Hindu province, and its population was chiefly Brahmins and Kshatriyas. Of these the most marked and universal feature was that of the village communities. The brotherhood which resided in each village was the only real proprietor of the soil, and among its members, the ancestral fields are divided. Each village was a separate little republic and having its accountant, public servants, the priest, the carpenter, the smith, the washer man, and the watchman, who were generally paid by dues claimable from the grain produce of each shareholder. The payment of a land tax was one of the oldest institutions of the country. It was levied from the several shareholders, by a rate upon the land, the shares, the ploughs, or the grain produce, and was paid to the Government officer through the head man of the village. As the numbers of these communities increased, their land no longer afforded them a

sufficient maintenance, and numbers leave their villages to seek service, returning on the leave of absence to visit their families; and retiring when pensioned to live and die in their ancestral home. Such were the features which distinguish the class from which the Sepoys were drawn. They were originally proprietors of the soil, and they valued this right of property in the land above all earthly treasure. Gubbins, pp. 66-67)

35. Savarkar, p. 5

Chapter 10

General Uprising or Popular Perspective

The general uprising or popular perspective seeks much attention of the nationalist scholars. The scholars, such as Maulana Abul Kalam Azad, Jawahar Lal Nehru, R.C Majumdar, Bipan Chandra, etc. supported this theory by calling it as discontent of different classes of Indian society. R.C. Majumdar holds a different view point and states that it is difficult to avoid the conclusion that so-called first National War of Independence of A.D. 1857 was neither first nor national, nor a War of Independence. It was the first attempt of the Indian people to organize them against a foreign rule, though on a limited scale. The Revolt of 1857, to Bipan Chandra, was much more than a mere product of Sepoy discontent. It was, in reality, a product of the character and policies of colonial rule, the accumulated grievances of the people against the company's administration and of their dislike for the foreign regime.

There was a discontent among the people much before and also during the Uprising of 1857. All the classes irrespective of caste and religion joined for the single objective to uproot the foreign yoke. The British scholars call the repression in the positive way that they were repressed by the law of the British rule. Every class found itself curbed and subjected to law, with curtailed privileges. The rule of law of course for years before the outbreak was the cause of growing disaffection towards the British rule. After British occupation, there was control of the predatory habits of the lawless and fighting classes, checking the unlawful practices of the landed classes and wealthy Rajas. People of the Hindu race, the Brahminical class, found their influence fading, their priestly dignity lowered, privileges which they had enjoyed under Native dynasties curtailed. Muslims were dreaming of the past glories of their Emperors, and were daily praying for the restoration of their power. The professional thieves, robbers, and dacoits found their occupation becoming more and more hazardous. Thugs and prisoners, smugglers and distillers of illicit spirits, slave-dealers, forgers and perjurers, coiners and cattle-lifters, all had for years felt the strength of the British administration. There were repression and control over every class of society, in every grade of the population.[1]

There was no doubt that the bad elements of the society were very much affected with the British rule of law but the repressive, discriminatory and humiliating policy in general against the landed aristocracy reduced them into a status of beggars and ultimately forced them to jump into the fire of rebellion with the do-or-die intension. The general public followed them as usual and revenged with the British. That's why wherever the rebellion started, the above-mentioned classes of people played their part and more actively engaged in loot plunder and murder.

Another important reason of dissatisfaction, which could not be avoided, was neglect of the position of general population by the British authorities. The distinctive feature of Indian official life was that the higher the grade of an officer the less he was likely to hear of what was going on around him. Members of Council and Lieutenant-Governors derive direct information only from the higher class of Natives, of whom a few pay them visits of courtesy, or from their Secretaries. By this negligence, the common people understood that whatever happening with them was basically due to the British Government.[2]

The events at Meerut based on the greased cartridges even after satisfying the British military officers was merely an excuse for revolt. According to John William Kaye, "If the fear had been only a fear of the fat of cows and swine, it might have been removed by the substitution of one grease for another; or if the external application of any kind of animal grease were objected to, oil and wax might be employed in its place; or if the touching of the unclean thing with the lips were the grievance, the end of the greased cartridge might be pinned off by the hand, and that objection removed. But to this fear of the paper used in all the cartridges issued to the Army, greased or dry, there was practically no antidote that would not have been both an admission and a concession, very dangerous for Government to make. It remained only that the English officer should persuade the Sepoy that he was wrong."[3]

John William Kaye again writes that General Hearsey, who was having large-hearted sympathy with the Sepoys in their affliction, on the afternoon of Monday, the 9th of February at Barrackpur, paraded the Brigade, using good vernacular Hindustani, addressed the assembled regiments. Earnestly, and emphatically he explained to them that they had laid hold of a foolish and a dangerous delusion; that neither the Government which they served, nor the officers who commanded them, had ever thought for a moment of interfering with their religious usages or depriving them of their caste; and that it was but an idle absurdity to believe that they could by any means be forced to be Christians.[4]

In addition to the greased cartridges, the mystery of chapati and lotus distribution was common among the Indians, and it was presumed a signal of untoward happening or rather superstitious act of the Natives. Ever since the middle of 1856, indeed, the final arrangements for the annexation of Awadh, these chapatis were known to have been from hand to hand. The chapati distribution was continued until the outbreak of the Uprising. It was reported that a village headman, carrying the chapatis, had to run up another village, and passed its headman the two chapatis and asked him to prepare the similar chapatis and to forward it to the nearest hamlet. Along with the chapatis they also passed the threatening message, "*Sub lal ho jaega*" (Everything will become red). What precisely was meant by these chapatis nobody knew. The British officers smiled scornfully at what they considered a silly and superstitious practice. But it was evident that some strange secret was in their midst, of which they were entirely in ignorance.[5]

George Dodd says that the number of chapatis was six and asserted that from the Sutlaj to Patna, throughout a vast range of the thickly populated country. It was the secret correspondence through the chapati distribution. These were to be eaten in the presence of the giver, and fresh ones made by the newly initiated one, who in his turn distributed them to new candidates for participation in the mystery. The chapatis were limited to civilians; and lotus flowers, the emblem of war, were in like manner, handed about among the soldiery.[6]

Savakar says about another conspiracy among the Sepoys, popularly known as the lotus conspiracy. Here, a messenger of the revolutionaries used to go to the cantonments with a red lotus flower and give it to the chief Native officer of a regiment. The chief would pass it on to the nearest Sepoy. The Sepoy would pass it to the one next to him, and so the red lotus would pass from Sepoy to Sepoy through the hands of all the thousand Sepoys, and then the last Sepoy would return it back to the revolutionary messenger. It was quite a strange that without a whisper or a word, the messenger would pass on like an arrow and as soon as the next regiment was in sight, he would give the red lotus in the hands of its chief officer. This strange process occurred throughout nearly all the military stations where regiments of the Bengal Native army were cantoned. Various speculations were made by Europeans as to the import of this extreme activity in the circulation of these occult harbingers of the mutiny, but they subsided into an impression that they formed some portion of the Native superstitions.[7]

Many have argued that lotus flowers, and chapati were the signals for the popular unrest or for the Uprising which was being planned for some time or months before. John William Kaye states, "one great authority wrote to the Governor General that he had been told that the chapati was the symbol of men's food and that its circulation was intended to alarm and to influence men's minds by indicating to them that their means of subsistence would be taken from them, and to tell them, therefore, to hold together. Others, laughing to scorn this notion of the fiery cross, saw in it only a common superstition of the country. It was said that it was no unwonted thing for a Hindu, in whose family sickness had broken out, to institute this transmission of chapatti in the belief that it would carry off the disease; or for a community, when the cholera or other pestilence was raging, to betake themselves to a similar practice. Then, again, it was believed by others that the cakes had been sent abroad by enemies of the British Government, for the purpose of attaching to their circulation another dangerous fiction, to the effect that there was bone-dust in them, and that the English had resorted to this supplementary method of defiling the people. Some, too, surmised that, by a device sometimes used for other purposes, seditious letters were in this manner forwarded from village to village, read by the village chief, again crusted over with flour, and sent on in the shape of a chapati, to be broken by the next recipient."[8]

Regarding the matter of chapati, Sherer also comments in his 'Havelock's March to Cawnpore, 1857' which needs to be mentioned here. He says, "We had had the celebrated "chapatis" in our district; but I am almost inclined to think more has been made of them than was their due. The village watchmen received them, and forwarded them, or similar ones, elsewhere, as they were requested to do; but all agree that the watchmen had no definite idea of what was meant. If the transmission of these cakes was only intended to create a mysterious uneasiness, that object was gained. But if the affair was a signal for united action, it failed altogether, and ended in a bungle, for no united action took place. And it must be remembered that the circulation of chapatis is a superstitious practice not unknown in Central India, resorted to, we are told, in the hope of passing on epidemics." He further says that the circulation of chapatis preceded the Mutiny of Vellore in 1806. However, that event was purely a military affair, in which the people did not join.[9]

Another contemporary chronicler Sir Syed Ahmad Khan has also given his opinion and condemned any type of sedition regarding distribution of the chapatis. He argues that, rather than an orgnaised conspiracy, this was merely evidence of widespread rural unrest caused by the diseases. Cholera happened at that time to be raging in Hindustan. Some have imagined that these chapatis were used as a kind of Talisman to keep off the Cholera. He traces that the exchange of chapatis to the traditional technique of disease prevention through transference.[10]

Whatever was the reason but it was rumour at that time that through the chapati distribution, the Muslims are hatching the conspiracies against the British. Even the British authorities were alarmed over the chapati distribution. The circulation of the chapatis before the outbreak was an exact repetition of what happened before the Marathas invaded Northern India, only in place of goat's flesh a sprig of millet had accompanied the bread. Before the Santhal rebellion, a branch of the sal tree had been sent from village to village. Hindus being vegetarians, it seems probable that a bit of raw flesh had a Muslim origin. British considered all these rumours as an alarm of rebellion and presumed the Muslims as the main conspirators.[11]

In Farrukhabad district, another story or fable was added which was never heard in any other district. According to the rumour, it was believed that the English Government had issued rupees of leather silvered over to represent the ordinary coinage of the country. John William Kaye gives an example of a British officer's interview with a Native banker (Baniya) who was inquiring about the fables circulated freely in the Farrukhabad district. Major Weller, of the Engineers, who was in Fatehgarh military cantonment in Farrukhabad district encountered with a Native banker or Baniya, who was called upon to inquire into the truth of the several stories about the bone-dust and other vile designs of the British to destroy the religion of the people. The British officer explained to him the absurdity of these rumours. However, the man was not convinced. "But you know," he said, "that Government are issuing leather rupees, and intend to gather up all the silver of the country." Major Weller laughed at this story. Nevertheless, the credulous banker shook his head, and said that he had seen the leather rupees, and had some in his possession. "Bring them to me," said Weller, "as many as you can, and I will give you fourteen annas for each of them." The Native banker took his departure, but never produced a leather rupee.[12]

In the provinces of Bengal and Bihar, the Permanent Settlement made the local magnates or zamindars as hereditary landlords with all the implied legal rights and restrictions. Within twenty years, this settlement became fatal and instead of assuring loyalty and dynamism it encouraged stagnation. Both the zamindars and cultivators suffered a lot and reached to the status of and starvation, bankruptcy and repression of the arrears. Tax rates were higher, and the collections were much rigorous. The high taxes on the peasantry and extortion, violence, cruelty and torture applied by the tax collectors was the general phenomena in British rule. Torture became an organ of British financial policy in India, and yet no part of the taxes gathered was spent on public works. The farmers fell into the clutches of the creditors popularly called Baniyas. In the North West India, Mahalwari system removed the provision of middlemen like zamindars and a collective responsibility of paying the revenue fell upon the village headman. However, in this system due to the over assessment of the revenue collectors, the cultivators suffered as under the Permanent Settlement. During the Uprising, these groups, firstly, attacked on the Baniyas, destroyed and burnt the records of debt and reinstated the traditional hereditary proprietors. After the moneylenders, the British officers and Government record rooms were the main targets of the revolutionaries.[13]

British officers were not in touch of the Natives in general so there was a big gap between the Government and the governed. British maintained relations and friendships with only a few prosperous people of the society. British just forgot that the stability of a Government depends upon the treating of its subjects with honour and thus gaining their affections. The phrase applied to the people that the wound that given by a sword can be healed, but that inflicted by a contemptuous word cannot be healed. Enemies even, if treated courteously, become a friend and strangers, if treated in a friendly manner, are no longer strangers. Nevertheless, the British were always remained the stranger for Indians and in the Uprising, the Natives tried to uproot the strangers from their Native land.[14]

Another great reason for the dissatisfaction of the Natives of India was the exclusion of the Natives from high appointments. Lord Bentinck did most for the advancement of the Natives in this respect, but the high appointments which he bestowed upon a select few were utterly inadequate to the wants of the people. English officers of the highest rank have often admitted through passing of an examination in England. Even the lower jobs were also not filled with common Natives of India. That's why when the leaders of the rebellion called for recruits, thousands of poor men, wanting service, flocked in and took it.[15]

Under the Regulation X of 1829, the price of stamped paper was enhanced, and it was certainly an additional burden on the Indian economy and its people. Indian people, who were being more and more impoverished every day, could never hope to bear up under that expense. The system of using stamped paper was one, which had been disapproved of by most men of reflection. Even some Englishmen such as Mr. Mill and Lord Brougham expressed their disapproval of the system.[16]

The British trade policy was totally unfavourable for Indians as lead to dissatisfaction and resentment among the cash crop farmers, weavers, and artisans. Millions of artisans were condemned to starvation through the break-up of local industries or de-industrialization policy of the British Government. Especially the hand-weaving and the hand-spinning industries suffered a lot and stood little chance of competing with the flood of cotton fabrics manufactured in the mills of Lancashire in England. This policy marginalized the workforce of rural and urban areas. That's why they participated in the Uprising in bulk and tried to uproot the British administration and throw out the Englishmen from Indian subcontinent.[17]

The annexation of Awadh also affected a lot to the artisans of the luxury item producers as the demand of their items reduced rapidly. Many artisans which were living the luxurious life were reduced to the beggars. They were the innocent sufferers by the change of Government. As stated by Gubbins, "Thousands of citizens found employ in providing for the ordinary wants of the Court and nobility. There were several hundreds of manufacturers of hooquah snakes. The embroiderers in gold and silver thread were also reckoned by hundreds. The makers of rich dresses, fine turbans, highly ornamented shoes, and many other subordinate trades, suffered severely from the cessation of the demand for the articles which they manufactured."[18]

All the above statements prove or rather support the Marxist historian's claim of the popular or general uprising theory about the revolt of 1857. They claim that the subaltern's participation in the Uprising was well known, which included farmers, peasants, craftsmen, artisans, and the labourer. Their motive in participation of the revolt was more economic and to some extent, social than any other. Their participation in the Uprising was mostly due to heavy land revenue policy of the British Government and indebtedness of the moneylenders. Farmers find their local monopolies being challenged by cheaper imports from Britain into India. The Britain made goods could be imported far more cheaply and efficiently than the locals could produce themselves. The gap between the Government and the governed, the immoral behavior of the British officials further added to the grievances of the public. Severe strains which were being placed on the existing economic systems and hate against the British forced the general public to jump into the war against the British in that very opportunity provided by the Sepoys.

Many types of rumours spread throughout the city, town and countries of the Northern India. John William Kaye states that it was rumoured in the public that the British officers had mixed ground bones with the flour and the salt sold in the markets; that they had adulterated all the ghees with animal fat; that bones had been burnt with the common sugar of the country; and that not only bone-dust flour, but the flesh of cows and pigs, had been thrown into the wells to pollute the drinking water of the people. The story also ran that the "Gora Sahibs," or great English lords, had commanded all the princes, nobles, landholders, merchants, and cultivators of the land, to feed together upon English bread.[19]

Governor General Lord Canning refuted all the rumours through a proclamation on 16th of May, "One of the last reports rife in the Bazaar is that I have ordered beef to be thrown into the tanks, to pollute the caste of all Hindus who bath there, and that on the Queen's birthday, all the grain-shops are to be closed, in order to drive the people to eat unclean food. Men, who ought to have heads on their shoulders, are gravely asking that each fable should be contradicted by proclamation as it arises, and are arming themselves with revolvers because this is not done. I have already taken the only step that I consider advisable, in the sense of a refutation of these and like rumours, and patience, firmness, and I hope a speedy return of the deluded to common sense, will do the rest." All the rumours were spread due to the hatred against the Europeans and definitely a great signal of warning and preparation that something great and portentous was about to happen, and to prompt the people to be ready for the crisis.[20]

From all the analysis and investigations, it becomes clear that the greased cartridge affair was mere illusion, and it was kept alive to play an instrumental role in the popular Uprising. When the Sepoys revolted at Meerut, they immediately found response from the civil population. The Sepoys, after loot and plunder left their work upon the insurgents of the neighbouring villages who attacked upon the Europeans and deliberately engaged the British garrison and rather prevented the Europeans to follow the rebellious Sepoys who had rushed towards Delhi. John William Key says, "The sweepings of the gaols and the scum of the Bazaars; all the rogues and ruffians of Meerut, convicted and unconvicted, and the robber tribes of the neighbouring villages; were loose in the cantonment, plundering and destroying wherever an English bungalow was to be gutted and burnt. The Sipahis had left the work, which they had commenced, to men who found it truly a congenial task. Day dawned; and those who survived the night saw how thoroughly the work had been done."[21]

As quoted in the *District Gazetteers of the United Provinces of Agra and Oudh*, "About 10 p.m. the Gujars of the neighbouring villages crowded in thousands to attack those parts of the station which had hitherto been spared. They set fire to the lines of the Sappers and Miners; a fine barrack for Europeans and the Native huts were destroyed and the sergeants' bungalow. ....." Edward Gilliat states that the markets and private houses were all night in the hands of thousands of Gujars (plundering gypsies) and badmashes (rogues). He continues to say that in the next morning, soldiers were sent around to collect the dead bodies and find that the ladies, lying naked on the ground, hacked with sabres and almost unrecognizable. They were picked up from smoking ruins or from streets and ditches. Everything was rifled and stolen; not by the Sepoys, for they rode away to Delhi, but by the released gaol-birds and bad men from the lowest classes of the Native city.[22]

About the remaining areas of the Meerut District, the *District Gazetteers of the United Provinces of Agra and Oudh*, says that in the meantime the Gujars and bad characters commenced the same system of plunder throughout the district that had been so successfully inaugurated in the city. Ramdajal, a prisoner confined in the civil jail for debt, was released on the night of the 10th, and hastening to his village of Bhojpur, in the Muradnagar tahsil, collected a party, and murdered the money-lender which had the decree against him. On the 11th and 12th, the tahsil of Sardhana was attacked by Rangars and Rajputs, who were beaten off from the tahsil, but they succeeded in plundering the market. Qalandar Khan, a Havaldar of Nirpura in pargana Barnawa, set himself up as Raja of that part.[23]

In this revolt the peasants, as well as section of the zamindars and the tallukdars were also involved and turned it into a popular movement. Through different proclamations, the Princes and the Maulvis invited the attentions of the public and appealed them to wage war against the British. The proclamation of Azamgarh of Emperor's grandson Firoz Shah on 25th August 1857 was much alarming for the British. It left far-reaching effect on the minds of all sections of Indian population.[24]

In Awadh, after its annexation, both the peasants and the landed classes were afraid of the same land revenue system as prevailing in all over Northern India and joined hands in the rebellion against the British Government. All the zamindars and the taluqdars including the peasants and artisans joined the war.[25]

Some examples of subalterns or general public revolts as quoted by Gautam Bhadra, which supported the theory of popular uprising need to be mentioned here. He says that there were many established local leaders and numerous individuals took up arms on their own initiative without waiting for the Emperor's appeal, or for feudal aristocrats to tell them what to do. He points out three examples of popular revolt:[26]

"Shah Mal, a Jat resident of the village of Bijraul in Baghpat area, which had suffered from over-taxation by the British in the months before the Uprising. Shah Mal put together a combined force of Jat and Gujar peasants, and attacked and plundered the tahsil of Barout and the bazaar at Baghpat.

"Another subaltern insurgent, Devi Singh, was acting entirely on his own, without any contact with outsiders. He came from a Jat dominated region centred around the small rural town of Raya in Mathura district. When zamindars and villagers in the locality heard of the King of Delhi's proclamation, they rose up against the moneylenders and attacked the town. Devi Singh was dressed in yellow, the traditional symbol of royalty, and declared by popular acclaim to be the Jat 'peasant King' of the 14 villages in the locality. Upon entering the town, he set up a Government upon the English model and tried the moneylenders. When Mark Thornhill, the Collector of Mathura arrived in mid June with a contingent of troops from Kota, Devi Singh was quickly captured and executed.

"Another was the example of a Kol adivasi and cultivator Gonoo from the Singhbhum district of Chotanagpur, who led the Larkha Kol insurrection in reaction to attempts by the British to interfere with traditional institutions. The arrow of war was circulated, and the insurrection kicked off with a mutiny by the Sepoys at Ramgarh but then escalated into a wholesale Kol insurrection with the Raja of Porahat forced to assume the customary role as their head. Bhadra's final example is the Maulvi Ahmadullah Shah, who had popular support in Faizabad and Lucknow, fought the battle of Chinhut, and formed his independent government at Mohammadi."

The hate was such an extent that to keep the communication open between their scattered forces; the English could not rely either on their Sepoy troops or on the Natives. In one word, disaffection on the one side and panic on the other were spreading throughout the whole Presidency of Bengal, even to the gates of Calcutta, where painful apprehensions prevailed of the great fast of the Moharram, when the followers of Islam, wrought up into a fanatical frenzy, go about with swords ready to fight on the smallest provocation, being likely to result in a general attack upon the English, and where the Governor General has felt himself compelled to disarm his own body-guard.[27]

The principal motive powers behind the insurrection were the masses, which rose in vast numbers against unbearable colonial oppression. The agricultural labouring classes or the peasants and artisans were the most hostile to the continuance of British rule and joined the Uprising, along with the feudal lords and Sepoys, with great enthusiasm. Karl Marx in *New York Daily Tribune* mentioned that the mutiny had not been confined to a few localities; and lastly, that the revolt in the Anglo-Indian army has coincided with a general disaffection exhibited against English supremacy on the part of the great Asiatic nations, the revolt of the Bengal army being, beyond doubt, intimately connected with the Persian and Chinese wars.[28]

There are many places in Northern India where the mass outburst was seen and the Sepoys, under the British, suppressed them brutally although they also mutinied after a time span. The masses having old hatred against the white men and wanted to extirpate them, root and branch, from the land. For them, the appointed time had come after the outbreak of mutiny from Meerut. John William Kaye mentions one of the such events of Farrukhabad district where the masses were in rebellion in the month of May, but the 10th Native Regiment had not then mutinied. He quotes a statement of a trustworthy informer, "I traversed a great portion of the district during the first week of June, and I saw villages on fire, and being plundered on all sides. At that time the Tenth Native Infantry had not revolted. The rebellion had existed for a full month before the corps mutinied."[29]

The horrible outrages committed by the inhabitants of some of the largest cities in Upper India, upon defenceless women and children, as soon as the revolt of the Native armed force had left them at their mercy, has encouraged the idea of a general disaffection and revolt. However, it should not be forgotten that these atrocities were not shared by the masses of the citizens, as Gubbin narrates, but were the work of the "badmashes," or loose characters, which abound in all large Native towns. They were more generally Muslims, though Hindus were found among their number.

Gubbin says, "They live by gambling, thieving, and swindling; or by extorting money out of the more respectable Natives by threatening insult and abuse. They pass much of their time in our gaols, but too generally escape punishment by availing themselves of our legal technicalities. They revel in a time of riot or disorder; and it is not surprising, that, as soon as civil power was at an end, we should have suffered so severely at their hands." He emphasizes that the Native gentry and local noblemen and chiefs have shown little attachment to our rule; but nothing has transpired to show that these were leagued together in any conspiracy before the army mutiny broke out.[30]

Therefore, the Uprising of 1857 was a popular war in which agrarian people as well as the people of cities like Delhi, Lucknow, Bareilly, Kanpur, Jhansi and other towns also joined the rebellion. The year 1857 was a time of liberation and an opportunity for the Indian masses to settle accounts with their oppressors and exploiters. Consequently, the Uprising was an expression of the popular uprising with national consciousness to save the religion and culture of the Indian people from the despised colonial rule. The Sepoys were merely the tools behind which stood the people of India, who rallied to the struggle and provided the motive power for it.

References

1. Sherer, John Walter, *Havelock's March on Cawnpore, 1857*, London 1910, pp. 65-66&150
2. *Two Native Narratives*, pp. 6-7&20
3. Kaye, John William, *A History of the Sepoy War in India, 1857-58*, Vol. I, London 1875, p. 524
4. *Ibid*, p. 525
5. Surridge, Victor, *Romance of Empire, India*, London, 1909, pp. 247-248, (The secret sentimental expression "*Sab Lal Ho Jayega*" was also attached to the Red Lotus distribution. According to V.D. Savarkar, 'the red lotus really made all the people one; for, in Bengal, both the Sepoys and agriculturists were found giving expression to this one sentiment, 'All is going to be red!', with a movement of the eyes which betrayed an extraordinary, mysterious pregnancy of meaning". Savarkar, p. 78)
6. Mowbray Thomson, *The Story of Cawnpore*, London 1859, p. 24, see also Dodd, pp. 35-36
7. Savarkar, p. 77
8. Kaye, John William, *A History of the Sepoy War in India, 1857-58*, Vol. I, London 1875, p. 571-572
9. Sherer, John Walter, *Havelock's March on Cawnpore, 1857*, London 1910, pp. 26-27
10. *Asbab-e-Baghawat-e-Hind*, p. 3

11. *Two Native Narratives*, pp. 6-7
12. Kaye, John William, *A History of the Sepoy War in India, 1857-58,* Vol. III, London 1876, pp. 292-293
13. Anderson, Clare, *The Indian Uprising of 1857-8: Prisons, Prisoners and Rebellion,* London, 2007, pp-7-8
14. *Asbab-e-Baghawat-e-Hind,* p. 41
15. *Ibid,* pp. 44-45
16. *Ibid,* p. 31
17. Anderson, Clare, *The Indian Uprising of 1857-8: Prisons, Prisoners and Rebellion,* London, 2007, p. 9
18. Gubbins, p. 78
19. Kaye, John William, *A History of the Sepoy War in India, 1857-58,* Vol. I, London 1875, p. 568
20. Kaye, John William, *A History of the Sepoy War in India, 1857-58,* Vol. II, London 1874, p. 118
21. Kaye, John William, *Kaye's and Malleson's History of the Indian Mutiny of 1857-58,* Vol. II, London, 1910, p. 53
22. Nevill, H. R., *District Gazetteers of the United Provinces of Agra and Oudh,* Vol. IV, Allahabad, 1904, p. 167, see also Gilliat Edward, *Heroes of the Indian Mutiny; Stories of Heroic Deeds,* London 1914, pp. 133-134
23. *Ibid,* p. 167
24. *Peoples Democracy, (Remembering 1857-* Irfan Habib) Vol. XXXI, No. 4, January 28, 2007. (It is well known to all, that in this age the people of Hindustan, both Hindus and Muslims, are being ruined under the tyranny and oppression of the treacherous and infidel and treacherous English. ..... several princes belonging to the royal family of Delhi, have dispersed themselves in the different parts of India, Iran, Turan, and Afghanistan, and have been long since taking measures to compass their favourite end; and it is to accomplish this charitable object that one of the aforesaid princes has, at the head of an army of Afghanistan, etc., made his appearance in India-and I, who am the grandson of Abul Muzuffer Sirajuddin Bahadur Shah Ghazi, King of India, having in the course of circuit come here to extirpate the infidels residing in the eastern part of the country, and to liberate and protect the poor helpless people now groaning under their iron rule, have, by the aid of the *Mujahideens,* or religious fanatics, erected- the standard of Mohammad, and persuaded the orthodox Hindus who had been subject to my ancestors, and have been and are still accessories in the destruction of the English, to raise the standard of Mahavir.

Several of the Hindu and Muslim chiefs who have been trying their best to root out the English in India.......... Therefore, for the information of the public, the present *Ishtahar*, consisting of several sections, is put in circulation, and it is the imperative duty of all to take it into their careful consideration and abide by it. Parties anxious to participate in this common cause, but having no means to provide for themselves, shall receive their daily subsistence from me; and be it known to all, that the ancient works both of the Hindus and the Muslims, the writings of the miracle-workers, and the calculations of the astrologers, pundits and rammals, all agree asserting that the English will no longer have any footing in India or elsewhere. Therefore it is incumbent on all to give up the hope of the continuation of the British sway, side with me, and deserve the consideration of the Badshahi, or imperial Government by their individual exertion in promoting the common good and thus attain their respective ends. ....

Section I - Regarding Zemindars.-It is evident the British Government, in making zamindari settlements...... In litigations regarding zamindaris, the immense value of stamps, and other unnecessary expenses of the civil courts, which are pregnant with all sorts of crooked dealings, and the practice of allowing a case to hang on for years, are all calculated to impoverish the litigants. Besides this, the coffers of the zamindars are annually taxed with subscriptions for schools, hospitals, roads, etc., such extortions will have no manner of existence in the Badshahi Government.... The zamindary disputes will be summarily decided according to the *Shurrah* and the *Shasters*, without any expense; and zamindars who will assist in the present war with their men and money, shall be excused for ever from paying half the revenue. Zamindars aiding only with money, shall be exempted in perpetuity from paying one-fourth of the revenue; and should any zamindar who has been unjustly deprived of his lands luring the English Government, personally join the war, he will be restored to his zamindari, and excused from paying one-fourth of the revenue.

Section II. -Regarding Merchants.- It is plain that the infidel and treacherous British Government have monopolised the trade of all the fine and valuable merchandise, such as indigo, cloth, and other articles of shipping, leaving only the trade of trifles to the people.........When the Badshahi Government is established, all these aforesaid fraudulent practices shall be dispensed with, and the trade of every article, without exception both by land end water, shall be open to the Native merchants of India, who will have the benefit of the Government steam-vessels and steam carriages for the conveyance of their merchandise gratis; and merchants having no capital of their own shall be assisted from the public treasury. It is therefore the duty of every merchant to take part in the war, and aid the Badshahi Government with his men and money, either secretly or openly, as may be consistent with his position or interest, and forswear his allegiance to the British Government.

Section III. - Regarding Public Servants.-It is not a secret thing, that under the British Government, Natives employed in the civil and military services, have little respect, low pay, and no manner of influence and all the posts of dignity and emolument in both the departments, are exclusively bestowed upon Englishmen; for Natives in the military service, after having devoted the greater part of their lives, attain to the post of Subedar.......... and in future the foot soldiers will be paid at the rate of eight or ten rupees, and sowars at the rate of twenty or thirty rupees, per month and on the permanent establishment of the Badshahi Government, will stand entitled to the highest posts in the state, to jagirs and presents.

Section IV. - Regarding Artisans. - It is evident that the Europeans, by the introduction of English articles into India, have thrown the weavers, the cotton-dressers, the carpenters, the blacksmiths, and the shoemakers, &c., out of employ, and have engrossed their occupations, so that every description of Native artisan has been reduced to beggary. But under the Badshahi Government the Native artisan will exclusively be employed in the services of the Kings, the Rajas, and the rich; and this will no doubt insure their prosperity. Therefore the artisans ought to renounce the English services, and assist the *Mujahdeens* engage in the war, and thus be entitled both to secular and eternal happiness.

Section V.-Regarding Pundits, Fakirs, and other learned persons.- The pundits and fakirs being the guardians of the Hindu and Muslim religions respectively, and the European being the enemies of both the religions, and as at present a war is raging against the English on account of religion, the pundits and fakirs are bound to present themselves to me, and take their share in the holy war, otherwise they will stand condemned according to the tenor of the *Shurrah* and the *Shasters*; but if they come, they will, when the Badshahi Government is well established, receive rent-free lands......' *Delhi Gazette*, 29ᵗʰ September 1857)

25. *Peoples Democracy*, (Remembering 1857- Irfan Habib) Vol. XXXI, No. 4, January 28, 2007

26. Ranjeet Guha (ed.), *Subaltern Studies IV*,(Gautam Bhadra '*Four Rebels of 1857*'), New Delhi, 1985, pp. 254-267

27. *New York Daily Tribune*, October 3, 1857

28. *Ibid*,, July 15, 1857

29. Kaye, John William, *A History of the Sepoy War in India, 1857-58*, Vol. III, London 1876, p. 292

30. Gubbins, p. 61

Chapter 11

War of Religion or Religious Perspective

Sir James Outram and William Tayler and a modern scholar William Dalrymple have treated the Uprising of 1857, as the combined conspiracy of Hindus and Muslims based on religion. Despite them, many scholars have given same theory with different modes, such as the Uprising was a conflict between the black and white; a religious war against Christianity; tug of war between civilization and barbarism and an elitlst movement. Dalrymple firmly proves this Uprising as war of religion on the basis of original documents.

According to the above-mentioned authorities and scholars, the religion was the central characteristic of the revolt, the factor of Uprising, and the common thread that tied most of the factors together and bringing an unlikely alliance between the Muslims and Hindus. Very surprisingly, even the scholars who support different perspectives of the Uprising, bounds to prove that the religious factor was one of the chief secondary factors of the Uprising.

Among the Hindus, the Brahmans were leading in the society. They suffered a lot from the British Government's policies. Formerly, they had ruled all the social life of the Hindus. They got fees for marriages, births, and deaths; education, law, and religion. Every kind of business was in their hands. However, during the British rule the telegraphs, railways, European education, and worst of all, a Court of Appeal, were breaking down their privileges and power. They skillfully played on one supposed grievance, by spreading about reports that the Government intended to abolish caste and religion. Among the Hindus, these reports became the principal incitement to revolt. The violation of the arbitrary rules of caste appeared to all was a step towards forcible conversion to Christianity.[1]

The Muslim Ulema also suffered by the same above mentions reasons. They thought that the introduction of English medium of instruction in the schools, changing of Court language, propagation of Christianity, were the direct attacks on their religion. In the schools, run by the Christian Missionary or the British Government, the boys heard much about the Christian religion, of which the parents disapproved, but they were unable to withdraw their boys in the desire of Government jobs. Any measure of development started by the British was considered as a prelude to the conversion into Christianity.

In 1856, Lord Canning promulgated the law, legalising the remarriage of Hindu widows, and off course this was an act of the purest benevolence from a British point of view. However, the publication of this law was coincident with increased missionary activity, which added the proof of polluting the caste and forcible conversion.

The new research of the modern historians proved the religious factor as one of the strongest factors and became one of the natures of Uprising in the form of 'war of religion' or *Jihad*. The term *Jihad* is of course to be stated is a richly ambiguous one, that it varies according to context, and that the struggle referred to can take many forms. Primarily, the *Jihad* is a term to wage war against the infidels to save the religion, and generally it was used by the Muslims but in 1857 during the Uprising this term was also used by the Hindu Sepoys against the British. In the Mutiny Papers in Delhi, there are two of the Hindu Sepoy Generals, General Sudhari and Hira Singh using the term of *Jihad* to describe their fight against the British.[2]

The modern historians prove this fact of religious perspective of the Uprising based on the very authentic contemporary documents. Particularly Dalrymple's research which emphasizes the religious factor based on Urdu documents in the National Archives. The words din and dharma (the Muslim and Hindu words for religion) appear constantly in rebel proclamations, and were used as war cries by the revolutionaries. These facts show the extent to which religious feelings drove the revolutionaries; it goes well beyond the question of greased cartridges.

The revolutionaries issued different proclamations to invite the general people against the British. Many of these proclamations were written by Mirza Mughal, who endeavoured to take charge and unite the chaotic rebel force in Delhi. Others were written by outlying mansabdars and supporters of the revolt who endeavoured to rally supplies and troops by invoking the authority and name of the Emperor. The famous Azamgarh Proclamation of August 1857, issued by the Feroz Shah, the grandson of Mughal Emperor Bahadur Shah Zafar, invites the both Hindus and Muslims to fight against the British.[3]

The Sepoys from Meerut mutinied and shouted the religious slogans like Muslims as Ali! Ali! And Hindus and Sikhs as Jai! Jai! When they reached at Delhi, told Mughal Emperor Bahadur Shah Zafar on 11 May 1857, "We have joined hands to protect our religion and our faith." Later, they stood in the Chandni Chowk, the main street of Delhi, and asked people: "Brothers: are you with those of the faith?" When the Uprising started, the British men who had converted to Islam were not hurt but Indians who had converted to Christianity were cut down immediately.[4]

Bahadur Shah Zafar's eldest surviving legitimate son Mirza Mughal was most likely behind a circular letter sent out in Zafar's name to all the Princes and Rajas of India, asking for them to join the Uprising and appealing for their loyalty on the grounds that all faiths were under attack by the British. The letter refers specifically to the laws banning sati and allowing converts to inherit, and Company's facilitation of Missionary activity and the alleged conversion of prisoners locked in British jails:[5]

"The English are people who overthrow all religions," it states. "You should understand well their object of destroying the religions of Hindustan... It is now my firm convictions that if the English continue in Hindustan they will... utterly overthrow our religions. As the English are the common enemy of both (Hindus and Muslims), we should unite in considering their slaughter... for by this alone will the lives and faiths of both be saved."

Even Mughal Emperor Bahadur Shah Zafar himself articulated the Uprising as a religious war. As late as the 6th September, 1857 at the very end of the siege when calling the people of Delhi to rally against the coming assault by the British, a proclamation issued in the name of Bahadur Shah Zafar spelled out very plainly as follows:[6]

"This is a religious war, and is being prosecuted on account of the faith, and it behoves all Hindus and Musalman residents of the imperial city or of the villages in the country... to continue true to their faith and creeds."

When the news of Uprising at Kanpur reached at Delhi, a letter or rather proclamation reached to Kanpur in June 1857. That was a religious proclamation addressed to all the Hindus and Muslims, Citizens and Servants of India, from the Officers of the Army now at Delhi and Meerut, was sent as greetings. The proclamation was as follows:[7]

"It is well known that in these days, all the English have entertained these evil designs; first to destroy the religion of the whole Hindustani army, and then to make the people Christians by compulsion. Therefore, we, solely on account of our religion, have combined with the people, and have not spared alive one infidel, and have re-established the Delhi dynasty on these terms, and thus act in obedience to orders and receive double pay. Hundreds of guns and a large amount of treasure have fallen into our hands; therefore, it is fitting that whoever of the soldiers and people dislike turning Christians should unite with one heart and act courageously, not leaving the seed of these infidels remaining. For any quantity of supplies delivered to the army, the owners are to take the receipts of the officers; and they will receive double payment from the Imperial Government. Whoever shall in these times exhibit cowardice, or credulously believe the promises of those impostors the English, shall very shortly be put to shame for such a deed; and rubbing the hands of sorrow, shall receive for their fidelity the reward the ruler of Lucknow got. It is further necessary that all Hindus and Musalmans unite in this struggle, and following the instructions of some respectable people, keep themselves secure, so that good order may be maintained, the poorer classes kept contented, and they themselves be exalted to rank and dignity; also, that all, so far as it is possible, copy this proclamation, and dispatch it everywhere, so that all true Hindus and Musalmans may be alive and watchful, and fix in some conspicuous place (but prudently to avoid detection), and strike a blow with a sword before giving circulation to it. The first pay of the soldiers of Delhi will be 30 rupees per month for a trooper, and rupees 10 for a foot-man. Nearly 100,000 men are ready, and there are 13 flags of the English regiments and about 14 standards from different parts now raised aloft for our religion, for God, and the conqueror, and it is the intention of Kanpur to root out the seed of the Devil. This is what we of the army here wish."

The State Papers printed by the order of Nana Sahib, dated 8th Hijri, 1275 find at Bithur, narrates, ".... previously to the distribution of the cartridges for the purpose of taking away the religion and caste of the people of Hindustan, a council was held, at which it was resolved that, as this was a matter of religion, it would be necessary to employ 7,000 or 8,000 Europeans, and to kill 60,000 Hindustanis, and then all Hindustan would be converted to Christianity.... A petition to this effect was sent to Queen Victoria and the opinion of the council was adopted. .... When this petition was perused in England, 35,000 European troops were embarked in ships with the utmost rapidity and dispatched to India. Intelligence of their dispatch was received in Calcutta, and the gentlemen of Calcutta issued orders for the distribution of cartridges. Their real object was to make Christians of the army under the idea that when this was done there would be no delay in Christianizing the people generally. In the cartridges the fat of swine and cows was used......... the Ambassador of the Sultan of Constantinople at the Court of London sent information to the Sultan that 35,000 English troops were to be dispatched to India to make Christians of that country. The Sultan sent a farman to the Pasha of Egypt .... if the English succeeded in making Christians of the people of Hindustan, they would attempt the same in his country. On the receipt of this farman of the Sultan, the Pasha (of Egypt), before the arrival of the English troops, made his arrangements and collected his troops at Alexandria... and on the arrival of the English army the troops of the Pasha of Egypt began firing on them with cannon from all sides, and destroyed and sank the ships so that not a single Englishman of them remained. ....God, by the exercise of His Almighty power, settled their business there....."[8]

Another letter bears the same religious feelings, "As, by the kindness of God and the ikbal of good fortune of the Emperor, all the Christians who were at Delhi, Poona, Satarah, and other places, and even those 5,000 European soldiers who went in disguise into the former city and were discovered, are destroyed and sent to hell by the pious and sagacious troops, who are firm to their religion; ....that it is the incumbent duty of all the ryots and landed proprietors of every district to rejoice at the thought that the Christians have been sent to hell, and both the Hindu and Mohammedan religions have been confirmed....."[9]

By all the proclamations, letters and handbills, it becomes clear that it was the religion which goaded the people against the British. Right from the beginning of the Company rule there was a constant attack on the religions of both Hindus and Muslims. The religious matter affected the Indian people on two sides. The first was the civil side in which the rules and regulations of the British Government which was considered as promotion of Christianity were affected to the civil population of Hindus and Muslims of India. The other was the military side in which the rules and orders of the Government affected the religions of Hindus and Muslim Sepoys employed in the British army. On the civil side Dalhousie as a governor general encouraged Christian Missionaries and societies to provide missions to care for the needy and low caste Indians. The passing of Act XXI of 1850 further intensified the doubt of the conversion. According to this Act, to such men, however, as became Christians it offered great advantages. Hence this act was said not only to interfere with people's religion but to hold out strong inducements to conversion. Act 15 of 1856 relating to Hindu widows was also an attack upon Hindu religion.[10]

On the military side, the promotion of Christianity was too dangerous. As the Christian Missionaries promoted and encouraged the conversion into Christianity, it was rapidly spreading among the British army officers. They readout the verses of Bible before the Sepoys while the daily parade. There was also the demolition of mosques and temples on the petty pretext. The Government financial aid was also stopped to the *Madarsas* and *Pathshalas* (Muslim and Hindu schools) which were being received since long back. The Mughal Emperor's helplessness and powerlessness further enraged the Indian population. It is evident that the Mughal Emperor was still considered as their national symbol by both Hindus and Muslims.[11]

The British Government's step to cancel the Persian as the Government official language and adopting the English in that place greatly infuriated the Muslims. The period when the war broke out was the month of *Ramadhan,* and every Muslim was filled with religious zeal. The Uprising provided the chance to the people, particularly the Muslims to get the maximum religious benefits by waging war against the *Kafirs* (infidels). Muslim theologians declared that their religion was in danger, and everyone should wage war against the British to save the religion. That's why band after band of *Jihadis* (freelance religious revolutionaries) joined the Sepoys against the British.[12]

Sir Syed Ahmad, although directly did not accept it as war of religion, declared the religious factor as one of the important causes of the Uprising. All the people of India irrespective of their caste, religion and social status were in firm conviction that the English Government was bent on interfering with their religion and with their old established customs and intended to force the Christian religion and foreign customs upon both Hindus and Muslims. The people thought that the Government would change their religion through indirect steps, such as doing away with the study of Arabic and Sanskrit, and reducing the people to ignorance and poverty. By depriving the Indians from the knowledge of their faith and religion the Government would compel them to turn to books of the Christian Creed and also to the employment in its services on the conditions of abjuring their faith.[13]

Regarding Christian Missionaries, Indian masses were also having a lot of objections. Sir Syed Ahmad Khan wrote, "The Missionaries, moreover, introduced a new system of preaching. They took to printing and circulating controversial tracts, in the shape of questions and answers. Men of a different faith were spoken of in a most offensive and irritating way....In violent and unmeasured language they attacked the followers and the holy places of other creeds: annoying, and insulting beyond expression, the feelings of those who listened to them." He continues, "In the Missionary schools, the principles of the Christian faith were taught...... Examinations were held in books which taught the tenets of the Christian religion. Lads who attended the schools used to be asked such questions as the following: "Who is your God?" "Who is your Redeemer?" and these questions they were obliged to answer agreeably to the Christian belief; prizes being given accordingly."[14]

In 1855, a letter written by Mr. Edmond was circulated publicly from Calcutta to all the principal officials and other government employees. This letter further strengthened the doubt of conversion. The people presumed it a direct message of conversion from the Government. It was to the effect that all Hindustan was now under one rule, that the telegraph had so connected all parts of the country that they were as one, that the railroad had brought them so near that all towns were as one, the time had clearly come when there should be but one faith; it was right therefore, that everyone should become the Christians.[15] Although the British Government tried to subsidise the matter in fear of religious uprising but this dissatisfaction was delayed rather than controlled.[16]

In the House of Commons in England, a debate was held regarding the Uprising in India in which Mr. Vernon Smith, President of the Board of Control, in opposing the some petition of the Missionaries in Bengal told the House, "It could not be disguised that considerable disaffection prevailed among the troops, in consequence, of a prevalent notion that a compulsory conversion of the Natives was intended."[17]

The British policies and orders that affected the religious sentiments of the Sepoys were more serious than the policies which affected the civilian population. William Dalrymple along with Mahmood Farooqi used the 20,000 rebel documents in Urdu and Persian, which survive from the Sepoy camp and palace in Delhi, all of which were found in the National Archives. In the rebels' own papers, they refer over and again to their Uprising being a war of religion. There was no doubt a multitude of private grievances, but it is now unambiguously clear that the rebels saw themselves as fighting a war to preserve their religion. The words din and dharma (the Muslim and Hindu words for religion) appear constantly in rebel proclamations, and were used as war cries by both the civil and military revolutionaries.

Both the Sepoys and civil population were severely affected by the rumours of the bone-dust factor along with greased cartridge episode. In a letter of Mrs. Keith Young to her sister in London, she writes, "I hear that there is a general feeling among the Natives that our Government is trying to make Christians of them by these unclean cartridges, and by mixing with their atta (flour) beef and pig's bones finely ground. Some months ago I was sending some whole wheat to a little mill on a stream a short distance from Simla to be ground and it makes such nice brown bread. We had often found our bread gritty with dust. My Aya, when she heard that I was sending this wheat, asked me to send some for her also, as there was a report in the bazaar that all the flour was mixed with the bones, finely ground, of cows and pigs. I laughed at her, and said, Aya, what nonsense! Who says so? 'She replied, 'It is quite true; all the bazaar people say so.' I thought it meant merely that the Baniyas (local merchants) did it to increase the weight of their flour."[18]

In the areas of Awadh, as Gubbins stated, bone dust and cartridge factor aroused the sentiments of both the Sepoys and common people. Although the rumour of bone-dust was baseless, but as it was fanned by the followers of ex-Nawab of Awadh, it became most burning factors for common peoples' resentment. It was said that the British Government at Lucknow had sent up cart-loads and boat-loads of bone-dust, which was to be mixed with the flour and sweetmeats sold in the bazaar, whereby the whole population would lose their caste. The public mind became greatly excited. On one day, at Sultanpur, it was spread over the station that a boat had reached a certain ghat on the river Gomti laden with bone-dust. A few days later, at the station of Salone, two camels, laden with ammunition, arrived at the house of Captain Thompson, the commandant. It was rumoured that the packages contained bone-dust, and a panic spread through the station. Not only, the Sepoys in their lines, but the domestic servants about the officers' bungalows, and the villagers and zemindars attending court, hastily flung away, untested, the food which they had cooked, and fasted for the day. The Sepoys of Kanpur refused to accept the Government flour, which they alleged had been mingled with the dust of cow bones so that the caste of the Hindus might be destroyed. At Lucknow, the rumours which were whispered about were perpetual, and the public mind was never allowed to rest. If it was at one shop, the next day in another bazaar, that dispatches of bone-dust had, it was asserted, been received.[19]

In the real sense, all the Indian masses, irrespective of their caste and creed, were maligned with the British policies. The rumours of greased cartridges and bone-dust flour, added the further filth. Even the economic class, Baniya or trader was unsatisfied with the Europeans. It was also rumoured that besides the bone dust flour, the British were also mixing bone dust into the salt and polluting the well by throwing flesh in them. All the above rumours affected, both the Hindu and Muslim communities, a lot.[20]

Besides Sepoys and civilians, there was another front of revolutionaries. This third front was of the Muslim fanatics, generally called by the British as *Ghazis* or *Jihadis* and *Mujahideen*, who were unpaid bind with religious ties rose in open rebellion following the Sepoys and civilians. They were led by Muslim Ulema. A number of sources prove that along with the '*Purbeas*' (rebel Sepoys of Awadh Province) who entered Delhi after fleeing their cantonments, were followed by a large number of 'freelance' and 'untrained' Muslims or *Mujahideen*.

A noted *Mujahid* Maulvi Ahmadullah Shah played the most important role in mobilizing the Muslim masses against the British during the Uprising. He was radicalised by the preaching of Sayyad Ahmad Shaheed of Rae Bareli. Ahmadullah Shah's ideas for a *Jihad* against the British were initially ridiculed by the Ulema in Delhi, and he was soon after captured and imprisoned by the British. However, when the Sepoys released him from jail in Faizabad, he had immediately cleaved to the side of the rebels in Lucknow and became an influential adviser to the Begam Hazrat Mahal.[21]

There are sufficient proofs of active participation of Ulema in the Uprising, but some scholars give a slight different theory and stressed that their participation was not for relieving the country from the British. Marina Carter and Crispin Bates in their article 'Religion and retribution in the Indian rebellion of 1857' says that most of the Ulemas sided the Sepoys on the decree of *Jihad* either to save the Muslims from British oppression or to quell the excesses of rebel troops. Maulana Muhammad Qasim Nanautawi and Maulana Rashid Ahmad Gangohi, the famous scholar of the Deoband Islamic seminary, were initially hostile to the revolt, only took up the rebel's cause after being persuaded of the injustice of the English in their campaign of repression. Mirza Firoz Shah, the Mughal Emperor's grandson, who for some time commanded, the rebel forces in Delhi, invoked the concept of *Jihad* in order to curb and quell the excesses of Sepoys, who had indulged in plundering and looting and had failed to protect women, children, and the innocents.[22]

No doubt the main aim of the revolutionaries of both Hindus and Muslims was to save their religion and country from the British oppressions. For that very cause, they adopted different methods, which were perhaps misunderstood by a few European scholars but majority believes in the religious motives of the revolutionaries.

References

1. Gubbins, p. 61
2. Evelyn Wood, *The Revolt in Hindustan 1857-59*, London, 1908, pp. 4-5
3. *Biblio*, Vol, XII, No. 3&4, March-April 2007, p.7
4. *Ibid*, p.6
5. Tracy, Louis, *The Red Year; A Story of The Indian Mutiny*, New York 1907, p. 22, see also *Biblio*, Vol,XII, No. 3&4, March-April 2007, p.6
6. *Biblio*, Vol,XII, No. 3&4, March-April 2007, p.7 taken from Salimuddin Quraishi, *Cry for Freedom: Proclamations of Muslim Revolutionaries of 1857*. Lahore 1997
7. *Biblio*, Vol, XII, No. 3&4, March-April 2007, p.7
8. Mowbray Thomson, *The Story of Cawnpore*, London 1859, pp. 143-144
9. *Ibid*, pp. 144-146
10. *Ibid*, pp. 146-147
11. The suspicion arose that this act was intended to free widows from all restraint, and to give them the power of doing whatever they might think proper, even the married women were also recognized to the Criminal Courts as competent. (*Asbab-e-Baghawat-e-Hind*, pp. 24-25)

12. *Secular Qayadat*, Delhi, 21 August, 2007
13. *Ibid*
14. *Asbab-e-Baghawat-e-Hind*, pp. 16-17
15. *Ibid*, pp. 18-19
16. *Ibid*, p. 22 (**Extract of E. Edmond's Letter-** "The time appears to have come when earnest consideration should be given to the subject, whether or not all men should embrace the same system of religion. Railways, steam vessels and the electric telegraph are rapidly uniting all the nations of the earth: the more they are brought together, the more certain does the conclusion become that all have the same wants, the same anxieties, the same hopes, the same fears, and therefore, the same nature and the same origin. It is also very certain that death universally closes the scene..... Now Christianity is a system which professes to have come by direct revelation from God Himself, as the only system by which happiness can be secured in this world or in that other world which it reveals. It has this peculiarity to distinguish it from every other system of religion in the world that it appeals to the reason as well as to the heart of man, and it is the only system in the world which has spread by the mere force of argument. .... we are anxious that others should be induced to receive them, and therefore, this solemn and earnest appeal is made to you to examine this important subject for yourself..... We urge you, therefore, as you value your own happiness forever, to examine this great subject, and to ask God himself to enable you, by His Holy Spirit's teaching to do so aright. ....be courageous and embrace it publicly: for He said Himself "whosoever shall be ashamed of me and of my words, in this adulterous and sinful generation, of him also shall the Son of Man be ashamed when He cometh in the Glory of His Father with the Holy Angels." .... Why not in this generation? Would it not be an infinite improvement upon the foolish, degrading and wicked idolatry, which now defiles the land? "We speak as to wise men, judge ye what we say." *Asbab-e-Baghawat-e-Hind*, pp. 55-59)
(**Extract of Eng, Trans. of a Persian notice, issued by the Lieutenant Governor of Bengal-** "His Honor the Lieutenant Governor of Bengal, having heard that the people of the country are unnecessarily apprehensive and uneasy on account of certain unreasonable and unfounded stories, fabricated and spread by people equally unreasonable and prejudiced, with regards to the religious rites and ceremonies of the Hindus and Mohammadans, hereby notifies that Government has no intention of interfering in the matters of religion, rites and ceremonies of the country, nor can it ever have such an intention. His Honor is sorry to find that the people of this country are unnecessarily alarmed at stories invented by seditious persons...The principal objection of the Government is and ever shall be to protect the life, honor and

property of its subjects, to respect their laws and customs and to do what it can to promote their welfare. Some of the Calcutta missionaries have, as is their wont, but without the sanction of the Government, published religious discourses and circulated them amongst the Natives who have wrongly understood them to have come indirectly from the Government. The Government has, however, had no hand in the affair. No attempt was ever made on behalf of Government to persuade the Natives to embrace the faith professed by the Government..... His Honor has been further given to understand that the inhabitants of this country regard the establishment of schools and colleges for the education of the Natives in arts and sciences and in the English language as a means to mislead them from their faith, and that for this reason they are disinclined to send their children to school. This is undoubtedly a great mistake of theirs. The step has been misunderstood by the people. .... It is a matter of great regret that the people have misunderstood the policy and the good intentions of Government in matters of education. His Honor, however, believes that the origin of all these evils is a misapprehension on the part of the Natives, and that they do not proceed from prejudices or ill feelings. Be it known that by the spread of English education Government is simply desirous of opening to the people of India a path to all arts and sciences, and not to mislead them from their religion and time-honoured customs and habits. It must however be well borne in mind that works relating to all arts and sciences at present exist only in English language, and new discoveries and inventions are every day being brought to light. Moreover, English being the language of the rulers of the country, it is one of the duties of the subjects to learn it along with Urdu or Bengali, so that they may rise in honor and live in greater ease and comfort...... (*Asbab-e-Baghawat-e-Hind*, pp. 60-63)

17. *The Living Age*, Volume 0055, Issue 702, New York, November 7, 1857, p. 321

18. Norman, Henry Wylie, *Delhi - 1857; The Siege, Assault, and Capture as given in the Diary and Correspondence of the Late Colonel Keith Young*, London 1902, pp. 17-18

19. Gubbins, p. 280

20. *Eight Days*, p. 93

21. *Leidschrift*, Leiden, Netherlands, No. 24, December 3, 2009, p. 53

22. *Ibid*

Chapter 12

Failure of the Uprising

The Indian Uprising, starting from Meerut on 10th May 1857, to the fall of Nana Sahib and Bakht Khan in June 1859 is full of chivalry and patriotism along with confusion and suspicion that led to at last a failure. There are a lot of reasons, which lead to the failure of the more than two years long Uprising by losing lakhs of people, and the property estimated in crores. It was due to a lot of reasons such as, lack of able leadership; lack of arms and ammunitions; military and strategic failure; failure to gather intelligence; unable to control the spying from the British agents; lack of communication or to coordinate effectively with other rebel centres such as Kanpur and Lucknow; unable to persuade most of the independent Rajas of Central India and Rajputana to come off the fence and join in the cause. Apart from the above all, the most important deficiency was the lack of food and money or failure of administrative and financial organisation.[1]

The failure of the Uprising does not mean that the revolutionaries had any lack of courage or bravery, but they always proved hard nut for the British. They defended Delhi for more than four months, Lucknow for almost ten months, repulsing the first invasion by General Campbell himself. The Gwalior contingent defeated the British troops and occupied Kanpur. The bitter defence of Jhansi under its brave Rani remained memorable. The role of Kunwar Singh of Jagdishpur and Tatya Tope and Ahmadullah Shah is too well known.[2]

The revolutionaries, including the Sepoys, *Mujahideen* and general public had enough enthusiasm and passion to fight against the British but due to above mentioned reasons their enthusiasm dimmed, and they lost the game with a heavy price. Mughal Emperor Bahadur Shah Zafar was in advanced age when the Uprising broke out, and he unwillingly accepted to command the same. Until the arrival of General Bakht Khan on 1st July 1857, there were chaos and anarchy and there was no proper direction for the revolutionaries. Slowly, and gradually the food and money were shortened, and the paid Sepoys began to return their homes without settling the aims of insurrection. Whoever remained in the front never followed orders from the Subedar of any other regiment, so they fought in a disconnected and uncoordinated fashion.[3]

Their failure to establish a well-governed 'liberated area' or Mughal realm from which they could draw tax revenue, manpower and most of all food supplies, ultimately proved the Delhi rebels' single most disastrous failure. No food was coming in, so prices rose dramatically, and starvation soon set in. By the time the British finally assaulted the city on 14th September, the number of Sepoy defenders had sunk from a peak of 100,000 down to 25,000. In addition to the Sepoys there were over 25000 *Mujahideen* in Delhi at that time. Most of the Sepoys left for their home because of hunger. The national administration was failed to provide them either food or pay or munitions.[4]

The other reason of the failure of the Uprising which could not be avoided was the lack of able leadership from the side of the revolutionaries. The Sepoys neither attained unity of command, nor they had single high command, because the Sepoys had no experience of being officers; they were only soldiers, though their leaders might now be called Generals or Colonels. In Delhi, they formed the famous Court of Administration, which in every way was modeled after British practices. However, these organs of power were no substitute for a unified command for the whole movement, which was not only a political but a military necessity. The British devised strategies and plan according to need while the Sepoys could decide only on tactics, and could not concentrate their military strength at vital points. That's why despite their large numerical strength, they could not become successful to overpower the British.[5]

After the capture of Delhi, the European military force was cantoned on a Ridge overlooking the great city, at a distance of about two miles from it. Nevertheless, the Sepoys were busy in loot and plunder than getting rid of the Europeans who were stationed on the Ridge. Even the *Mujahideen* and the Sepoys who were about one lakh in the number could not dare to attack the entire British garrison of 7521 including the Brigadier Nicholson's re-enforcement which arrived in August 1857. Around one-third of their forces were covered by the loyalist Sepoys who could change the side after a decisive battle. Undoubtedly, Bakht Khan was the able leader but in that fateful time perhaps both the Sepoys and *Mujahideen* handled the strategy in their own way and passed the time in defending the capital city except some battles around the huge wall and the gates of Delhi. Emperor Bahadur Shah himself exhausted by the delaying fight of the revolutionaries, remarked, "We have here 60,000 men in the city, but they have not been able to win a clod of dirt from the English". On another place while replying the *Jihadis* of Nasirabad, the Emperor said, "there are 60,000 men in Delhi, and they have not yet driven the English away from the Ridge; what can your 6,000 do?" The defensive policy of the revolutionaries chanced the British forces for further re-enforcement of 3000 in the same month of August.[6]

Delhi was covered one side with river Jumna, and on the three sides, there was a huge wall covering over seven miles in distance. The British force was not enough to guard the long wall of the city and resist the small skirmishes and battles with the revolutionaries. The success of the British was only possible on the internal dissensions breaking out among the rebels, their ammunition being spent, their forces being demoralized, and their spirit of self-reliance giving way. There was an awkward situation before the British in lack of the forces. For them, it became a question, whether their force should retreat from before Delhi, because it was too much harassed by daily fighting to support overwhelming fatigues much longer. However, that intention was strenuously resisted by Sir John Lawrence, who plainly informed the Generals that their retreat would be the signal for the rising of the populations around them, by which they must be placed in imminent danger. This counsel prevailed, and Sir John Lawrence promised to send them all the re-enforcements, he could muster.[7]

The ration was too insufficient for the revolutionary; it was not proper even for the royal household. On 7th June, its employees were complaining that they had received no rations for a month. In the following week, the deputy kotwal wrote to his assistants begging them to find some food for the new battalions from Haryana who had just marched into Delhi. In the third week of this month, the officers of the different regiments were coming to the Fort and complaining that their troops could not attack the British on empty stomachs, and that their Sepoys had begun returning. On 28th July, Kishan Dayal and Qadir Baksh, Subedars of the Meerut Sepoys, came to court to say that their men were now starving. In contrast, the British were famous for paying their troops as regularly as they promised. It was the food and money factor that allowed the British to recruit a brand new mercenary army from the Punjab and send it to Delhi.[8]

Another important reason of the failure was the spying system of the Company. Hodson was the in charge of Intelligence Department with 100 Horse and 50 Foot as his personal escort. He was also working as Assistant Quartermaster General on Commander-in-Chief's personal staff and used his influence in the spying and even superseded his personality over the others in the decision making matters. He allured the dubious peoples of Delhi and won over to his side and successfully maintained the spying network in the Royal city of Delhi. These spies not only provided information about Indian troops' preparations and movements to the British but also advised them how and when to attack. There were many spies working overtime for the British forces, and they were employed to sow the seeds of dissension within Indian Forces, between Delhi residents and defenders of the city and also between Hindus and Muslims. Maulvi Rajab Ali, Mirza Ilahi Baksh, Hakim Ahsanullah, Jeewan Lal, Mukund Lal, Turrab Ali, Gauri Shankar, Jawahar Singh, Mamraj, Ramji Dass, Mir Mohammad Ali, Nawal, Achhu, Gopal, Fateh Mohammad Khan, Ami Chand, etc. were the trusted spies of the British. They misguided the Emperor Bahadur Shah Zafar and supplied the information related to the strategies and planning of the revolutionaries.[9]

Hodson, who had been appointed executive chief of the Intelligence Department, had done his work quite well. He approached the traitors or dubious type people of Delhi and collected information of revolutionary activities. Maulvi Rajab Ali was made the chief of the informers or spies and was rewarded Rs. 10,000 for his services during the siege. Jeewan Lal was also one of the main informers whose family was always attached to the Mughals and one of his forefathers was prime minster of Aurangzeb. He was made honorary Magistrate and a Municipal Commissioner for providing critical information to the British during the siege. Mirza Ilahi Baksh, another sagacious, was very close to the Emperor Bahadur Shah Zafar, and one of his daughters was married Emperor Bahadur

Shah Zafar's son Mirza Fakhru. He had no dream of the restoration of the lost honours of the House of Delhi and planned for the fall of Delhi by other nobles of the city, including Queen Zeenat Mahal. On one occasion, Mirza Ilahi Baksh saved the life of Jeewan Lal when rebels arrested him for spying for the British. He also successfully convinced Bahadur Shah Zafar not to leave the city with Indian forces when Bakht Khan and other chiefs of the Indian Army met Emperor and the Princes at Humayun's Tomb and requested them to join them. Mirza Ilahi Baksh persuaded the Emperor to not even listen the ungrateful Bakht Khan and brought about the surrender of the King and the princes. Thus, Mirza Ilahi Baksh had got the whole Royal Family in his toils, and held them in gentle bondage at the Humayun's Tomb with its surrounding structures, a suburb in itself, beyond the modem city.[10]

The spies who operated in Delhi could be divided into three categories. The first category was of those Sepoys with the British army who were sent for gathering information of the rebel activities. They were known as guides. The second category was of those spies who were hired from the city or its vicinity and were known as *Harkaras*. The third and the most dangerous category was of those spies who were old loyalists of the British, very close to Mughal Emperor who either belonged to Delhi elite or brought from outside Delhi as civilians and planted here. The third category spies whose identity was hided and generally referred as 'unknown' were not only expected to gather information of the rebels but to sow the seeds of dissension within the rank of the rebel, between the rebels and Delhites and even between Hindus and Muslims.[11]

Some reporting of the spies are as follows, which ultimately shattered the all hopes of the revolutionaries:

Turrab Ali reported to the British in mid August, "Mirza Ilahi Baksh Sahib is trying to break up the army and is awaiting an answer to his communication to you."[12]

Gauri Shankar advised the British on August 14th 1857, "In the writer's humble opinion, as the rebels always move out in the Taliwara and Subzi Mandi direction, and the fights are generally in that neighbourhood, a Battery to check them should be planted in Kala Pahar."[13]

An unknown spy on 29th July 1857 reports to the British, "There are now 50000 Mutineers in Delhi, and at the very least 20000 will go out to the next attack. They are all ready to fight, some out of natural hatred of Europeans, some by force of example."[14]

An unknown spy on 31st July 1857 reports to the British camp, "250 Khalasees are employed everyday to make up Cartridges and Gun Chargers. There are 400 mounds of Native Powder…. There is talk of new Gun Cap. Kallu mechanic of the magazine made up some sample for approval and Mazhar Ali Superintendents of Roads of Delhi has offered to prepare the detonating powder. It is possible to bribe these rascals; however, nothing will be done without you."[15]

The Cief *Harkaras*, Ami Chand reported on 16th Septenber, 1857, two days after the British attack on Delhi, "I went to Teliwara and Kishanganj suburbs and saw that the rebels had evacuated the positions. They had abandoned their batteries and fled, taking the light guns with them."[16]

Fateh Mohammad Khan narrated the scene of Delhi on the same day, "The Bareilly and Neemuch Brigades, who belonged to distant parts of the country have resolved and send their entire luggage ….. on the Gwalior road escorted by light guns and some Sepoys of infantry. The rest of the force to remain in Delhi and to fight for four days and then to abscond and overtake their baggage….. The troops in the Palace are ready to die at their posts."[17]

The master spy Rajab Ali also reports on 16th September, 1857, "A vigorous force is maintained at Salimgarh and Palace. The Sepoys leave Delhi by Ballabhgarh and Rewari roads. The rebels in the town keep up an incessant musketry for the day and night. They gradually vacate their positions and retreat towards Delhi Gate and take the opportunity of the night to escape."[18]

Another important factor of the failure of the Uprising was the lack of trust among the revolutionaries. Even the Sepoys of Meerut and Delhi were not in good terms. In the mere suspicions, many authorities of the Delhi administration were robbed and punished. On 16th May the Sepoys assembled and went to the Palace in great anger, and said to the Emperor that they had seized a messenger with a letter, cursing the revolutionaries. They also accused the Emperor for saving the lives of European men, women and children and concealing them in the Fort, and through them communicating with the Europeans at Meerut. The Sepoys also threatened to kill Ahsanullah Khan and Nawab Mahboob Ali Khan, and to take away Zeenat Mahal Begam Sahiba and keep her as a hostage for the King's loyalty. In order to appease the revolutionaries, Mahboob Ali Khan took an oath that he was not the author of that letter, nor had it been written with his knowledge. The Emperor Bahadur Shah Zafar and his assembled councilors stood like dumb puppets. The Emperor Bahadur Shah Zafar ordered the Sepoys to separate themselves into two parties, Muslims and Hindus, and he appealed to each to consult their religious advisers to see if there were any authority for the slaughter of helpless men, women, and children. However, no effort became fruitful, and the Europeans slaughtered.[19]

In another incident, the suspicion again arose when the Islamgarh Magazine was suddenly blasted, and it was discovered that somebody had mixed the "kankar" (gravel) in the gunpowder. About fifty mounds of gunpowder blew up and destroyed five hundred workmen. Suspicion fell upon Hakim Ahsanullah Khan, and he was charged before the King of collusion with the English. The revolutionaries threatened to kill the Hakim, together with Mahboob Ali Khan. Both men swore that they were innocent. The King shielded the accused and appeased the anger of the soldiery. Mirza Abu Bakr was also accused of disloyalty and tampering with the guns. Finally, a Havildar was suspected of having filled the guns with gravel and iron nails. He was apprehended, tied to one of the guns, and blown up. Munshi Jeewan Lal narrates that certain Sikhs presented a petition to the Emperor complaining that they were in the habit of attacking the English entrenchments, but had to return, as the *Purbeahs* would give them no assistance and would not co-operate; they prayed the Emperor to form a regiment of Sikhs from among the regiments of Delhi.[20]

The nature and character of the Sepoys assembled from different areas was another cause to the failure of the Uprising. The Sepoys' loot, plunder, and extortion on the pretext of collecting war fund, created a state of anarchy, which slowly deviated them from their national cause. The innocent people were generally terrorized on their behaviour. The *New York Daily Tribune* reports that merchants of Delhi, had become averse to the rule of the Sepoys, who plundered them of every rupee they had amassed, the religious dissensions between the Hindu and Mohammedan Sepoys, and the quarrels between the old garrison and the new re-enforcements, sufficed to break up their superficial organization and to insure their downfall. Henry Wylie Norman quotes a letter, "I was speaking to some of the men of the Gwalior contingent that have come over, and they say that the Sepoys are committing all kinds of atrocities in the city, and that the city people are all ready to rise on them when we go in. The Sepoys have lots of money; one man killed to-day had eighty gold mohurs on him, and another thirty-three."[21]

Even the rural peoples were much fearful of the loot and plunder of the Sepoys or rebels. The villagers generally left their residences on the arrival of the rebels. They had no sympathy with the rebels and were always suffered with the extortions and demand of money. It created a lack of confidence and mutual understanding among the citizens of India and eventually resulted the failure of the Uprising. Gubbins narrates an event by saying, "Clark and I have ridden out this morning some six miles towards the rebels, with a small body of cavalry. As we returned home, we crossed a small river, and came over the high ground of its bank. The instant we were seen from the first village, coming from the direction of the rebels, we heard shrieks and cries; — everybody put his plough on his shoulder, and drove his two oxen before him, — women rushed off headlong into the nearest wood, the whole village was deserted. As we got closer to it, we saw a man lurking about, and called to him. He uttered a shout, rushed inside and brought out the zemindar, (owner of the village), who came running towards us, half laughing. 'Oh! Sahib,' said he, 'we thought you were the rebels!' 'What,' I said, laughing, 'do I look like a badmash? 'No, Sahib,' was the reply, 'but we couldn't distinguish, and we took you for Bisram Singh!' The moment they found out we were English, the whole village returned at once; and in half an hour, twenty ploughs were going merrily sain. The same happened with the next village; and returning home, we overtook its two zemindars, who were on their way to our camp at Bunnee, to tell us that Bisram Singh (a rebel leader of note) had come."[22]

The inhuman torture of the revolutionaries and innocent Indians by the cruel British soldiers was another cause of the failure of Uprising. The British retribution policy to the people of conquered territories terrorized the Indian people that they think at least hundred times to join the revolutionaries. The torture, hanging and publicly blowing from the guns was not only for the Sepoys but also for the ordinary men. They went to their deaths unbowed and hardly anyone craved pardon. This type of retribution and holocaust if not completely routed, then at least dimmed the Uprising.

One more important cause of the failure of the Uprising was the help and assistance of the Native Rajas to the British Government. According to Karl Marx, Sindhia was loyal to the "English dogs," not so his "troopers"; Raja of Patiala for shame! sent large body of soldiers in aid of the English!" Elliot and Dowson mention the details of the assistance of the Native Rajas of Punjab. According to them, the Raja of Patiala placed in the hands of young Charles Metcalfe the keys of his fort, and said that all he possessed was at the service of the British Government. The Maharaja of Patiala supplied 5,000 men, horse and Foot and three guns under his brother, to Thaneswar on the Grand Trunk Road between Ambala and Karnal before Delhi for a distance of 120 miles. The Nawab of Karnal, a Muslim nobleman and land-owner of large influence in that part of the country, threw the weight of his personal power into the scales on British side. The Raja of Jind was actually the first man, European or Native, who took the field against the mutineers. He openly declared at once that he could side with the British. He marched with a contingent of 800 men to Karnal, and cleared the road as the British troops advanced upon Delhi. Raja of Jind was also instructed to collect supplies and carriages for the field force, to protect the station of Karnal. The Raja of Nabha sent a contingent of 800 strong, occupied the fort of Ludhiana, and escorted the siege train from Phillaur. Nawab of Maler Kotla marched with his men to Ludhiana, and the Raja of Faridpur was desired to place himself under the orders of the Deputy Commissioner of Firozpur. The Raja of Kapurthala furnished a contingent of 2,000 men who took the place of the mutinied troops at Jalandhar and, headed by the Raja in person, afterwards marched to Awadh and fought in six actions on the side of the British.[23]

Maharaja Jiyaji Rao Sindhia of Gwalior proved a strength for the British during the crisis of 1857. The Gwalior contingent under Maharaja was composed of four field batteries of artillery, a small siege train, two regiments of cavalry, and seven of infantry, aggregating eight thousand three hundred and eighteen men. The greater portion of his force was stationed at Gwalior, under the command of Brigadier Ramsay. At this crucial juncture Maharaja Jiyaji Rao Sindhia was sure to the gravity of the entire Native army, yet he was ready to meet the fate along with the British. He was, however, doubtful about the fidelity of his own army; even then he supported the British cause whole heartedly. He warned the British political agent at his Court, Major Charters Macpherson that the disaffection was universal, and that the men of his own contingent, sooner or later, would follow the example of the regular army. When Mr. Colvin asked him for assistance, Jiyaji Rao Sindhia promptly responded and at once dispatched to Agra a battery of six guns under Captain Pearson, Captain Alexander's regiment of cavalry, and a little later Captain Burlton's regiment. Later on, the remaining Sepoys of the Gwalior contingent revolted on 14th June 1857, and the Maharaja took refuge in the British protection.[24]

Maharaja Jashwant Singh of Bharatpur also prompted a faourable response on the call of Mr. Colvin. He sent Captain Nixon to occupy the station of Mathura with a detachment of infantry. Mathura was only thirty-five miles from Agra where three companies of Native Infantry belonging to two regiments stationed at Agra, mutinied on the 30th of May. They shot down one officer, wounded another, plundered the treasury, fired the houses of the English, released the prisoners from the jail, and went off to Dehli. However, the Bharatpur troops under Nixon occupied the position at Hodel, a small town lying between Mathura and Delhi. On 31st, a position was marked out, and the troops were ordered to take it up. However, here occurred an unexpected difficulty. The Sepoys of the Raja of Bharatpur not only refused to obey, but they warned the British officers to depart.[25]

Maharaja Tukoji Rao Holkar of Indore also favoured the British during the Uprising of 1857. Apart from his uncordial relationship with the political agent Durand, Holkar placed three companies of his troops and three of his field-guns, for the protection of the Residency. Holkar had shown that he was well aware of the disorder fomenting around him. He had candidly told Durand that he mistrusted his own troops. Taking the above facts into consideration, he had sent away from Indore, his most uncontrollable troops, prior to the start of the mutiny. However, Saadat Khan, one of the cavalry troops of Holkar organized the discontented troops and made a call, "Get ready, come on to kill the Sahibs; it is the order of the Maharaja." Following the call of Saadat Khan, mutiny erupted on 1st July 1857. Holkar sent into Mhou Fort, by the hands of Ganpat Rao, his agent at the Residency, a letter addressed to Colonel Piatt to inform him of the mutiny, and stating that his own troops refused to act against the revolutionaries. On the same day, he wrote also to the Governor of Bombay, Lord Elphinstone, telling him of what had occurred. On the 4th of July, mounted, and spear in hand, Holkar confronted the revolutionaries boldly at the Residency. They received the Maharaja at first respectfully, but afterwards reminded him of the martial character of his ancestor, Yashwant Rao, and reviled him as a degenerate Holkar. He absolutely refused his countenance, and rejected all their demands.[26]

Following the days of the Uprising, Maharaja Tukoji Rao Holkar refused the threatening demands of the revolutionaries from Mhou to deliver up the Europeans and other Christians, who had taken refuge in his palace. He stated himself that he offered to them his own person rather than the heads of those under his protection.[27]

The rulers or Native Chiefs of Rajputana also supported the British during the Uprising. The whole of Rajputana was ruled by eighteen Native States; seventeen of which were ruled by Hindus, and eighteenth, Tonk, by the Muslim descendant of the famous freebooter, Amir Khan. The other seventeen States were, Karauli, Kishangarh, Dholpur, Udaipur (Mewar), Jaipur, Bharatpur, Alwar, Bikaner, Jodhpur (Marwar), Bundi, Jaisalmer, Sirohi, Dungarpur, Kota, Jhalawar, Banswara and Partapgarh. Most of the States were assigned a political officer, but the chief of all these, the Govemor General's

Agent for the general control of entire Rajputana, was Colonel George St. Patrick Lawrence. Colonel Lawrence on the 23rd of May issued a proclamation to the Native Rajas of Rajputana. In this proclamation, he called upon them to preserve peace within their borders, to concentrate their troops on the frontiers of their respective States. So that they might be available to aid the British, to show zeal and activity in dealing with anybody of rebels who might attempt to traverse their territories. [28]

Due to the non-cooperation of the Native States, the Sepoys and civilians of Rajputana could not involve in the Uprising. Only Naseerabad, which was the British army cantonment, in the British territory of Ajmer revolted and played important role in the Uprising.

A most powerful Native ruler of India at that time, Afzal-ud-Daula, the Nizam of Hyderabad, and his influential minister Salar Jang, fully cooperated the British during the Uprising. He arrested the fanatic leaders, from the Makka Masjid, who made a call to kill the Europeans. However, on 17th of July, about four hundred Rohela troops followed by about four thousand mobs of Hyderabad rose in insurrection and marched towards residency by demanding the release of the prisoners. The Resident Major Davidson was duly informed due to the cunningness of Salar Jang, and the mob faced the heavy firing and lastly repulsed. Many revolutionaries were killed and several of them arrested. Among the arrested were Torbaz Khan and Maulvi Alauddin. The first was shot dead while attempting to escape, and Maulvi was tried and send to Andaman.[29]

The role of John Lawrence in controlling Punjab and his effort to get support of Punjabi forces could be added another cause of the failure of the Uprising. Punjab garrison consisted, on May 12, of some 60,000 men, of whom 10,000 were Europeans, 36,000 *Purbeas* of the Regular Army, and 14,000 Punjab Irregulars. They were broken up into two sections at the extreme ends of the province; one in the Peshawar valley, and the other in the Simla Hills. The arrogance of the *Purbeas* towards the vanquished soldiers of the Khalsa had made them hated. Between the Sikh and the Muslims, there was ancestral hatred. A true Sikh was damned if he place on his head anything belonging to a Muslim. He was required by his Holy Book to fight a Muslim face to face whenever he meets him. The British officers fully utilized the chance of the animosity. Henry Lawrence also got support of Maharaja Jang Bahadur of Nepal and his 10,000 Gorkha soldiers, who were more martial and trustworthy than the Punjabi forces. Both the martial communities fought tooth and nail to crush the rebellion.[30]

The sympathy of the Sikhs was in favour of the British. They didn't want to see the Mughas, their ancestral enemy, on the Delhi throne. According to Frederick Cooper, The Sikhs generally were most eager to aid in the capture of Delhi, from the existence of a most remarkable prophecy, — that they, in conjunction with "topi wallahs" (hat wearers, or the British), who should come over the sea, would reconquer Delhi, and place the head of the King's son on the very spot where the head of Guru Teg Bahadur had been exposed, one hundred and eighty years before, by order of Aurangzeb, the Great Mughal.[31]

George Campbell also writes by appreciating the fidelity of the Sikh soldiers. He writes, "As respects the effect of Lord Dalhousie's annexations, I do not think anyone will now doubt that the Punjab as a British possession saved India; that without the Punjab and the Punjabis we must inevitably have failed before Delhi, and lost all Northern and Central India — and then who knows what would have happened?"[32]

After the failure of the Uprising in India, thousands of revolutionaries belonging to both Hindus and Muslims galloped in the neighbouring country Nepal and appealed to the King Jang Bahadur for help. The King as one of the allies of the British ordered the revolutionaries to leave his country within ten days. The fugitive Sepoys numbering about 10,000 appealed to the King of Nepal, Jang Bahadur, in February 1859, "we fought for the Hindu religion, the Maharaja being a Hindu should help us." They also petitioned to the King, who in case of his denial of the support, they would lend a Gorkha officer to command each Hindustani Battalion.[33]

Perhaps their intention was to reorganize themselves in Nepal and with the Gorkha support attack, the British India from afresh. However, the last effort of the revolutionaries also could not become successful due to the non-cooperation of the Jang Bahadur.

References:

1. *Biblio*, Vol, XII, No. 3&4, March-April 2007, p.9
2. *Peoples Democracy*, (Remembering 1857 - Irfan Habib), Vol. XXXI, No. 04, January 28, 2007
3. *Biblio*, Vol, XII, No. 3&4, March-April 2007, p.9
4. *Ibid*
5. *Peoples Democracy*, (*Remembering 1857* - Irfan Habib), Vol. XXXI, No. 04, January 28, 2007
6. *New York Daily Tribune*, October 23, 1857, (According to the narrations of Munshi Jeewan Lal, the revolutionaries were more bend for their salaries rather fighting the foes. They had also lack of courage and patriotism. He says, "In the absence of the English, the mutineers were as lions, but on hearing of their approach, they sought places of refuge like rats in the presence of a cat." *Two Native Narratives*, p. 102, 179 &181)
7. *New York Daily Tribune*, October 23, 1857
8. *Biblio*, Vol, XII, No. 3&4, March-April 2007, p.9
9. The names of the British agents or spies were collected from different pages of the book, Shamsul Islam, *Letters of Spies: And Delhi was Lost,* New Delhi, 2008
10. Kaye, John William, *A History of the Sepoy War in India, 1857-58,* Vol. III, London 1876, pp. 643-645

11. Shamsul Islam, *Letters of Spies: And Delhi was Lost,* New Delhi, 2008, p. 37

12. *Ibid,* p. 38

13. *Ibid,* p. 40

14. *Ibid,* p. 41

15. *Ibid,* pp. 42-43

16. *Ibid,* p. 50

17. *Ibid,* p. 50

18. *Ibid,* pp. 50-51

19. *Two Native Narratives,* p. 94

20. Cave-Browne, pp. 36-37, see also *Two Native Narratives,* pp. 103-5 & 183 (According to Munshi Jeewan Lal, more than hundred cavalry troopers hunted Hakim Ahsanullah in the Palace on the suspicion of his negotiations with the Europeans and explosion of gunpowder, and returned by the denial of the Emperor about his presence in the Palace. They turned towards his house and plundered. The females happily managed to get away, and eventually escaped violence at the hands of these soldiers. Mirza Mughal, on the instructions of the Emperor, arrived on the spot, and with some cavalry drove the plunderers away. At night, the Sepoys surrounded the Palace, and demanded Hakim Ahsanullah to be given them. For hours, the Emperor resisted their demands. At last, Emperor Bahadur Shah Zafar agreed, on the condition that his life was spared. This was agreed to, and the Hakim was handed over to the soldiers, and confined by them under custody in the room of the Crown jewels. The King then summoned all his sons around him, and told them to remain by him and protect his life. Mirza Kizr, Mirza Mehdi, and Mirza Abdullah remained with him all night. Begam Zeenat Mahal also complained to the Emperor that she, too, was suspected of negotiating with the English, and that she had been warned that the soldiers intended to plunder the Palace. *Two Native Narratives,* pp. 186 & 190)

21. *New York Daily Tribune,* November 14, 1857, see also Henry Wylie Norman, *Delhi - 1857; The Siege, Assault, and Capture as given in the Diary and Correspondence of the Late Colonel Keith Young,* London 1902, p. 55

22. Gubbins, pp. 80-81

23. Marx, Karl, *Notes on the Indian History (664-1858),* Russian Edition, Moscow, 1947, p. 152, see also Kaye, John William, *Kay's and Malleson's History of the Indian Mutiny of 1857-8,* Vol. II, London, 1910, pp. 121-122, Aitchison, Charles, *Rulers of India: Lord Lawrence,* Oxford, 1892, p. 83, and Gibbon, pp. 260-261

24. Malleson, George Bruce, *History of the Indian Mutiny of 1857-58, Commencing from the Close of the Second Volume of Sir John Kaye's History of the Sepoy War,* Vol. III, (Contemporaneous with Sir John Kay's Third Volume), London, 1878, pp. 154,169 & 174

25. *Ibid,* pp. 164-165

26. *Ibid*, pp. 227-229 & 231-232, see also Shrivastawa, P.N., *Madhya Pradesh District Gazetteer, Indore*, Bhopal, 1971, p. 100
27. *Ibid,* p. 232
28. *Ibid,* p. 245 & 251
29. Malleson, George Bruce, *Kay's and Malleson's History of the Indian Mutiny of 1857-8,* Vol. V, London, 1911, pp. 81-83
30. Gibbon, pp. 256-258, see also Aitchison, Charles, *Rulers of India: Lord Lawrence*, Oxford, 1892, pp. 76-77
31. Cooper, Frederic, *The Crisis in the Punjab, The 10th of May until the Fall of Delhi*, London, 1858, p. 32
32. Campbell, George, *Memoirs of My Indian Career,* Vol. I, (edited by Charles E. Bernard), New York, 1893, p. 212
33. Wood, Evelyn, *The Revolt in Hindustan 1857-59*, London, 1908, pp. 7& 21

Chapter 13

Retribution in the Uprising

The overall course of Uprising witnessed a brutal retribution which may be described as inhuman and highly condemnable on the part of both Europeans and Indian revolutionaries. These brutalities were due to the highest level of hatred and hostility developing from many decades in both the Europeans and Indian masses. The whole period of Uprising and after, there was a systematic use of violence as this was a time of bloody savagery on both sides because both were desperate to win, and believed violence to be the only language their enemy understood. Tatya Tope, originally just a Maratha gunner, rose to be the Commander-in-Chief of the forces led by Nana Sahib, during his march to central India ordered that village officials who had collaborated and collected taxes for the British should have their ears, and noses cut off as an example to others. It was argued by the scholars that there was a holocaust where millions disappeared. It was a necessary holocaust in the British view because they thought the only way to win was to destroy entire populations in towns and villages. It was simple and brutal. Indians who stood in their way were killed. However, its scale has been kept a secret. This holocaust caused the deaths of almost 10 million people over 10 years beginning in 1857.[1]

Atrocities Committed by the Indians

The newspaper, *New York Daily Tribune* on 16th September, 1857 starts with the words, "The outrages committed by the revolted Sepoys in India are indeed appalling, hideous, ineffable — such as one is prepared to meet – only in wars of insurrection, of nationalities, of races, and above all of religion." In India, there was intense hostility developing against the British from the last few decades, but it was 24th April 1857, a petty riot against them started at Meerut city, spread throughout Northern and Central India and broken all barriers of brutality. *New York Daily Tribune* continues, "The Indian revolt does not commence with the Ryots, tortured, dishonored and stripped naked by the British, but with the Sepoys, clad, fed, petted, fatted and pampered by them. To find parallels to the Sepoy atrocities, we need not, as some London papers pretend, fall back on the middle ages, not, even wander beyond the history of contemporary England."[2]

On the 10th May, evening around 30 Sepoys of 3rd Light Cavalry intoxicated in bhang mutinied with the intention of revenge of the punishment and humiliation to their 85 Sepoys. They, along with the Meerut city rioters, galloped the jail, overpowered the guards and liberated their 85 comrades. They were joined by 11th and 20th regiments, commenced an indiscriminate attack on European residences and set their houses on fire.

Many officers, including Colonel Finnis were shot dead. The Sepoys along with the city rioters started loot and slaughter. A total of about 50 European men (including soldiers), women and children were killed. The height of the atrocity was committed and a lady Mrs. Chambers, who was pregnant; her unborn child was ripped from her womb by a local butcher. Louis Tracy records that the sky flamed red in a thousand fires, and the blood of unhappy Europeans, either civilian families or the wives and children of military officers, was being spilt like water. The mutineers commanded their fellow Sepoys, "quick brother quick! The white men are coming!" "To Delhi! That is our only chance!" [3]

When the revolutionaries reached at Delhi, they committed the same type of atrocities. The revolutionaries were immediately joined by the Native corps of Delhi and Mr. Frazer the Civil Commissioner of Delhi with all the European residents who could be found were slaughtered without mercy. The Commissary of ordnances Liutenant Willoughby fired and blown up himself as a result many Sepoys who came to seize were also blown. As the revolt progressed, the atrocities also reached its peak. According to the British records, the officers were murdered and their dead bodies were stripped and mutilated. Ladies were violated in the presence of their husbands, parents and children and then cruelly mangled and slain. Children were thrown up in the air and received on the point's bayonets as they fell; others had their limbs cut off and scattered on the roads. [4]

Many of these atrocities might have been committed by the thieves and camp-followers that rose in the wake of the Sepoys but the fact could not be avoided that the Native soldiery both Hindus and Mussalmans were at the head of all.

About the murder of the European, John William Kaye states that on 11th May, and its following days, that a crowd of insurgents killed all the Christians, who could not effect their escape. They also destroyed the house and its contents, taking away all the type that they could carry, to turn to another and a deadlier use. Everywhere the Christian people were butchered; their property was plundered or destroyed, and then their houses were fired. He further narrates, "Nor less surprising was it, that, with all these shameful proofs of the great crimes which had been committed… The Bazaars on that Monday morning must have been full of the plundered property of our people, and of many dreadful proofs and signs of complicity in the great crime of the preceding night." He continued, "Cutting down every European they could find, and setting fire to their houses, they doubled back towards the Calcutta Gate, where they learnt that Commissioner Fraser, Douglas of the Palace Guards, and other leading Englishmen would be found. As they rode on, with the cry of '*Deen- Deen!*' they were followed by an excited Mohammedan rabble." So there was not, after that 16th of May, a single European left in Delhi, either in the Cantonment or in the City. [5]

At sunset on 11th of May, about 49 Christians surviving in Delhi, adults and children of both sexes, were brought to the Palace and placed in a dungeon. Five days later they were led out into the courtyard and butchered and their bodies were thrown to river Jumna, although the Emperor was not in favour of this massacre.[6]

Not only, the Europeans but the Natives who were suspected to be sympathizers of English were killed brutally, and their properties were plundered. Munshi Jeewan Lal narrates that Buldeo Sing, the brother of Lachman Sing, Thanedar of Alipur, was seized and brought to the Kotwali. He was accused of sympathizing with the English. He was shot, and his body suspended from a tree. Thirteen bakers residing at the Kabul Gate were dragged from their houses and killed, on being suspected of supplying bread to the English. Several persons were killed by cannonballs falling in the city. A mine was discovered being dug, near the Kashmiri Gate. The man caught was hung before the Kotwali on a tree. A proclamation was issued that all friends of the English would be treated in this manner.[7]

The cantonments at Kanpur contained one of the great Native garrisons of India. Dhondu Pant alias Nana Sahib of Bithur supported the rebel Sepoys and declared himself as ruler of Kanpur. The Europeans numbering more women and children than fighting men shut themselves up in an ill-chosen hasty entrenchment. On 27th June, 1857, Europeans surrendered on the condition of being allowed to depart on boats down the Ganges to Allahabad. About 450 of them embarked in boats on the Ganges, but the British had hardly put out into the middle of the stream when guns opened upon them from the right bank of the Ganges (Satichaura Ghat). They destroyed 39 boats only a single boat carrying four men escaped. Many of the embarked Europeans were caught, and the men were separated from women and children. The men were shot down immediately, and the ladies and children were saved. It is said that the horror was suddenly happened on hearing the news of General Neil's outrages at Allahabad and the rumours that the daughter of Nana Sahib had been captured and burnt alive by the British. The British women and children who survived from the massacre were, about 210 in the number, (163 survivors from the Kanpur garrison, and 47 refugees from Fatehgurh) imprisoned in Sawada House and later on shifted to Bibighar. After Nana's defeat from General Havelock on 15th of July, he decided to massacre the captives of Bibighar. For that purpose, he selected two Muslim butchers, an Afghan, and two out-caste Hindus, to do his bidding. Armed with long knives these five friends entered the shambles, and massacred the captives and their bodies were thrown down a well. Nana Sahib along with his associates fled from Kanpur after his defeat.[8]

John William Kaye states, "All who had not been burnt, or bayoneted, or sabred, or drowned in the great massacre of the boats on the 27th of June, had been swept up from the Ghat and carried to the Savada House.... to Bibighar (which) was scanty accommodation in it for a single family. In this wretched building were now penned, like sheep for the slaughter, more than two hundred women and children. ..... They were taken out, two at a time, to grind corn for the Nana's household... as it enabled them to carry back a little flour to the Bibighar to feed their famishing children."[9]

When Kanpur fell again into the hands of the British, by a train of operations hereafter to be described, there were found among other wrecks two small pieces of paper, covered with blood, and containing a few words in pencil; they appeared to have been written by two persons, both females. One gave a brief and confused narrative of some of the events in the entrenchment; while the other consisted simply of a record of the dates on which members of the writer's family were struck down by the hand of death. The written record on paper was, "Mamma died, July 12' 'Alice died, July 9' 'George died June 27' 'Uncle Willy died, June 13' 'Aunt Lilly, June 17." The other piece of paper contained, "Entered the barracks, May 21' 'Cavalry left, June 5' 'First shot fired, June 6."[10]

Another example of atrocities, more or less as of Kanpur, could be noted in a village Sundarpur near Fatehgarh cantonment in Farrukhabad district. The European officers and troops, including women and children escaped in the night and embarked in the boats through the adjoining river. Colonel Smith, Colonel Goldie, and Major Robertson commanded severally the three boats on 4th of June 1857. However, after sailing some distances the three boats were reduced to two as Colonel Goldie's boat ran upon a shoal, and the rudder was smashed. A vain attempt was made to repair it, the result of which was that the villagers of Sundarpur around three hundred in the number (according to some account, four hundred to five hundred in the number) came down and fired upon them. The blood of the Englishmen was stirred by this assault. Then a little band of five Christian officers namely Captain Vibart, Major Munro, Lt. Eckford Lt. Sweetenhani and Henderson, went out and charged a upon the Natives and drove them back to their village with the loss of some of their leaders. The occupants of Colonel Goldie's boat betook themselves to Colonel Smith, and they pursued their perilous journey down the river. The villagers again attacked the Europeans with equal ferocity. The Sepoys also were coming down upon them in their boats, and the banks of the river were lined with revolutionaries.[11]

At Lucknow, the capital of Awadh, the British garrison found themselves nearly in the same plight which had proven fatal to their comrades at Kanpur. They shut up in a fort, surrounded by overwhelming forces, straitened for provisions, and deprived of their leader.[12]

In Awadh area at Mohammadi, there happened a terrible tragedy. The Europran fugitives from Shahjahanpur reached at Mohammadi on 1st of June but on the 4th, here too, the soldiery mutinied. The Europeans who were increased at Mohammadi headed towards Aurangabad but in the way they were massacred by the Awadh Irregular soldiery. One was somehow escaped to tell of the butchery. He explains, as quoted by Kaye, "We all collected under a tree, and took the ladies down from the buggy. Shots were firing from all directions amidst the most fearful yells. The poor ladies all joined in prayer, coolly and undauntedly awaiting their fate. I stopped for about three minutes among them, but thinking of my poor wife and child here, I endeavoured to save my life for their sakes. I rushed out towards the insurgents, and one of their men, Gurdhan, of the Sixth Company, called out to me to throw down my pistol and he would save me. I did so, when he put himself between me and the men, and several others followed his example. In about ten minutes more they completed their hellish work. Poor Lysaght was kneeling out in the open ground, with his hands folded across his chest, and though not using his firearms, the cowardly rascals would not go up to the spot until they shot him; and then rushing up they killed the wounded and children, butchering them in a most cruel way. With the exception of the drummer-boy, everyone (of the Shahjahanpur party) was killed, and besides poor good Thomason and one or two clerks. They denuded the bodies of their clothes for the sake of plunder."[13]

The same thing happened with the fugitives of Faizabad. After the rebellion broke out in the city, the Europeans fled away through Ghaghra River, but they had scarcely gone thirty miles down the stream, the Sepoys (Azamgarh revolutionaries) lined on the banks of the river and opened fire. Colonel Goldney, the Commissioner ordered the companions to fly with their lives. He himself could not run due to his old age and was shot dead. Others from the two leading boats perished in the attempt to escape. Lieutenant Currie, of the Artillery, and Lieutenant Parsons, of the Awadh Irregulars, were drowned. It was supposed that Major Mill also was drowned. Adjutant Bright, of the Twenty-second, shared the fate of Colonel Goldney. The rest seemed to have escaped to Araorah, where they were joined by the fugitives from another boat. The party then consisted of eight. In the morning of the 10th of June, they reached Kaptanganj in safety. Thence they pursued their hazardous journey, with good hope of ultimate deliverance. When they passed through the village Mahua Dabar, the people rushed out, armed with swords and matchlocks, and fell mercilessly upon the fugitives. Only one Sergeant Major Busher outran all his companions, saved his life.[14]

Alaxendar Duff writes, ".....the Native regiments having openly mutinied, killed nearly all their officers, and plundered or destroyed the whole property of the British residents. Being in military possession of the city, they have been indulging in excesses, the nature and extent of which cannot yet be fully known; but some of the details authentically brought to light are truly heart-rending. One European family they caught, and having stripped father, mother, and children, they chopped off their toes and fingers, tied them to trees, and burned them alive! Their treatment of any European females that have fallen into their hands has been too horrible to be expressed by me."[15]

No doubt there were atrocities against the British because there was the matter of revenge and a fixed mission of ousting the foreigners. However, it was not so as narrated by the Europeans. If there was genocide at any place surely it was the reaction of the cruelties and butchery committed by Europeans. No doubt there were the anarchy and lawlessness at the independent centres and even in Delhi. However, the revolutionaries were in control of their leaders who were more humane than the Europeans. The example of Native kindness could be seen at Bijnor where Nawab Mahmud Ali Khan allowed all the Europeans to go with their baggage in full security.[16]

The Indian nationalist chroniclers V.D. Savarkar and other nationalists narrate that the Sepoys and rebellious people never committed such atrocities as quoted by the English historians. The revolutionaries were more humane and merciful during the Uprising than British oppressors. Accounts of the Europeans also seem to be exaggerated as they never mentioned any instance of European atrocity, which was well-known among the people. They always pose the Indians as most barbaric and cruel and Europeans as most civilized and innocent.

Atrocities Committed by the Europeans

There was a kind of hate among the Europeans against Indian Natives and that hate was due to the infidelity of the Indian subjects, and cruelties committed to their women and children. A British historian John William Kaye while defending the European atrocities, shamelessly says, "But when we come to weigh the heavy burden of unutterable guilt, of which our women and children were the victims, against the cruelty and inhumanity of the avenging power, we see how light were our reprisals.".[17]

According to Karl Marx, who has commented in *New York Daily Tribune*, 15th April 1858, that after the rebellion was suppressed, despite the English assiduously trying to find evidence against the rebels for molesting English women nothing by way of evidence could be found. However, the cry that "the Natives have dishonoured our women," was a very important piece of hate propaganda spread in England against the Mutineers and used to justify all barbarities perpetrated.[18]

Act No. XIV. 1857 was passed on the 6th of June 1857, to legalise all types of retributions. In this Act, the provision was made for the punishment of persons convicted of exciting mutiny or sedition in the army, the offender was rendered liable to the punishment of death and the forfeiture of all his property; and persons guilty of harbouring such offenders were made liable to heavy punishment. Power was also given the general court-martial to try all persons, whether amenable to the Articles of War or not, charged with any offence punishable by this or the preceding Act; and the Supreme and Local executive governments were authorised to issue commissions in any district, for the trial by single commissioners, without the assistance of law officers or assessors, and with absolute and final power of judgment and execution, of any crime against the state, or any 'heinous offence' whatever; the term 'heinous offence' being declared to include every crime attended with great personal evidence', or committed with the intention of forwarding the designs of those who are waging war against the State."[19]

Atrocities reached a climax on 14th of September 1857 and after, when British forces attacked and besieged the Delhi city. They proceeded to massacre not only the rebel Sepoys and *Jihadis*, but also the ordinary citizens of the Mughal capital. In one neighbourhood alone, Kucha Chelan, over 1400 unarmed citizens were cut down. Delhi, a sophisticated city of half a million souls, was left an empty ruin. John William Kaye states about the Delhi massacre, "Many who had never struck a blow against us, who had follow their peaceful pursuits and who had been plundered and buffeted by their own armed countrymen, were pierced by our bayonets, or cloven by our sabres, or brained by our muskets or rifles......all else were, in our eyes, the enemies and persecutors of our race...... during the first days of our occupation of Delhi, many innocent men were shot down or otherwise massacred." He continues, "I know only one instance of slaughter on a large scale, which was made the talk of the Camp. Major James Brind, Brind of the Batteries, was sent into the city on the most ungrateful duty of burying the rotting carcasses which were polluting the atmosphere of certain parts of Delhi........ Among the traitors were 'Syeds and various classes of debauchees.' Many of the enemy were slain on the spot, and others, 'against whom blood-proofs, as also relics of our murdered countrywomen, children, and other Christian residents' were to be found on their persons or in their houses, were reserved for more humiliating punishments. Following the example set by Neill at Cawnpore, he kept these men 'to labour in cleansing our polluted lines before their final punishment.' The number slain by Brind's detachment ranged from a hundred and fifty to two hundred men. As a pleasant set-off to this, Brind had the satisfaction of reporting that he had 'sent out of the city many hundreds of women, children, and helpless male inhabitants — blind and decrepit.' It is not clear whether the men thus 'slain' were our revolted Sepoys or civil inhabitants of Delhi......"[20]

The atrocities committed in Delhi after its siege was a blot on the name of any civilized community in the world. About the atrocities committed by the British after the siege of Delhi, a 19-year-old British officer Edward Vibart recorded, "The orders went out to shoot every soul. It was literally murder ..... The women were all spared but their screams, on seeing their husbands and sons butchered, were most painful.....I feel no pity, but when some old grey bearded man is brought and shot before your very eyes, hard must be that man's heart I think who can look on with indifference..."[21]

About Delhi massacre after its siege by the British, Charles Raikes writes, "In the evening I went out with General Penny on his elephant, to see the side streets of the city. For miles not a creature saved a half-starved cat, and here and there an old hag groping about amidst the bones, old papers, and rags with which this once wealthy and populous place is strewed. It is as a city of the dead."[22]

Gorkha and Sikh regiments were most active in the massacre of the innocents of Delhi. The Sikhs got a chance of revenge of the execution of their Guru. As there was a cherished prophecy among the Sikhs that God was to grant them revenge for the death of their martyred Guru; and that the time would come, when they would storm and sack Delhi. Even for a long period after the capture of Delhi executions by hanging were of common occurrence in the city. 60th Rifle and some Gorkhas formed a firing party and massacred the innocents as much as they could. According to the Griffiths, the disguised

Sepoys and inhabitants taken with arms in their possession had short shrift, and were at once consigned to the gallows, a batch of ten one day suffering death opposite the Kotwali.[23]

After fully cleansing the population of Delhi by the British, there naturally emerged a lot of mosquitoes and insects and definitely the British and their forces were under their attack. It was the height of their shamelessness that they ridiculed over flow of the mosquitoes and insects that these wasps probably were the ghosts of the Sepoys who had been killed, their bodies, by the transmigration of souls, having taken the shape of these malignant insects in order to wreak vengeance on their destroyers.[24]

The height of retribution starts from June 1857, when Col. James Neill committed a horrible bout of atrocities during his expeditions. At Banaras the villages were burnt and both the revolutionaries and innocents were killed en masse. About the retribution at Banaras, Kaye & Malleson writes, "Already our military officers were hunting down criminals of all kinds, and hanging them up with as little compunction as though they had been pariah-dogs, or jackals, or vermin of a baser kind. One contemporary writer has recorded that, on the morning after the disarming parade, the first thing he saw from the Mint was a 'row of gallowses.' A few days' afterwards military courts or commissions were sitting daily, and sentencing old and young to be hanged with indiscriminate ferocity. ...... On one occasion, some young boys, who, perhaps, in mere sport had flaunted rebel colours and gone about beating tom-toms, were tried and sentenced to death. .... as all brave men are, towards the weak and helpless, went with tears in his eyes to the commanding officer, imploring him to remit the sentence passed against these juvenile offenders, but with little effect on the side of mercy. And what was done with some show of formality, either of military or of criminal law, was as nothing, I fear, weighed against what was done without any formality at all. Volunteer hanging parties went out into the districts, and amateur executioners were not wanting to the occasion. One gentleman boasted of the numbers he had finished off quite 'in an artistic manner,' with mango-trees for gibbets and elephants for drops, the victims of this wild justice being strung up, as though for pastime, in 'the form of a figure of eight'."[25]

After Banaras, Allahabad fell under cruel clutches of Col. James Neill. John William Kaye writes about British retribution at Allahabad that Martial Law was proclaimed; those terrible Acts passed by the Legislative Council in May and June were in full operation; and soldiers and civilians alike were holding Bloody Assize, or slaying Natives without any assize at all, regardless of sex or age. Afterwards, the thirst for blood grew stronger still. In papers sent home by the Governor General of India in Council, that "the aged, women, and children, are sacrificed, as well as those guilty of rebellion." They were not deliberately hanged, but burnt to death in their villages. Englishmen did not hesitate to boast, or to record their boastings in writing that they had spared no one, "peppering away at niggers" was very pleasant pastime, "enjoyed amazingly." And it has been stated, in a book patronised by high official authorities, that "for three months eight dead-carts daily went their rounds from sunrise to sunset to take down the corpses which hung at the cross-roads and market-places," and that "six thousand beings" had been thus "summarily disposed of and launched into eternity."[26]

Colonel Neill sent a detachment to Kanpur under Major Kenaud of the Madras Fusiliers, with the instructions of brutal retribution at Fatehpur town, "Attack and destroy all places en route close to the road occupied by the enemy, but touch no others; encourage the inhabitants to return, and instill confidence into all of the restoration of British authority." In his letter, certain guilty villages were marked out for destruction, and all the men inhabiting them were to be slaughtered. All Sepoys of mutinous regiments not giving a good account of themselves were to be hanged. The town of Fatehpur, which had revolted, was to be attacked, and the Pathan gunners destroyed, with all their inhabitants. Neill further instructed, "All heads of insurgents, particularly at Fatehpur, to be hanged. If the Deputy-Collector is taken, hang him, and have his head cut off and stuck up on one of the principal (Muhammadan) buildings of the town."[27]

Following the instructions of their Colonel, the British forces committed genocide in their way to Kanpur. They first settled the disturbances at Fatehpur and committed all the cruelties they could. John William Kaye has quoted the narration of Mr. Sherer, "Many of the villages, had been burnt by the wayside, and human beings there were none to be seen. . . . The swamps on either side of the road; the blackened ruins of huts, now further defaced by weather stains and mould; the utter absence of all sound that could indicate the presence of human life, or the employment of human industry, such sounds being usurped by the croaking of frogs, the shrill pipe of the cicala, and the under him of the thousand winged insects engendered by the damp and heat; the offensive smell of the neem-trees; the occasional taint in the air from suspended bodies, upon which, before our very eyes, the loathsome pig of the country was engaged in feasting; — all these things appealing to our different senses, combined to call up such images of desolation, and blackness, and woe, as few, I should think, who were present would ever forget."[28]

Col. James Neill, when conquered the Kanpur, committed the same type of atrocities and torture. He forced the Hindus and Muslims to eat beaf and pork, sewed them in the skins of the pigs, and forced them to lick the blood of the Europeans which were shed during the rebel occupation. John William Kaye quotes the words of General Neill, "The first culprit was a Subedar of the Sixth Native Infantry, a fat brute, a very high Brahmin. The sweeper's brush was put into his hands by a sweeper, and he was ordered to set to work. He had about half a square foot to clean; he made some objection, when down came the lash, and he yelled again; he wiped it all up clean, and was then hung, and his remains buried in the public road. Some days after, others were brought in; one a Mohammedan officer of our civil courts a great rascal, and one of the leading men, he rather objected, was flogged, made to lick part of the blood (at Bibighar) with his tongue. No doubt this is strange law, but it suits the occasion well, and I hope I shall not be interfered with until the room is thoroughly cleansed in this way. ..."[29]

There are a lot of stories were in circulation in Anglo-Indian and continental journals, regarding the revengeful carnage. It was stated that ten thousand of the inhabitants had been killed in the city of Kanpur by the British forces. John William Kaye says that this was a tremendous assertion, representing rather what might have been than what was. Some wished that it was so, for vengeance' sake; others, that there might be a pretext for maligning the English.[30]

The mutinous Sepoys left Meerut after the murder and plunder. However, the British, in the reprisal of the 10th May episode, started retribution to the suspected Sepoys and civilians at Meerut. According to Munshi Jeewan Lal's report, more than 200 Sappers and Miners were shot dead by the Europeans. The remaining Sepoys fled towards Delhi and occupied the place at Salimgarh.[31]

In Lucknow, the barbarism and cruel retribution of the British were repeated after Delhi. The murder and destruction of the property were prevalent throughout the day and night. The objective of the cruelty was to strike terror among the people. The entire layout of the city was transformed. A large part of the densely populated area around Macchi Bhawan, the traditional centre of the city, was demolished. Nearly two-fifths of the entire city was destroyed, and the residents uprooted. The socio-religious and cultural life of the city was severely affected by the British policy of retribution. The military occupation of the Jama Masjid robbed the area of its life and vitality. The city was never the same again.[32]

A British officer Julius George narrates a story of the terrible fighting at Lucknow, which was fought three months before in November. He says, "I rode off, and found my way to the Sikander Bagh, where a working party of Sappers, under two of our officers, had already proceeded. This place, rendered memorable by the terrible fight that occurred here on the Chiefs first advance to Lucknow, was, as its name denotes, a Native garden, with an enclosure wall and various buildings, and summer houses inside. The breach by which the Chief had entered nearly three months before was still unrepaired...... see the courtyard in which 1,800 Sepoys were killed, having shut themselves up with no outlet of escape...... Volley after volley from the Enfield was poured in through the doors and windows by our men, until at length a writhing mass of half dead men and corpses, piled five and six deep, showed that the massacre at Cawnpore was at last partially avenged. We found quantities of human hair and bones still lying about, and the smell, even now, was intolerable."[33]

An army officer from Peshawar gave a description of the disarming of the 10th irregular cavalry for not charging the 55th Native infantry when ordered to do so. The defaulters were not only disarmed, but stripped of their coats and boots and there embarked in boats and sent down the Indus to be drowned in the rapids. Another officer narrated that some inhabitants of Peshawar having caused a night alarm by exploding little mines of gunpowder in honor of a wedding. In the next morning, the persons concerned were tied up and received such a flogging as they would not easily forget.

Another tells from Allahabad, "Not a day passes but we string up from ten to fifteen of them." From Banaras there was the information, "Thirty zamindars were hanged on the mere suspicion of sympathizing with their own countrymen, and whole villages were burned down on the same plea." An officer from Banaras, whose letter is printed in *The London Times,* says: "The European troops have become friends when opposed to Natives."[34]

Frederick Cooper, the Deputy Commissioner of Amritsar, states in his account, "About 150 having been thus executed, one of the executioners swooned away (he was the oldest of the firing-party), and a little respite was allowed. Then proceeding, the number had arrived at two hundred and thirty-seven; when the district officer was informed that the remainder refused to come out of the bastion, where they had been imprisoned temporarily a few hours before. Expecting a rush and resistance, preparations were made against escape; but little expectation was entertained of the real and awful fate which had fallen on the remainder of the mutineers: they had anticipated, by a few short hours, their doom. The doors were opened, and, behold I they were nearly all dead! Unconsciously, the tragedy of Holwell's Black Hole had been re-enacted."[35]

Hodson's merciless execution to the two sons of Bahadur Shah Zafar, Mirza Mughal, Mirza Khizr Sultan, with the grandson, the son of Mirza Mughal, by name Mirza Abu Bakr, was globally condemned by the history scholars. For several weeks after its recapture, Delhi resounded to the sounds of gunfire as the British looted and wreaked revenge with a series of horrific executions of mutinous Sepoys, hundreds of whom were shot or hanged each day on a gallows especially constructed in Chandni Chowk or occasionally blown from the mouths of cannons. The destruction within the city, which reduced the buildings of the Red Fort alone to one-fifth of their former area, brought to a complete end not only a dynasty but the dominance of Muslim, Urdu culture in North India.

Europeans charge Nana Sahib for the Kanpur massacre, but even before they could have possibly known of the Kanpur massacre that took place later, the English had begun committing atrocities on Indian men, women, and children. Such atrocities undertaken by the English from the beginning of the Uprising enflamed the revolutionaries and hardened their hearts.

Irfan Habib quotes Angels that the English violated all laws of war in killing the prisoners of war; and they did so by ever imaginable, fiendish means, like hanging after binding their victims in contorted forms or blowing the captives from mouths of their guns. Every subsequent success of the British was marked by a general massacre and plunder of civil populations.[36]

The atrocities and cruelties committed by the Europeans, the so-called most civilized community in the world, had no parallel at least in the history of Indian sub-continent. The British practice of executing rebel soldiers and officers by tying them to the mouths of cannons, so that the crowds of onlookers would be spattered with blood and the corpses dispersed over a wide area, was intended to shock. It was furthermore, a deliberate offence, because blasting the body to pieces in this manner prevented either cremation or a proper burial. The British also carried out hundreds of arbitrary hangings in Northern India as the fighting progressed almost hand to hand through the villages, until they were finally retaken. It is said that cutting of noses, breasts, etc., in one word, the horrid mutilations committed by the Sepoys, were of course more revolting to European feelings.[37]

Harper's Weekly gives the account of the terrible retribution at Firozpur in Punjab. The morning of 13th of June, at Ferozepore was fixed upon for the execution. A gallows was erected on the plain to the North side of the fort, facing the Native bazaars, and at a distance of some 300 yards. On this two Sepoys were to be hanged, and at the same time their comrades in mutiny were to be blown away from guns. It is said that when they were about to be blown from canon some of them cried, "Do not sacrifice the innocent for the guilty!" Two of them rejoined, "Hold your sniveling: die men and not cowards — you defended your religion, why then do you crave your lives? Sahibs! They are not Sahibs; they are dogs!" Finally, they were blown. *Harper's Weekly* further quotes the account of an eye witness, "The scene and stench were overpowering......the consequence was that they were greatly bespattered with blood, and one man, in particular, received a stunning blow from a shivered arm!"[38]

There were pursuits, trials, and executions. Confiscations of lands and properties followed. Not only individual rebels, but whole families, whose members were suspected of having been involved in any way in the Uprising were deprived of their lands. The confiscated lands were given to British families, and to such 'Natives' as could claim to have rendered service against their own compatriots.[39]

It was published in the press in England that for every Christian church destroyed, fifty mosques should be destroyed, beginning with the Juma Masjid at Delhi; and for every Christian man, woman, and child murdered, a thousand rebels should bleed.[40]

After the suppression of the Uprising, the Viceroy Lord Canning requested his ministers and counselors to submit a report on how to entrench British rule in India. Abdul Hamid Ishaq in his *Ulema of Deoband* quotes Sir William Muir, the in charge of the intelligence department, stated in his report:[41]

"Of the entire population of India, the Muslims are the most spirited and vigilant. The Battle of Independence was fought by Muslims. As long as Muslims cherish in them the spirit of *Jihad* we shall not be able to vanquish them. It is therefore, imperative to first and foremost snuff out this spirit by eliminating the 'Ulema and the Qur'aan."

Giving expression to this advice, the Government in 1861 launched a campaign to destroy copies of the Qur'aan. 300,000 copies of the Qur'aan were set alight by the Government. The heavy hand of the British was fallen upon the Ulema who were considered responsible for waging Holy War against the British. About the policy of eradicating Ulema from 1864-1867, Abdul Hamid Ishaq in his *Ulema of Deoband* quotes an English historian Thompson, as follows:[42]

"From 1864 to 1867 heart-rending acts of brutality and torture were perpetrated against the Ulema. The British executed 14,000 Ulema by hanging them on trees. From Chandi Chowk of Delhi up to Khaibar, not a single tree was spared the neck of the Ulema. Ulema were wrapped in pig skin and hurled alive into blazing furnaces. Their bodies were branded with hot copper rods. They used to be made to stand on the back of the elephant and tied to high trees. The elephant would then be driven away and they would be left hanging by their necks. A make shift gallow was set up in the courtyard of the Shahi Masjid of Lahore and each day up to 80 Ulema were executed by hanging."

"Sometimes Ulema were wrapped in sacks and dumped into the river Ravi of Lahore after which a hail of bullets were pumped into the sacks". Abdul Hamid Ishaq further quotes Thompson, "As I got into my camp at Delhi, I perceived a stench of putrefied flesh. As I stepped out and went behind camp I saw a blazing fire of live coals. I saw a group of 40 naked Ulema being led to the fire. As I was witnessing this scene, another group of 40 Ulema were brought onto the field. Right before my eyes their clothes were taken off their bodies. An English commander addressed them thus: O Maulvis! You will be roasted in this fire just as these Ulema are being roasted. To save yourselves, just one of you should say that you were not part of the 1857 Uprising. The moment I hear this proclamation, I shall release you all." Thompson continues: "By the Lord who has created me! Not a single one of the Ulema said anything of the sort. All of them were roasted on the fire. Then another group of forty was brought and roasted over the blazing fire. But not a single Alim surrendered to the demands of the British".

An Urdu poet has rightly said:

"*Naujawanon Ko Huein Phaansian Be Jurm-Wa-Qusur,*
Maardi Goliyaan Paya Jise Kuchh Zor Awar"

(Young people were hanged without having committed any crime; whosoever was found powerful was gunned down).

References:

1. *The Guardian*, New Delhi, August 24, 2007
2. *New York Daily Tribune*, September 16, 1857
3. *The Living Age*, Volume 0055, Issue 702, New York, November 7, 1857, p. 329, see also John William Kaye, *A History of the Sepoy War in India, 1857-58*, Vol. II, London 1874, p. 174, Louis Tracy, *The Red Year; A Story of The Indian Mutiny*, New York 1907, pp. 24-25, and Mackenzie, A. R. D., *Mutiny Memoirs: Being Personal Reminiscences of the Great Sepoy Revolt of 1857*, Pioneer Press, Allahabad, 1892, pp. 22-23
4. *The Living Age*, Volume. 0055, Issue 702, New York, November 7, 1857, p. 330

5. Kaye, John William, *A History of the Sepoy War in India, 1857-58,* Vol. II, London 1874, pp. 72, 77& 83

6. Wood, Evelyn, *The Revolt in Hindustan 1857-59,* London, 1908, p. 27

7. *Two Native Narratives,* p. 121 &131

8. Hunter, William Wilson, *A Brief History of the Indian Peoples,* Oxford, 1893, pp. 225-226, see also, Tracy, Louis, *The Red Year; A Story of The Indian Mutiny,* New York 1907, pp. 107-109 *New York Daily Tribune,* September 15, 1857, Surridge, Victor, *Romance of Empire, India,* London, 1909, pp. 264-266, and Thomson, Mowbray, *The Story of Cawnpore,* London 1859, p. 210

   (Kaye narrates the story, "Every boat that had been prepared for our people was intended to be a human slaughter-house.... He (Nana Sahib) knew how the founder of the Mahratha Empire... dug his wagnuck into the bowels of the Mohammedan envoy, and gained by foulest treachery what he could not gain by force..... Tatya Tope, who had been appointed master of the ceremonies, sat enthroned on a '*Chabutra*' or platform, of a Hindu temple, and issued his orders to his dependents. Azimullah, also, was there, and the brethren of the Nana, and Teeka Singh, the new Cavalry General, and others of the leading men of the Bithur party...... The signal had been given, and the butchery was to commence.... Then a murderous fire of grapeshot and musket-balls was opened upon the wretched passengers from both banks of the river. There was then only a choice of cruel deaths for our dear Christian people. ....." Kaye, John William, *A History of the Sepoy War in India, 1857-58,* Vol. II, London 1874, pp. 339-341)

9. Kaye, John William, *A History of the Sepoy War in India, 1857-58,* Vol. II, London 1874, pp. 349-355

10. Dodd, p. 136

11. Kaye, John William, *A History of the Sepoy War in India, 1857-58,* Vol. III, London 1876, pp. 300-301

12. *New York Daily Tribune,* September 15, 1857

13. Kaye, John William, *A History of the Sepoy War in India, 1857-58,* Vol. III, London 1876, pp. 459-460

14. *Ibid,* pp. 466-467

15. Duff, Alexander, *The Indian Rebellion: Its Causes and Results, in a Series of Letters,* New York, 1858, p. 24

16. Graham, G.F.I., *The Life and Work of Sayed Ahmed Khan,* Edinburgh, 1885, pp. 23-24

17. Kaye, John William, *A History of the Sepoy War in India, 1857-58,* Vol. III, London 1876, p. 636

18. *New York Daily Tribune,* April 15, 1858

19. Kaye, John William, *Kay's and Malleson's History of the Indian Mutiny of 1857-8,* Vol. II, London, 1910, p. 208

20. Kaye, John William, *A History of the Sepoy War in India, 1857-58,* Vol. III, London 1876, pp. 636-637

21. *New Statesman,* October, 16, 2006

22. Raikes, Charles, *Notes on the Revolt in the North-Western Provinces of India,* London, 1858, p. 82

23. Adam and Charles Black, *History of the Siege of Delhi,* Edinburgh, 1861, p. 7, see also Charles John Griffiths, *A Narrative of the Siege of Delhi with an Account of the Mutiny at Firozpur in 1857,* London, 1910, pp. 213-214

24. Griffiths, Charles John, *A Narrative of the Siege of Delhi with an Account of the Mutiny at Firozpur in 1857,* London, 1910, p. 216

25. Kaye, John William, *Kay's and Malleson's History of the Indian Mutiny of 1857-8,* Vol. II, London, 1910, p. 177

26. Kaye, John William, *A History of the Sepoy War in India, 1857-58,* Vol. II, London 1874, pp. 269-270, see also Kaye, John William, *Kay's and Malleson's History of the Indian Mutiny of 1857-8,* Vol. II, London, 1910, p. 203

27. Kaye, John William, *Kay's and Malleson's History of the Indian Mutiny of 1857-8,* Vol. II, London, 1910, p. 207

28. Ibid, p. 277

29. Kaye, John William, *A History of the Sepoy War in India, 1857-58,* Vol. II, London 1874, pp. 399-400

30. Kaye, John William, *Kay's and Malleson's History of the Indian Mutiny of 1857-8,* Vol. II, London, 1910, p. 291

31. *Two Native Narratives,* p. 96

32. *Peoples Democracy, (Lucknow in 1857-58: The Epic Siege-* Amar Faruqui) Vol. XXXI, No. 41, October 14, 2007

33. Medley, Julius George , *A Years Campaigning in India from March 1857 to March 1858,* London 1858, pp. 171-172

34. *New York Daily Tribune,* September 16, 1857

35. Cooper, Frederic, *The Crisis in the Punjab, The 10th of May until the Fall of Delhi,* London, 1858, p. 162

36. *Peoples Democracy, (Remembering 1857-* Irfan Habib) Vol. XXXI, No. 4, January 28, 2007

37. *New York Daily Tribune,* September 16, 1857

38. *Harper's Weekly,* New York, February 15, 1862

39. *Peoples Democracy, (Remembering 1857-* Irfan Habib) Vol. XXXI, No. 4, January 28, 2007

40. Martin, R. Montgomery, *The Indian Empire,* Vol. II, London, 1858, p. 22

41. Ishaq, Abdul Hamid, *Ulema of Deoband,* Madarsa Arabia Islamia, Azaadville, South Africa, 2011, p. 10

42. *Ibid,* pp. 10-12

Chapter 14

Conclusions

The Uprising of 1857, which awakened the Indian population, filled national consciousness in their hearts and minds, taught the communal harmony, has multifaceted character. It was perhaps first time in Indian history that the people of all class, caste, and creed rose together against one common enemy with national passion and religious enthusiasm. The national unity was such an extent that even the Hindu civilians and the Sepoys unhesitatingly surrounded under the Islamic green flag and frequently termed the "*Jihad*" to their war against the British.

First time in the Indian history, the world saw the depth of hate against a foreign race, and well organized unity against them. This type of unity shook the mighty British Empire and indirectly bound the British to not to provide such chances in the future by adopting divide and rule theory. As a mark of jealousy towards such unity, a contemporary British historian Louis Tracy has abused its own way. In his book, '*The Red Year*' he has termed this unity as 'a wolf and a snake make common alliance against a watch dog.' Louis Tracy again omits the racial poison that it was a life-and-death struggle between West and East, between civilization and barbarism, between the laws of Christianity and the lawlessness of Mohammad, supported by the cruel, inhuman, and nebulous doctrines of Hinduism. However, all the metaphor rakings of British intellectuals in their hundreds of books are unable to prove this prestigious holy national war into a mutiny or any other nature.

The Hindu Chiefs, Muslim rulers and Ulema and almost all the population of North and Central India actively participated for their nation and religion, which were in danger under the British rule. This type of unity was the most important and powerful weapon of the revolutionaries. After the suppression of the Uprising, in order to materialize their divide and rule policy, the British authorities, reminded the both communities of Hindu and Muslim that how Shivaji and Ranjit Singh had oppressed the Muslims and how Aurangzeb had crushed the Hindus. The Europeans also told the people that their religion was now safe only under British administration. They also addressed the Indian people that how could they rise against the British who provides religious freedom, peace and tranquility.

It is very sad and matter of grave concern that after the failure of the Uprising in 1858 and even after gaining independence in 1947, we the Indian people still believe the theories which the British had taught us during the Uprising of 1857. We still look each other's ancestors as oppressors and on those very grounds, we commit such heinous crimes by the name of communal riots which even Europeans hesitated to do during normal days in their regime.

If the Mughals were oppressors, then how the Sepoys of Meerut and all over North Indian headed towards Delhi and enthroned the Bahadur Shah Zafar of the same Mughal dynasty. If the Islam under Shivaji's rule was in danger, then Muslims of Kanpur and adjoining areas arrayed under Nana Sahib, and Rani Luxmi Bai, of the same Marathas. Why Azimullah supported and boosted Nana Sahib against the British. Almost all the propaganda made by the Europeans in their regime was due to break the Hindu-Muslim unity and spread hatred in the minds and hearts of both the communities.

After the short skirmishes at Damdam, Brahampur and Barrackpur, the first long lasting banner of revolt was raised against the oppressive British rule by both Sepoys and civilians of Meerut. Here the question arises why the Sepoys, who had massacred their own countrymen on the single order of the British commanders, rose against them? Whether it was only due to the greased cartridge issue? On the same time of the Sepoys discontent, the British Government issued the order that no pre-greased cartridges should be issued to the Sepoys, then why the Sepoys revolted against them? If the cartridges were the main matter of the revolt, then why the Sepoys frequently used the same cartridges against their old masters during the revolt. The only answer of the all the questions and other related queries is that en masse uprising of Indians, belonging to both military and civil population, was in order to save their motherland and religion, which were in danger under British rule.

During the Uprising, the centuries' old capital of Delhi was chosen as the centre of all over India and established a national government under Mughal Emperor Bahadur Shah Zafar. The first national Emperor, in order to respect the feelings of his Hindu subjects, banned the slaughter of cows even in the festival of Bakrid. Five Muslims were cut down on the charge of killing a single cow in the capital. No action was taken against the murderers as the cow killing was unlawful in the capital under the rule of Bahadur Shah Zafar. Even the sons of the Emperor were treated as common people and threatened by Commander-in-Chief, General Bakht Khan to cut their nose and ears on the condition of involving in misdeeds. Overall the Government at Delhi was having purely a national character and run by a council composed of both the military and civil authorities.

Other than Delhi, the most sensitive centre of Uprising was Awadh and its' headquarter, Lucknow. Here Begam Hazrat Mahal with the assistance of Maulvi Ahmadullah Shah guided the military and civil Uprising. It has been verily noted in this book that most of the Sepoys of the Bengal army were belonged to the Awadh region and annexation of their homeland greatly pained them. They waited a chance to revenge their masters, and the cartridge issue provided the opportunity to rise against the British Government. The rumours of popular prophesy of the end of the British rule after completion of hundred years from the Plassey episode, further boosted the power of the revolutionaries. Here also the matter of freedom of nation and religion was also in the fore.

Jhansi, Kanpur, and Jagdishpur were also the centres where the revolutionaries were arrayed in bulk. Although, Rani Luxmi Bai, Nana Sahib and Kunwar Singh had their own personal grievances but after Sepoys revolt, they joined them and their guidance became national in character. Their activities were not only confined to their respective dominions but all over North India. Rani Luxmi Bai with the assistance of Tatya Tope and Bala Sahib went to the Kalpi and Gwalior and established the revolutionary Government. Nana Sahib and Kunwar Singh went to the far-off areas of Azamgarh, Lucknow, Mohammadi, and Terai border of Nepal. Their movement to mobilize the Indian people to wage war against the British Government was undoubtedly a national in nature and character.

The Ulema class of Muslim society was in front in every battles, which were fought against the British. It was well known by the forensic report of the cartridges that these were greased with cow fats not the hog lard, then why these people sacrificed their cherished lives not only during the Uprising but even before and after the Uprising. The Ulema were the only organized class who not only declared *Jihad* against the British, fought in the battlefield, but goaded the Muslim population by the name of religion and prepared them for martyrdom by assuring better life after death. In the league of the other revolutionaries, they proved themselves very fruitful for the nation.

The mass level hanging, and blowing the revolutionaries by cannon balls, could not stop the en masse recruitment of the revolutionaries in the Uprising. In another way, it testifies strongly to the point of view with which the Indian regards death. Death to them was no great matter; the only question which did really matter was whether they were true to their religious traditions or not. The British author Sieveking has beautifully quoted in his book *The Turning Point of the Indian Mutiny* that during the court-martial of the revolutionaries and other suspects at Arrah, an old man, while awaiting his turn on the gallows, and witnessing the painful struggles of a man dying in the air, opening his Kummerbund, took out all his property three rupees and said calmly, "This is my will! I give one rupee for prayers for my soul, one I leave for charitable purposes, and the third I bequeath to the man who hangs me."

The Uprising, which was full of courage and positive intention, could not last long and after sacrifice of lakhs of people, the mighty British power became victorious. The revolutionaries were lost the ground but positively became successful in creating nationalism and the concept of one nation to the whole of India. The Indian people also learnt a lesson that the mighty British power could not be defeated by arms. That's why after few decades of Uprising, the Indian intelligentsia again rose against the British but this time they adopted the weapons of non-violent movements in place of battles and warfare. The well-organized non-violent movements were dead slow and took about seventy-five years to set India free from British rule, but this method was very effective and successful.

Bibliography

Newspapers, Journals, Magazines and Gazetteers

1. *Biblio*, Vol, XII, No. 3&4, March-April 2007
2. *Defense Journal*, Vol. 3, No. 9, Islamabad, December,1999
3. *Delhi Gazette*, 29th September 1857
4. *Harper's Weekly*, New York, February 15, 1862
5. *Leidschrift*, Leiden, Netherlands, No. 24, December 3, 2009
6. Nevill, H. R., *District Gazetteers of the United Provinces of Agra and Oudh*, Vol. IV, Allahabad, 1904
7. *Naya Daur*, Awadh Number, a Monthly Urdu Journal published by the Information & Public Relations Department of the Government of Uttar Pradesh, Lucknow, February-March 1994
8. *New Statesman, October, 16, 2006*
9. *New York Daily Tribune*, July 15, 1857, August 4, 1857, August 14, 1857, September 15, 1857, September 16, 1857, October 3, 1857, October 23, 1857, November 14, 1857, April 15, 1858, October 1, 1858
10. *People's Democracy*, Vol. XXXI, No. 41, October 14, 2007, Vol. XXXI, No. 18, May 6, 2007, Vol. XXXI, No. 10, March 11, 2007, Vol. XXXI, No. 04, January 28, 2007
11. *Secular Qayadat*, Delhi, August 21, 2007
12. Shrivastawa, P.N., *Madhya Pradesh District Gazetteer, Indore*, Bhopal, 1971
13. *Social Scientist*, Vol-26, No. 1-4, January-April 1998
14. *The Guardian*, New Delhi, May 10, 2007, August 24, 2007
15. *The Living Age*, Volume 0055, Issue 702, New York, November 7, 1857
16. *The Pioneer*, 6th May, 2007
17. *The United States Democratic Review*, Volume 0040, Issue 5, New York, November 1857
18. *Tilism*, Lucknow, December 19, 1856

Books

1. Adam and Charles Black, *History of the Siege of Delhi*, Edinburgh, 1861
2. Aitchison, Charles, *Rulers of India: Lord Lawrence*, Oxford, 1892
3. Anderson, Clare, *The Indian Uprising of 1857-8: Prisons, Prisoners and Rebellion*, London, 2007

4. Argyl, Campbell, George Douglas, Duke of, *India Under Dalhousie and Canning*, London, 1865
5. Bartlett, D.W., *The Heroes of the Indian Rebellion*, Columbus, 1859
6. Beveridge, Henry, *A Comprehensive History of India*, Vol. III, London, 1962
7. Browcher, George, *Eight Month's Campaign Against the Bengal Sepoy Army, During the Mutiny of 1857*, London, 1858
8. Campbell, George, *Memoirs of My Indian Career,* Vol. I, (edited by Charles E. Bernard), New York, 1893
9. Campbell, George, *Memoirs of My Indian Career,* Vol. II, (edited by Charles E. Bernard), New York, 1893
10. Cave-Browne, J., *The Punjab and Delhi in 1857*, Vol. II, Edinburgh, 1861
11. Charles, Allen, *A few words anent the Red' Pamphlet. By one who has served under the Marquis of Dalhousie*, London, 1858
12. Cooper, Frederic, *The Crisis in the Punjab, The 10th of May until the Fall of Delhi*, London, 1858
13. Cunningham, Henry Stewart, *Earl Canning*, Oxford, 1891
14. Dalrymple, William, *The last Mughal: The fall of a Dynasty: Delhi, 1857*, New Delhi 2006
15. Dodd, George, *The History of the Indian Revolt and of the Expeditions to Persia, China, and Japan, 1856-7-8,* London, 1859
16. Duff, Alexander, *The Indian Rebellion: Its Causes and Results, in a Series of Letters*, New York, 1858
17. Edward, Gilliat, *Heroes of the Indian Mutiny; Stories of Heroic Deeds*, London 1914
18. Fanshawe, H.C., *Delhi Past and Present*, London 1902
19. Forrest, George W., *A History of the Indian Mutiny; Reviewed and Illustrated from Original Documents,* Vol. I, London 1904
20. Forrest, George W., *A History of the Indian Mutiny; Reviewed and Illustrated from Original Documents,* Vol. III, London 1904
21. Forrest, George W., *Selections from the Letters Despatches and other State Papers Preserved in the Military Department of the Government of India 1857-58*, Volume I, Calcutta, 1893
22. Forrest, George W., *Selections from The Letters Despatches and other State Papers Preserved in the Military Department of the Government of India 1857-58*, Volume III, Calcutta, 1902
23. Forrest, Robert Edward, *Eight Days; A Tale of the Indian Mutiny*, London (ND)
24. Frazer, R. W., *British India*, New York, 1896
25. Gibbon, Frederick P., *The Lawrences of the Punjab*, London, 1908
26. Graham, G.F.I., *The Life and Work of Sayed Ahmed Khan*, Edinburgh, 1885
27. Grant, Hope, *Incidents in the Sepoy War 1857-58*, Edinburgh, 1873
28. Greathed, Harvey Harris, *Letters Written During the Siege of Delhi*, London, 1858

29. Griffiths, Charles John, *A Narrative of the Siege of Delhi with an Account of the Mutiny at Firozpur in 1857*, London, 1910

30. Gubbins, Martin Richard, *An Account of the Mutinies of Oudh and of the siege of the Lucknow Residency; With some Observation on the Condition of the Province of Oudh and of the Causes of the Mutiny of the Bengal Army*, London, 1858

31. Halls, John James, *Two Months in Arrah in 1857*, London, 1860

32. Handcock, Arthur Gore, *The Siege of Delhi in 1857: A Short Account*, Allahabad, 1897

33. Henry, Wylie, *Delhi - 1857; The Siege, Assault, and Capture as given in the Diary and Correspondence of the Late Colonel Keith Young*, London 1902

34. Hodson, George Herbert, *Hodson of Hodson's Horse or the Twelve Years of a Soldiers Life in India: Being Extracts from the Letters of the Late Major W. S. R. Hodson*, London, 1889

35. Hope, Ascott R., *The Story of the Indian Mutiny*, London, 1896

36. Hunter, William Wilson, *A Brief History of the Indian Peoples*, Oxford, 1893

37. Inglis, Julia Selina Lady, *The Siege of Lucknow: A Diary*, London, 1892

38. Innes, McLeod, *Lucknow & Oude in the Mutiny: A Narrative and a Study*, London, 1895

39. Innes, McLeod, *The Sepoy Revolt: A Critical Narrative*, London, 1897

40. Ishaq, Abdul Hamid, *Ulema of Deoband*, , Madarsa Arabia Islamia, Azaadville, South Africa, 2011

41. James F. Holcomb, and Helen H. Holcomb, *In the Heart of India: or, Beginning of the Missionary Work in Bundela Land, with a short chapter on the Charecteristics of Bundelkhand and its People, and four Chapters of Jhansi History*, Philadelphia 1905

42. Kaye, John William, *A History of the Sepoy War in India, 1857-58*, Vol. I, London, 1875

43. Kaye, John William, *A History of the Sepoy War in India, 1857-58*, Vol. II, London, 1874

44. Kaye, John William, *A History of the Sepoy War in India, 1857-58*, Vol. III, London, 1876

45. Kaye, John William, *Kay's and Malleson's History of the Indian Mutiny of 1857-8*, Vol. II, London, 1910

46. Keene, Henry George, *Fifty-Seven: Some Account of the Administration of Indian Districts during the Revolt of the Bengal Army*, London, 1883

47. Khan, Syed Ahmad, *Asbab-e-Baghawat-e-Hind*, (Eng. Trans.), Patna, 1999

48. Kofoid, Charles Alwood, *The Story of the Indian Mutiny, 1857-58*, Edinburgh, 1898

49. Louis Tracy, *The Red Year; A Story of The Indian Mutiny*, New York 1907

50. Mackenzie, A. R. D., *Mutiny Memoirs: Being Personal Reminiscences of the Great Sepoy Revolt of 1857*, Pioneer Press, Allahabad, 1892

51. Malleson, George Bruce, *History of the Indian Mutiny of 1857-58, Commencing from the Close of the Second Volume of Sir John Kaye's History of the Sepoy War*, Vol. III, (Contemporaneous with Sir John Kay's Third Volume), London, 1878

52. Malleson, George Bruce, *Kay's and Malleson's History of the Indian Mutiny of 1857-8*, Vol. IV, London, 1911

53. Malleson, George Bruce, *Kay's and Malleson's History of the Indian Mutiny of 1857-8*, Vol. V, London, 1911

54. Malleson, George Bruce, *The Indian Mutiny of 1857*, New York, 1891

55. Martin, R. Montgomery, *The Indian Empire*, Vol. II, London, 1858

56. Marx, Karl, *Notes on the Indian History (664-1858)*, Russian Edition, Moscow, 1947

57. Mead, Henry, *The Sepoy Revolt: Its causes and its Consequences*, London, 1858

58. Medley, Julius George , *A Years Campaigning in India from March 1857 to March 1858*, London, 1858

59. Metcalfe, Charles Theophilus, *Two Native Narratives of the Mutiny in Delhi*, (Eng. Trans. of *Roznamcha Mainudin Hasan Khan* and *Munshi Jeewan Lal*), London, 1898

60. Norman, Henry Wylie, *Delhi - 1857; The Siege, Assault, and Capture as given in the Diary and Correspondence of the Late Colonel Keith Young*, London 1902

61. Qasmi, Ataur Rahman, *Hindustan Ki Pahli Jang Azadi 1857 Me Musalmanon Ka Hissa*, New Delhi, 2008

62. Raikes, Charles, *Notes on the Revolt in the North-Western Provinces of India*, London, 1858

63. Ranjeet Guha, (ed.) *Subaltern Studies IV*, (Gautam Bhadra '*Four Rebels of 1857*'), New Delhi, 1985

64. Roberts, P.E., *A Historical Geography of the British Dependencies: India*, Vol. VII, London, 1914

65. Rotten, J.E.W., *Captains Narratives of the Siege of Delhi from the Outbreak at Meerut to the Capture of Delhi*, London, 1858

66. Savarkar, V.D., *The Indian War of Independence of 1857*, London, 1909

67. Sedgwick, F.R., *The Indian Mutiny 1857: A Sketch of the Principal Military Events*, London, 1920

68. Shamsul Islam, *Letters of Spies: And Delhi was Lost*, New Delhi, 2008

69. Sherer, John Walter, *Daily Life During the Indian Mutiny: Personal Experiences of 1857*, Allahabad, 1910

70. Sherer, John Walter, *Havelock's March on Cawnpore, 1857*, London 1910

71. Sieveking, Isabel Giberne, *A Turning Point in the Indian Mutiny*, London, 1910

72. Spear, Percival, *Twilight of the Mughals: Studies in Late Mughal Delhi*, Cambridge, 1951

73. Stewart, Charles Edward, (Edited by Basil Stewart), *Through Persia in Disguise with Reminiscences of the Indian Mutiny,* London, 1911
74. Surridge, Victor, *Romance of Empire, India,* London, 1909
75. Thomson, Mowbray, *The Story of Cawnpore,* London 1859
76. Tracy, Louis, *The Red Year; A Story of The Indian Mutiny,* New York 1907
77. Trevelyan, George, *Cawnpore,* London, 1910
78. Trevelyan, George, *The Competition Wallah,* London, 1864, p. 92
79. Vibart, H.M., *Richard Baird Smith: The Leader of the Delhi Heroes in 1857,* Westminster, 1897
80. Wagnor, Kim A., *The Great Fear of 1857, Rumours, Conspiracies and the MaKing of the Indian Uprising,* Witney (UK), 2010
81. Wilson, T.F., *The Defence of Lucknow: A Diary,* London, 1858
82. Wood, Evelyn, *The Revolt in Hindustan 1857-59,* London, 1908
83. Wright, Charles H.H., *Memoire of John Lovering Cooke,* London, 1873

Printed in Great Britain
by Amazon

83191777R00108